Quality Management Handbook

C I *m* A

Published in association with
the Chartered Institute of
Management Accountants

Books in the CIMA Professional Handbook series

Series Editor: Rob Dixon

IT Management Handbook
Edited by Rob Dixon and Ray Franks

Management Accounting Handbook
Edited by Colin Drury

Quality Management Handbook
Edited by Max Hand and Brian Plowman

Quality Management Handbook

Edited by Max Hand
and Brian Plowman

Butterworth-Heinemann Ltd
Linacre House, Jordan Hill, Oxford OX2 8DP

 PART OF REED INTERNATIONAL BOOKS

OXFORD   LONDON   BOSTON
MUNICH   NEW DELHI   SINGAPORE   SYDNEY
TOKYO   TORONTO   WELLINGTON

First published 1992

British Library Cataloguing in Publication Data
Quality management handbook.
I. Hand, Max   II. Plowman, Brian
658.562
ISBN 0 7506 0143 4

Printed and bound in Great Britain by
Billing & Sons Ltd., Worcester

Contents

Contributors

Max Hand Co-editor of The *Quality Management Handbook* and as a co-founder and director of Develin & Partners, Max Hand has spearheaded the consultancy's services in total quality management.

Prior to the formation of Develin & Partners, he spent 15 years in a variety of management positions. His eight years consulting experience has included total quality, organizational effectiveness and IT strategy assignments within the financial services, manufacturing, construction and retail sectors. He has written numerous articles on a range of management issues and he is joint author of the survey *The Effectiveness of Quality Improvement Programmes in British Business*.

Brian Plowman Co-editor of the *Quality Management Handbook* and a co-founder and Director of Develin & Partners, he began his career with a number of production engineering appointments in the UK and mainland Europe. He was latterly group managing director of a plastics manufacturer, before moving to management consultancy ten years ago.

He has specialized in developing total quality management methodologies and has successfully applied them in the financial services, energy, transport, retail and food industries, with particular emphasis on manufacturing industry. He is a Chartered Engineer, and a Fellow of the Association of Quality Management Consultants. He is joint author of the survey *The Effectiveness of Quality Improvement Programmes in British Business*.

David Baines obtained a first degree in Electrical and Electronic Engineering at Imperial College, London in 1972. He joined the Post Office (now British Telecom) as an engineer designing large public switches for six years, before embarking on a two-year MBA course at the London Business School which he completed in 1980.

Following appointments as Operations Manager at F&S Electronic Control Systems and as Marketing Manager at Rathdown Industries, he entered management consulting with the London office of A.T. Kearney, in 1984. He was promoted to manager in 1987.

He continued marketing studies with organizational work and has continued with this same mix of assignments with Develin & Partners, since its formation in May 1988.

Professor Tony Bendell is East Midlands Electricity Professor of Quality Management at Nottingham Polytechnic and Chief Associate Consultant of Services Limited, the Nottingham Quality and Reliability Consultancy. He is an experienced consultant and lecturer having been involved in progressing the achievements of quality and reliability within large and small companies for almost 20 years.

Tony graduated from the London School of Economics (London University) with a BSc (Econ) Statistics Honours degree in 1971 and obtained his MSc Statistics with Distinction from the same University in 1972. In August 1982 he was awarded a PhD for his thesis on reliability modelling, in collaboration with the National Centre for Systems Reliability – UKAEA, by the Council for National Academic awards.

He is Founding Chairman of the Quality Methods Association, which incorporates the UK Taguchi Club, and Founding Chairman of the East Midlands Quality Club. This club was formed by a joint initiative between the Quality Unit at Nottingham Polytechnic and major organizations within the East Midlands to promote and support quality improvement in all aspects of business life throughout the district.

Professor Bendell has been involved in Services Ltd since 1983. The company specializes in assisting companies to implement total quality management. In addition to in-house courses, public courses are run on numerous subjects including total quality management, the tools of quality, ISO9000, statistical process control, Taguchi methodology and reliability analysis.

Services Ltd have been awarded a grant by the DTI to produce a set of 6–7 training videos to assist British Companies implement total quality management.

A prolific author, Professor Bendell has authored or jointly authored more than 100 articles or papers on quality and reliability methods. Among the books he has published are: *Taguchi Methods: Applications in World Industry*, A Bendell, J Disney and W A Pridmore (Eds), IFS/Springer Verlag, 1989; *The Quality Gurus – What They Can Do For Your Company?* (booklet) A Bendell, DTI/The Enterprise Initiative, 1989, 1991; *Taguchi Methods Within Total Quality*, A Bendell, G Wilson and R Millar, IFS, 1990; *Japanese Quality Methods*, A Bendell, Elsevier Applied Science (to appear 1992).

Over the past few years Professor Bendell has given numerous presentations on TQM, quality methods and tools, reliability, etc throughout the UK, Europe and the World. These include presentations for the DTI, CBI and professional societies.

During 1991 at the invitation of the Indian Government and the Indian Institute of Directors he visited India twice, to participate in the World Congress on Total Quality and to run TQM seminars for industry. He also visited Hong Kong twice at the invitation of the Government to run seminars on TQM, SPC and the tools of quality for industry and to advise the Industry Department.

Richard Coleman has been with Rank Xerox for 20 years, and has been a member of the Quality Office within the company's International Headquarters since 1984, when work on implementing the Leadership Through Quality process was first started. His main responsibilities during that time have related to the development and implementation of training programmes which have supported the progressive evolution of the strategy.

Dr Barrie Dale is Senior Lecturer and Director of the University of Manchester Institute of Science and Technology Quality Management Centre. The centre is involved in three main activities: TQM research; the operation of a TQM Multi-Company Teaching Programme, involving at any one time eight industrial collaborators; and education and training in TQM, including the Ford Motor Company Regional Training Centre for training suppliers in SPC – some training is also carried out for the Motorola Corporation. Dr Dale is co-editor of the *International Journal of Quality and Reliability Management* and co-author of *Managing Quality* published by Philip Allan, *Quality Costing* published by Chapman and Hall and *Quality Improvement Through Standards* by Stanley Thornes. He is a Non-Executive Director of Manchester Circuits Ltd.

G Douglas Denyer was a wartime State Scholar, reading Metallurgy at the University of Wales. He spent 20 years in Industry working in research, pilot and production manufacture, technical service and personnel departments. He then spent 20 years in local government concerned with management training, information and intelligence, computing and quality consultancy before moving to the Institute of Quality Assurance where he has worked with the national Scheme for Assessor Registration (TickIT Officer), as Secretary of the British Quality Association and its BQ Awards Officer.

His interests include travel, gardening, crosswords and the occasional round of 'coarse' golf.

Dr David Lascelles is both Chief Executive of Q-MAS Ltd. (a total quality management consultancy linked to the UMIST Quality Management Centre) and the EFQM's Programme Manager for Research. Prior to this he was a lecturer in the Manchester School of Management at UMIST, and has held positions in sales, marketing and project management in the mechanical engineering and steel stockholding industries. Dr Lascelles received the 1989 European Quality Award for Best Doctoral Thesis on quality management.

Ted Merry CCol, ASDC, with 25 years' experience in production environment including 14 years in various management roles for Courtaulds Textile Division, Ted Merry joined Services Ltd in March 1991. In the field of total quality he worked in the UK branch of a Japanese textile company, as the quality improvement facilitator.

Suehiro Nakamura was born in April 1937 and after studying electro-communications at college joined Sony in 1959 as a design engineer.

Within three years, he gained his first overseas experience with Sony Corporation of America and returned to Japan in 1964 to take up a production engineering position in colour TV, manufacturing and design.

In 1966 he founded the Sony European Service Centre in Belgium and returned to Japan at the end of 1972 to take up a management position in production, planning and design for the Japanese market in Tokyo.

In 1980, Mr Nakamura joined Sony (UK) Ltd as Assistant General Manager at Bridgend, and in 1983 was promoted to General Manager. In February 1986, he was promoted to Director, and in 1988, he became Managing Director of Sony Manufacturing Company UK.

He has been a member of the CBI Welsh Council for three years and is a founder governor of the Welsh Quality Centre.

He and his wife live in Bridgend. His elder son, Tadashi, has recently returned to Japan after completing his degree at university in London, and is working as a semiconductor engineer at Sony Corporation. His younger son Kenji is attending university in Japan.

Mr Nakamura's main hobby is golf and he is both a member of the local golf club and President of the Sony Golfing Society. His regret is that work pressure and frequent foreign travel mean he is unable to play as often as he would like.

In January 1991, he was assigned to the position of Senior General Manager, TV Group and returned to Tokyo. In this position he has responsibility for TV manufacturing worldwide.

Dr Henry R Neave is Statistics lecturer at the University of Nottingham and Director of Education and Research in the British Deming

Association. He is author of *The Deming Dimension*, an eminently readable, comprehensive and up-to-date account of the Deming management philosophy. The British Deming Association is a not-for-profit educational and research organization dedicated to spreading awareness and deepening understanding of Deming's work both in Britain and further afield.

Peter Pring is Director, Customer & External Affairs for 3M United Kingdom PLC, based in Bracknell, Berkshire. He was born in 1939 in Surrey and now lives in Wokingham, Berkshire. He holds an MA in Modern History from Oxford University, and joined 3M in September 1961 as a sales coordinator, before being appointed export office supervisor, then production control supervisor at the Aycliffe Plant. He then moved into personnel as manager of that discipline at the Gorseinon Plant and was later appointed General Manager of personnel at 3M United Kingdom PLC in Bracknell.

In his current assignment he is responsible for customer service, public affairs and public relations.

Peter Pring is a fellow of the Institute of Personnel Management, a director of 3M Manufacturing Ltd and a member of the Southern Regional Council of the CBI.

David Procter, during his twenty year career in personnel management with British Steel, has held appointments in training and employee relations. In his previous appointment of Personnel Manager – Steelmaking and Flat products he had wide experience of the management of change. Since 1988 he has used this experience to manage the development of Total Quality at General Steels, Teesside one of the five major integrated Steelworks within the United Kingdom.

Bill Quirke is a consultant specializing in helping organizations use communication in the management of change. As Managing Director of *People in Business* he has worked internationally with blue chip organizations in both the public and private sectors, helping them achieve better results by changing employee attitudes and behaviour. He was a board director of Burson-Marsteller, one of the world's largest corporate communication consultancies, where he specialized in employee communication. He combines experience in organizational and management development from his initial training with TBA, a New York based human resources consultancy.

Ken Sanders became managing director of Texas Instruments Limited in June 1987, following two years as marketing director of TI's North European Semiconductor Division. After graduating from Queen Mary College, London, with an Honours degree in Physics, he spent four years at Marconi laboratories before joining TI in 1972 as a Process Engineer in the Quality Assurance department. In this role, and later as Engineering Manager for bipolar semiconductor products, he represented TI on numerous local and international standards committees for which he travelled to many countries including Russia, Taiwan, Canada and El Salvador.

In 1979 he became Video Products Manager, leading a team of engineers in Bedford who developed the first set of integrated circuits for the Teletext and Viewdata market. This led to his first operations management role and, subsequently, to assuming responsibility for Microsystem and Semicustom products before becoming manager for Linear IC products throughout Europe. He became TIL's Marketing Director for the North European Semiconductor division in 1985, and succeeded Peter van Cuylenburg as Managing Director in 1987.

Quality improvement: the motivation and means of starting the process

D. M. Lascelles and B. G. Dale

Introduction

During the last decade, organizations in the Western world have been subjected to a clarion call that the quality of products and services need to be improved to the level of their superior company counterparts. All the available evidence points to the fact that product and service quality is regarded by most producers, customers and consumers as more important than ever before in their manufacturing, service and purchasing strategies. Despite a notable activity devoted to the theme by a wide variety of dedicated people and organizations, there still exists a considerable number of firms where the prevalent attitude amongst the senior management team is 'Let us meet the production schedule first and then, if there is time, attend to quality', 'We do not receive many customer complaints so we can't have any problems with the quality of our products and service' 'Our priority is profits, accounts and systems', etc.

What motivates an organization's management to change such traditional attitudes, prejudices and practices to one in which product and service quality becomes their number one priority? Unfortunately there is no easy answer. Changing the behaviour and culture of an organization is extremely difficult; organizations by their very nature are not meant to change. They are social structures intended to make behaviour more predictable and efficient by rationalizing and depersonalizing it in the form of a bureaucracy. The bureaucratic sophistication of modern organizations works against change to the extent that organizations usually develop an inbuilt resistance to it over the years.

Organizational change can, therefore, never be spontaneous; good reasons must exist for it to happen. Strong forces or triggers must be present to precipitate the process of change, and these may be present both inside and outside an organization.

The quality improvement process often results from the existence of one or more forces or triggers. The chapter opens by discussing these agents of change and is followed by an outline of how companies start a process of quality improvement.

Forces/Triggers for Quality Improvement

An analysis was made by the authors of a considerable number of quality case histories presented at ministerial working luncheons as part of the then Department of Trade and Industry's (DTI) National Quality Campaign. From this analysis, a study of the literature, discussions with various managers and personal speculation, the hypothesis was advanced that the chief executive officer (CEO), competition, demanding customers, a greenfield venture and a restart situation are the main change forces or triggers that precipitate a process of quality improvement in an organization, whether it be involved in manufacture, commerce or service.

It was concluded from this piece of work that demanding customers are the most effective agent for change. In addition to providing tangible proof of the need for improvement they also have the potential for actually bringing about a more permanent change in supplier behaviour and attitudes towards quality improvement, by direct intervention and providing the resources to teach and help the supplier to implement and successfully use quality management tools and techniques.

To provide some quantitative evidence on the perceived influence of the five forces/triggers, respondents to three separate questionnaire surveys (suppliers to three major automotive companies[1] and CEOs[2] and respondents to the Second International Conference on TQM organized by IFS Conferences[3] were asked by the authors to identify the factors that provided the motivation to start a formal process of quality improvement. The response to this question (shown in Table 1.1) supports the earlier view that demanding customers are indeed the most effective.

The five forces/triggers are now described.

Table 1.1.   Factors which motivated the launch of a formal quality improvement process

Factor	Survey of automotive suppliers by Lascelles and Dale (1) (N = 246) Number	Survey of chief executives by Lascelles and Dale (2) (N = 41) Number	Survey of delegates at the TQM 2 Conference by Dale (3) (N = 85) Number	Total
Demanding customers	190	30	41	261
Need to reduce costs, etc.	164	26	47	237
Chief executive	142	24	38	204
Competitors	86	14	35	135
Others	26	4	12	42
Restart situation	10	2	3	15
Greenfield venture	4	0	0	4

The chief executive officer

Internationally famous authors on the subject of total quality management (TQM)[4-8] are all agreed that unless the CEO takes the lead in a process of quality improvement, any attempts and improvements made by individuals and departments will only be transient in nature. In the majority of cases CEOs will not be the sole trigger; they are more likely to be one of a combination of forces (typically with either or both competition and demanding customers).

The following factors are likely to influence the effectiveness of the CEO as a force for change:

1 Internal factors such as: personality and managerial philosophy; knowledge of TQM in terms of strategy and working practices; career background; newness to the job; organizational culture (e.g. history, ownership, people, location, management style), and the attitudes towards TQM within the parent company.

2 Environmental factors which produce a reaction on the part of the CEO and lead to positive action include: static profit levels; privatization; attractiveness of products to the market-place; type of production process; state of manufacturing technology; joint venture agreement, for example with an organization more advanced in its quality thinking and improvement activities; and the implications of other strategic actions on which the company may have embarked (e.g. diversification of products, technological innovation to maintain a market lead over competitors and image building to win customer credibility).

Competition

Competition is fierce in world markets and product and service quality is becoming increasingly recognized as the prime consideration in many purchasing decisions. Fitness for purpose and reliability are now an essential part of the marketing mix as companies seek ways to effectively differentiate their products from those of the competitors and use quality as the means of increasing their market share. Most successful companies (in market share terms) now advertise their product on the basis of quality and reliability rather than price; (e.g. the Ford Motor Company advertising slogan, 'Ford cares about quality', and that of Esso, 'quality at work'). On the other hand, in a number of markets quality performance of around 100 parts per million (PPM) or less is the accepted norm and organizations who fail to meet this level do not get orders.

Similarly, new technology, product innovation, attractiveness of products, short product development and market response times, cost-effectiveness, all combine to form the cutting edge of competition. Such competitive forces compel companies to deploy the latest state-of-the-art management techniques and methods throughout their operations; this includes a process of continuous quality improvement.

There are numerous well-publicized instances (e.g. the DTI's 'case for quality'[9] where intense competition has been the change agent driving companies to adopt the concept and principles of TQM and a process of quality improvement in order to improve product and service quality to a level which satisfies the needs and expectations of the marketplace. The alternative is to go out of business or, at the very least, to lose market share or withdraw from that market.

The effectiveness of competition as a force for change depends on its severity in a particular market or industry. The tougher the competition the greater the likelihood that companies will be motivated to improve product and service quality in a bid to maintain or increase market share. Contributory factors may be classed as either 'defensive' or 'offensive'. These factors should be recognized in planning quality improvement objectives.

Defensive factors result from competitive forces (or changes in them). These include: profits squeezed under competitive pressure; loss of market share due to entry into the market by overseas competitors committed to TQM and continuous quality improvement; changes in market structure; rationalization following market contraction due to economic recession; and the attitudes and behaviour of buyers in export markets.

Offensive factors are linked to some kind of proactive strategy designed to give a company a competitive lead. These include: breakthrough to improve product and service quality in advance of that of competitors; product innovation strategies; and corporate image building.

Demanding customers

A demanding customer with high product and service quality expectations can result in a supplier adopting a more effective quality system, developing advanced quality planning methods and systems, and introducing specific quality management tools and techniques to retain the business, especially if the customer provides a major part of the company's business and that this is profitable.

A number of major purchasers have now articulated and documented what is required from their supplier communities: (e.g. the Ford Motor Company's worldwide quality system standard Q-101 and Q1 requirements[10] and the Nissan Motor Manufacturing (UK)s 'the Nissan way'[11]. These documents describe fundamentals which must be incorporated in each supplier's quality planning methods and quality system to control and improve product quality on a continuous basis. Each supplier is responsible for building on these fundamentals to develop an effective quality system and provide products which are free from defects. Such companies have made it part of their business to help their suppliers improve product quality. Their staff spend time in suppliers' plants giving practical advice and assistance. Companies that take an active interest in the business of their suppliers are likely to provoke a far-reaching effect on the way that suppliers manage quality improvement.

The relevant contributory factors of demanding customers can be divided into the following four groups:

1   Nature of market (e.g. hi-tech, National Health Service, Ministry of Defence, Civil Aviation Authority, Pacific Rim).
2   Nature of the product/service (e.g. reliability essential, legal/other mandatory requirements, value and/or premium placed on product/ service).
3   Influence of major customers (e.g. strength of customer purchasing power, quality audits, adoption of a certain quality system standard, such as the BS5750/ISO9000 series[12]).
4   Marketing strategy (e.g. upgrading product quality specification to satisfy the target market segment, diversification into markets with more exacting quality requirements, exporting to Japan and her Pacific Rim neighbours, market research data, competitive benchmarking).

Greenfield venture

A greenfield venture may be defined as: a new company; a new operational direction for an existing company (e.g. creation of a new strategic business unit as part of a diversification programme); a company setting up in a new factory; and an existing company establishing a new operation in its old premises after a clearout of plant, product lines, manpower, etc.

A greenfield venture provides the opportunity for the introduction of an effective, unambiguous approach to TQM in a situation where the traditions of inadequate conformance levels and performance do not exist. In such a situation everything starts from scratch so there is no vested interest and inhibiting behaviour, attitudes and prejudices to overcome. The Japanese companies establishing a manufacturing base in the UK have followed this approach. It presents an opportunity for management to do all those things the experts and textbooks say should be done to make sure output is right first time in a cost-effective way from the outset.

The factors influencing the effectiveness of a greenfield venture as a trigger for change may be divided into two categories: endogenous and exogenous.

Endogenous factors include the personality/background of the CEO or founding entrepreneur; parent company's quality system and attitude towards TQM and quality improvement (if the greenfield venture is the offshoot of another company); and the reasons for establishing the venture (e.g. marketing strategy, research and development opportunity, organizational restructuring).

Exogenous factors include geographical location, perhaps in an area that has an attractive infrastructure (e.g. 'Silicon Glen' in Scotland or Telford in Shropshire, UK – an area in which a relatively large number of Japanese manufacturers are situated), or an area close to a major customer (e.g. the North East of England and Nissan Motor Manufacturing (U.K.) or Derby in the UK and Toyota Motor Corporation); the nature of the market or industry; and customer attitudes and traditional purchasing patterns (e.g. a new supplier sees the adoption of a demonstrable quality system or the use of a particular quality management technique as a way of gaining credibility with potential customers).

Restart after hiatus

A hiatus, no matter how brief, brought about by an interruption of the operation of a company or a manufacturing site, may present the kind of opportunity for a new start normally associated with a greenfield venture. Some form of financial or organizational restructuring, including a merger between two or more companies, a takeover by another company and management buyout, or a major catastrophe (e.g. the fire that in the late 1970s destroyed the Manchester Transmission Plant of Eaton Limited) could be the catalyst for such a change.

Overview

The five trigger forces were originally viewed as separate elements, however, from case study work carried out and reported elsewhere[13] it would be more realistic to see them as links in a chain. The 'market-led' paradigm of quality improvement causation competition acts as a catalyst setting off a chain reaction which enhances quality awareness in the market, resulting in demanding customers and the CEO behaving as change agents so that awareness and motivation is cascaded down through the organization as illustrated in Figure 1.

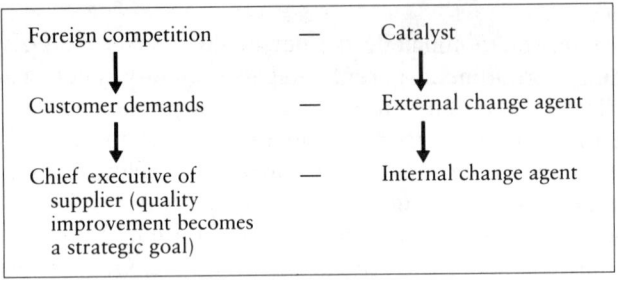

Figure 1.1   *Market-led paradigm of quality improvement*

The generally accepted definition[14] of a change agent is a person (or group of people) involved in the implementation of change. Our definition of a change agent is a person (or group of people) who causes change as well as implementing it. In both definitions, change agents are people. Therefore, the CEO and customers can be defined as change agents, but competition (that is a dynamic set of market forces), greenfield ventures and restart situations cannot.

If, by definition, competition cannot be regarded as a change agent it can still be regarded as a primary catalyst of quality improvement. In addition to the elevation of quality as a component of the marketing mix, a shift has occurred in the fundamental nature of international competition that involves the effectiveness of the management of quality improvement activities. For competition to be an effective catalyst, the CEO must recognize the nature of this paradigm shift and its strategic implications for the business, whether it is the need to fill a potential quality gap in the marketplace or as a means of exploiting a market opportunity. However, the effects of competition as a catalyst are probably indirect in many cases. The research evidence indicates that many companies do not bother to monitor the actions of their competitors very closely. For example, questionnaire survey evidence[1] reveals that out of 246 automotive suppliers with a formal quality improvement process only 62% evaluated competitors' products and only 32% engaged in market research. The structural shift in global competition has resulted in greater pressures on the cost structures of manufacturing industries, and it is this need to reduce costs (an outcome of competitive forces rather than the marketing activities of direct competitors) that is the real catalyst of change in most instances.

Demanding customers can be seen as the key external change agent and the CEO as the key internal change agent, and there is little doubt that most companies are reactive to direct customer pressure. However, demanding customers will not bring about change on their own. In a number of cases demanding customers have failed to effect lasting improvement because the CEO did not support the improvement process.

Greenfield ventures or restart situations are not in themselves change agents but opportunities for change acting as positive enhancers of the environment which is conducive to change. Both can also be used as techniques of change. To artificially create a greenfield venture can be very effective in aiding short-term change as no major shift in the overall organizational culture is required initially, although any gains will be relatively short lived without company-wide organizational change. Similarly, a restart situation in the form of an organizational or financial restructuring might be used as an expedient measure to eliminate traditional roadblocks to change which typically exist within organizations which have been in existence for a long time and have well-established traditions and culture.

To summarize, the motivators of quality improvement are seen as belonging to one of the following three categories:

1 Catalysts of change:
   (a) Competition;
   (b) Costs.
2 Change agents:
   (a) Demanding customers;
   (b) The chief executive.
3 Change opportunities:
   (a) Greenfield ventures;
   (b) Restart situation.

Starting Quality Improvement

Once an organization has been motivated to try and improve product and service quality how do they go about it? Unfortunately, there is no 'surefire recipe' for starting the process of quality improvement. If there was, some people would have earned considerable monies from providing and applying the 'recipe'.

When an organization's senior management team reach the stage where they want to translate their motivation and enhanced quality awareness into effective action they typically seek answers to questions such as: What should we do? What advice to we need? From who should we be taking advice? Can we get impartial advice? Which of the gurus' teachings should we adopt? What TQM packages/approaches should we buy? What TQM training courses/conferences should we attend? Should we call in a management consultant? Should we develop our quality system to meet the requirements of the BS5750/ISO9000 series? What quality management tools and techniques should we use?

Their dilemma is often compounded not just by a lack of knowledge of TQM and the process of quality improvement but also by a lack of experience in managing organizational change, because, this is exactly what TQM and quality improvement is about. The overwhelming quantity and variety of available advice, which is often conflicting and sometimes biased, simply adds to the confusion. It is not surprising then that there is sometimes inertia on the part of senior management teams who are faced with the task of introducing a process of formal quality improvement in their organizations. Smith[15] calls this 'total quality paralysis'. He says: 'Just deciding where to begin is so difficult that many never get off the starting block'. In addition, if the bulk of the responsibility for choosing the method and means of getting started rests with a manager to whom the task has been delegated then there is a certain amount of concern, in terms of future career prospects, about making the correct choice and as a direct result there is often a tendency to select the safest option which may not be the best for their organization. We believe the term 'total quality paralysis' is perhaps a little extreme. In our experience, whilst senior management may be uncertain how to structure and start a process of quality improvement, almost all have initiated some kind of quality improvement activity in their respective organizations.

It is interesting to note that some writers seem to cringe as they report half-baked organizational quality improvement initiatives. For example, Rohan[16] tells the story of one chief executive officer who bought 15,000 copies of Crosby's book *Quality is Free*, had them distributed to all his company's employees, and then six months later complained bitterly that nothing had happened.

There are four main ways in which an organization can typically start a process of quality improvement:

- By applying quality management tools or techniques.
- By applying the 'received wisdom' of any one of the quality management gurus.
- By awarding a contract to one of the major quality management consultancies and applying the purchased 'package'.
- By developing the existing quality system to meet the requirements of the BS5750/ISO9000 series or the quality system standard of a major purchasing organization.

Organizations are also likely to use a combination of these four methods to get started, in which they develop for themselves a vision, quality objectives, policy, strategy, an approach and a route map for quality improvement and TQM.

Table 2, based on a survey by Dale[3] of delegates attending the second

Table 1.2. *How organizations started the process of TQM*

Method	Number of respondents (N = 71)
Adopted the teachings of one of the quality management gurus	37
Crosby (23)	
Juran (14)	
Deming (6)	
Feigenbaum (4)	
The quality assurance system – obtaining accreditation to BS.5750	33
Developed their own quality objectives and strategy from the published literature on the subject, discussions with other practitioners, visits to other companies, competitive benchmarking, etc.	32
Used the services of a major quality management consultancy.	27
The use of a particular TQM tool and technique	21

International Conference on Total Quality Management (TQM-2), shows the ways in which organizations got started and/or plan to start on TQM. The most popular method was adopting the teachings of one of the quality management gurus, followed by quality system certification and organizations developing their own tailor-made approach after assimilating the available knowledge on the subject.

Applying Quality Management Tools and Techniques

One approach is for an organization to adopt and apply a specific quality management tool or technique, perhaps to satisfy the contractual requirements of a major customer, and use it to initiate and structure the process of quality improvement. However, irrespective of the TQM approach chosen by the organization they will undoubtedly need to use a selection of quality management tools and techniques to assist with the process of quality improvement, from introduction to its development and advancement.

It is important that organizations do not rush headlong into the use of a plethora of tools and techniques. The techniques used could be those specified as a contractual requirement by a major customer, they may be what management believe the marketplace will be expecting in the future, or the view may be taken that the use of a specific technique will give the organization an edge over the competition. As might be expected, customer pressure can influence the use of specific quality management techniques. For example, among the major automotive companies in the UK, the Ford Motor Company are leaders in the promotion and use of SPC by applying it in their own manufacturing plants, and in requiring that suppliers provide them with statistical evidence of process capability and demonstrate commitment to the pursuit of continuous improvement. The same is now happening with regard to 'failure mode and effects analysis' (FMEA) and other advanced quality planning methods.

Dale and Shaw[17] report that when a major customer insists upon the use of a specific quality management technique as a contractual requirement of its suppliers, two phases can be clearly identified in its use. Firstly, the technique in question is applied by the supplier just to satisfy the demands of the customer in order to maintain the business. During this phase the supplier often resorts to a number of camouflage measures, fakes and ruses to convince the customer that the technique is being applied in an effective and beneficial manner. The emphasis in this phase is on satisfying the customer's paperwork requirements. They go on to make the point that this phase is wasteful in terms of time and resources but suggest that suppliers appear to need this phase to develop their awareness and understanding of the technique which is being applied. The second phase begins when the supplier's management team starts to question how they might best use the technique to enhance the company's competitive position. This is when the quality improvement fuse has been lit. They also point out that motor industry suppliers appear to have reached this second phase in a shorter period of time with FMEA than they did with SPC, which is indicative of the learning experience.

The approach recommended by Dale and Shaw to suppliers in the use of quality management tools and techniques is that followed by the managing director of a printed circuit board manufacturer with whom they have close ties – 'Forget the Ford Motor Company and General Motors: we need SPC for our own corporate well-being.'

Quality management tools and techniques fulfill a number of roles. For example, planning for quality, improving the design of the product and process, listening to the voice of the process, improving the process, controlling the process, capturing and documenting quality system data, solving problems, involving people, motivating and promoting quality awareness. It is important that the management team are fully aware of the main purpose and use of a particular tool or technique. If not, they will soon become frustrated if the technique fails to produce the anticipated result.

We believe that a number of companies use quality management techniques without thinking through the implications for a TQM strategy or how the concept will be developed and advanced within the organization. This can give rise to misconceptions and misunderstandings that eventually become barriers to progress. The evidence we have acquired indicates that the majority of companies who use specific tools and techniques as the springboard to quality improvement usually single out a specific technique, sometimes apparently at random, and apply it with undue haste without giving sufficient thought to issues such as:

- How will the technique facilitate the quality improvement process?
- What is the fundamental purpose of the technique? Is it used to gather data or to facilitate continuous improvement? What will it achieve? Will it produce benefits if applied on its own?
- Is the technique right for the company's product, processes, people and culture?
- Are we receiving the right advice?

- What organizational changes are necessary to make the most effective use of the technique?
- What is the best method of introducing and then using the technique?
- What are the resources, skills, information, training, etc. required to introduce the technique successfully?
- Has the company the management skills and resources, and the commitment to make it work successfully?
- How will it fit in with, complement, or support other techniques, methods and quality systems already in place, and any that might be introduced in the future?
- What are the limitations, if any, of the technique?

It is important for managers to address such questions when considering the introduction of a quality management technique. Unfortunately, some managers are always looking for techniques as a quick-fix solution to the problems facing their organization at a particular point in time. In general, management teams who are 'technique reactive' tend to be unclear on the concept of TQM and the management of quality improvement. They often confuse the implementation of a particular technique with TQM and tend to use the technique as an end in itself rather than as a means to an end. This approach is also symptomatic of Western managers' desire for 'quick-fix' solutions, as described by authors such as Goldsmith and Clutterbuck[18] and Peters and Austin[19]. For example, one company we studied chose as its quality improvement drivers, high-profile 'glory' techniques (namely quality circles, SPC and Taguchi Design of Experiment methods in that order) as each came in vogue. Because each of these techniques was introduced in an *ad hoc* fashion, the long-term results were disappointing in spite of considerable managerial attention, training, resources, energy and money devoted to them. The senior management of this company have now realized that quality improvement cannot be 'implemented' in this way.

The benefits of starting with a limited number of quality management techniques is that the process of improvement gets under way relatively quickly, employees are involved and feel they are making a worthwhile contribution, quality awareness is enhanced, and behaviour and attitude changes start to happen, albeit slowly. When the process of quality improvement is begun in this way, it is important that: the senior management team ensures that they themselves have a good understanding of the techniques, to be employed, particularly in the case of statistical methods, so that they can have a common dialogue with people using the techniques; everyone in the company is aware that any technique is not an end in itself; that improvement objectives and strategies have been developed; that a quality awareness, education and training programme has been formulated and is in place; and that the organization has a route map for the techniques which it intends to apply.

The major danger with a preoccupation with specific techniques, without an adequate understanding of TQM and the quality improvement process, is that tools and techniques are picked up and discarded as fashion changes; an analogy can be made to a magician pulling magic balls out of the air or rabbits out of a hat. When this happens and the techniques fail to meet expectations, disillusionment sets in and the company will experience considerable difficulty convincing their employees they are serious about product and service quality improvement. This, of course, has an adverse effect on the future use of techniques in the organization. One of the main reasons that companies fall into this trap is that they have undue high expectations of the benefits arising from the use of a single technique, much of this is a result of the hype which often accompanies specific techniques. Organizations should never attempt to isolate the benefits arising from any one tool or technique. In general, on its own a single technique will produce only a small incremental improvement. It is only the result of the cumulative effect of a series of techniques within a strategic framework of TQM that the organization starts to see some real long-term benefits from its quality improvement endeavours.

Because of the variety of starting points and motivations for quality improvement it is not possible to identify a universal implementation plan detailing the order in which specific techniques should be used by an organization. However, one piece of advice which we can offer is that organizations should start with the simpler techniques such as the seven original quality control tools[20] and techniques to facilitate teamwork. Simple tools and techniques can be just as effective as the more complex ones. In the West we do have the tendency to ignore the simple techniques in our haste to use what are perceived to be the more complex, fashionable and 'high-powered' techniques. We, also have the tendency to use techniques in isolation, a case in point is control charts. This should be contrasted to the case in Japanese companies: they tend to use the seven original quality control tools together and visibly display the results on a quality control notice board (termed an MQ station); in this way they are not only listening to the process through control charts but taking action to improve it and this combined use of the seven tools obviously facilitates problem resolution and improvement action.

When selecting quality management techniques there are two factors which organizations should keep in mind. Firstly, the application of any tool and technique in isolation without a TQM strategy and long-range management vision will only provide short-term benefits. For tools and techniques to be effective over the longer-term major organizational changes in behaviour and attitude are needed. Secondly, no one tool or technique is more important than another, they all have a role to play at some point in the quality improvement process. It is a mistake to single one out for special attention; the Japanese make the point that a warrior should never have a favourite weapon.

Our research evidence indicates that there is an approximate hierarchy of quality management technique usage. This progresses from the basic techniques, such as inspection and keeping of records, then as a company starts to develop its quality management system and approach to a quality improvement, more sophisticated tools and techniques are used; this corresponds to the phases of inspection, quality control and quality assurance in the evolution of TQM.

Applying the 'Received Wisdom'

Another approach is for an organization to assimilate and then adopt the writings and teachings of one of the internationally recognized quality management experts[4, 5, 6 and 8] and follow whole-heartedly the advice and methods expounded by the chosen expert. The rationale is that this approach provides a coherent framework and gives discipline to the process, enabling people to have a common language and understanding and in this way helping to reduce confusion. Moreover; because they are all well-proven packages they represent security. To facilitate this, some companies have purposely opted for the simplest package. Dale[3] in his survey of TQM-2 delegates found that Crosby and Juran were the most frequently used experts. It is interesting to note that the approach of Crosby is generally recognized as being the easiest to follow.

All the companies we have studied that took this approach did utilize the work of the other quality management experts once their quality improvement process had got underway. This is understandable because none of the experts has all the answers to the problems facing an organization; despite each guru and their supporters stressing the exclusivity of their approaches/methods.

As with quality management tools and techniques, whichever expert's 'package'/approach is adopted it should be treated as a means to assist the quality improvement process and not as an end in itself. It is not unusual for a company to buy a guru's package, and then allow it to fall into disuse once the initial enthusiasm wears off. This is usually because the management team fail to see real-life in-company applications and benefits. For example, in one of our case studies a company had purchased the Juran package[21] but had not used it to any great extent, they were now introducing SPC. Until it was pointed out, senior management did not see the connection between the use of SPC, and the problem-solving techniques and team work skills which can be fostered from the use of the Juran training methods.

The ways of approaching quality management as suggested by Crosby, Deming, Feigenbaum and Juran are variations on a theme, the essential difference is the focus of their approach. Several commentators, for example Fine[22], Main[23], Geeruliet[24], and Bendell[25] have compared and contrasted the approaches of the four gurus. Broadly speaking, the teaching of these four gurus can be characterized by the main focus of their approach, as follows:

- Crosby company-wide motivation
- Deming statistical process control
- Feigenbaum systems management
- Juran project management

Is there any sure-fire route TQM for those seeking, the 'philosopher's touchstone'? Are these really conflicting or mutually exclusive choices? The short answer is that there is no quick-fire solution and that these four approaches are compatible.

Advocates of each guru are apt to claim that 'their man's' approach is the only one likely to work. This is an arrogant and myopic stance to adopt; each approach has its strengths and weaknesses and they are all proven packages. It is also worth remembering that all four gurus are consultants and it is in their business interests to distinguish their approach from that of their peers and appear to have all the answers. McBryde[26] says that the 'golden thread' running through the philosophies of all four (and other, unnamed) gurus is the concept of adopting quality as a fundamental business strategy permeating the culture of the entire organization. Fine[22] concludes that the teachings of Crosby, Deming and Juran (Feigenbaum is not included in his comparison) have four points in common:

- The importance of top management support and participation.
- The need for workforce training and education.

- Quality management requires careful planning and a philosophy of company-wide involvement.
- Quality improvement must represent permanent, ongoing activities.

In the final analysis, irrespective of the approach, package, system, etc., it is the senior management team's commitment to making quality improvement work and understanding what they are doing which is the key to long-term success.

As a final point on this discussion of gurus we suggest that any person interested in learning about any of these quality management gurus goes to the source of the original work rather than that of their disciples.

The Japanese wisdom

In discussions concerning the use of quality management experts in quality improvement it would be an oversight not to mention the TQM wisdom and experience which is undoubtedly possessed by the Japanese. In recent years the work and ideas of a number of Japanese quality management experts have been published in English and, therefore, made more accessible to the majority of Western managers and scholars. They, include Imai[27], Ishikawa[7], Mizuno[28], Nemoto[29], Shingo[30], Suzaki[31] and Taguchi[32].

The Japanese typically treat the management of quality as waste reduction in its broadest sense and their goal is continual improvement towards perfection. They allocate responsibility for quality improvement among all employees. The shopfloor workers are primarily responsible for improvement activities. Managers do less maintaining and more on planning and improving. At the highest levels, the emphasis is on breakthrough activities and on teamwork throughout the organization.

The 'loss function' concept of Taguchi[32] typifies the target-focused approach of the Japanese quality management philosophy. Taguchi defines the quality of a product as: '. . . the loss imparted to society from the time the product is shipped.' Among the losses he includes consumers' dissatisfaction, warranty costs, loss of reputation and, ultimately, loss of market share. He maintains that a product does not start causing losses only when it is out of specification, but when there is any deviation from the target value. Further, in most cases the loss to society can be represented by a quadratic function, i.e. the loss increases as the square of the deviation from the target value. This leads to the important conclusion that quality (as defined by Taguchi) is most economically achieved by minimizing variance, rather than by strict conformance to specification.

There are a number of now-familiar concepts associated with Japanese total quality control (TQC). These include; the next person or process is the customer, listening to the voice of the customer, commitment to improvement and perfection, elimination of waste, insistence on compliance to procedures and correcting one's own errors. Various practices facilitate TQC in Japanese corporations – quality policy deployment, quality function deployment, use of statistical methods (simple and advanced), daily management control, housekeeping, successive and self-check systems, mistake-proofing, detailed quality assurance procedures, the just-in-time (JIT) philosophy, total productive maintenance (TPM) and quality control circles (QC circles).

In the West, there is a fascination with Japanese management styles and techniques. However, many admirers of 'Japan Incorporated' stand accused of wanting to copy directly without properly assimilating and understanding the lessons of Japanese business. Snowdon[33] calls this the 'factory tour' or 'read a book about Japan' approach. As he points out, the Japanese have developed their present industrial structures over a period of four decades; so it is not surprising that it takes more than a few days to assimilate the results. There is also the added danger of substantive issues being confused with cultural issues. Dorsky[34] cautions readers not to blindly emulate Japanese practices; Japanese problems and responses may, out of necessity, be different from those of the West. A number of writers on the Japanese approach to quality management[35–38] agree that there is one fundamental lesson to be learned: it requires commitment, patience and tenacity.

Applying a Consultancy Package

Some companies (usually large concerns) decide to adopt the programme of one of the major quality management consultancies on the grounds that it is a self-contained package which can be suitably customized for application throughout their organization. Some companies are very comfortable with consultants, others not so.

It is important for a company to understand that the use of a consultant organization does not relieve the board of their own responsibilities for TQM, it is their responsibility to own the improvement process and to exercise leadership. The company should never allow the consultant to become the 'TQM champion'. The consultants should be perceived by the organization as an 'implementation tool' and not as an initiator of TQM and the improvement process. More often than not the consultant is learning on the job and any ideas, proposals and decisions should always be scrutinized carefully by the TQM steering committee for their applicability to the company's operations.

These quality management consultant organizations bring their expertise to the company and provide the resources and catalyst for getting the process started. The consultants are usually involved in a wide range of activities from planning through to training and project work and implementation of specific improvement initiatives.

A company intending to use a consultant organization must carefully consider the method for selecting the management consultancy and sometimes the individual consultant who is most suited to their needs. There are a number of factors to be taken into consideration including, personality of consultant and the perceived interaction with the people with whom they will work, presentation and proposal made, previously published material, reputation of the consultancy organization and individual consultant with existing clients, their knowledge of TQM and its application in practice in similar or related companies – not just in consulting and/or teaching, and the extent to which the consultant organization is prepared to assist in tailoring the package to suit their individual needs. The decision to use a consultant organization is usually made by the chief executive officer with support from the quality director. It is dangerous for the consultant to assume that other board members will contribute more than vocal support to the process of improvement.

The company needs to be very careful on what they are buying from a consultant organization. It is often difficult to define in precise detail what is required in a TQM assignment with the consequence that the terms of reference are vague. This sometimes results in a difference between what was ordered and delivered; wrangling over the outputs arising from a TQM contract is a major detractor in a process of continuous improvement. The company should also be wary that a TQM assignment is not used to open the door for other consultancy work in problem areas such as manufacturing management, human resources, organization development, accountancy and business management. The easiest way of selling consultancy is on the back of a short-term successful assignment; this might have a negative influence on the long-term success of TQM.

For those considering the purchase of a consultancy package, it is well worth heeding Fine's[16] advice, that individual programmes should be designed to address each of these seven areas:

- Goals and objectives
- Philosophy and strategy

- Allocation of responsibilities
- Decision tools
- Measurement systems
- Managerial style
- Plan for transition management

Developing a Quality System

In the UK, during the last decade or so, many organizations have developed their quality system to meet the requirements of the BS.5750/ ISO 9000 series[12] or equivalent third-party assessment scheme. Many more have developed an approach to quality management based on the quality system requirements of a major purchasing organization (e.g. Ford Motor Company's Q-101 Quality System Standard[10]).

Possession of a documented quality system encompassing quality management objectives, policies, organization and procedures to demonstrate compliance with an internationally recognized standard which has been assessed by either a third party, or a reputable second party, provides an effective managerial framework on which to develop a company-wide approach to continuous quality improvement; one of the main vehicles for this is the corrective action procedure. However, possession of such system certification may demonstrate an organization's capability to deliver to the customer conforming products and services but does not guarantee the management team's intent to do so; indeed possession of certification often results in a sense of complacency. In most cases there are some system lapses after approval.

Implementing a quality system which satisfies the requirements of a major customer is an effective stimulus to initiate action to achieve a short-term quality improvement objective. Furthermore, most major purchasing organizations are prepared to assist suppliers to achieve the required system certification status. However, the gains may be short-term if system certification is perceived as a contractual condition rather than as a base for further improvement activity. It is not unusual for suppliers to adopt the practice of 'stratified quality assurance' by grading their products or services according to their perception of customer purchasing power or quality system requirements. Such organizations miss the point that a documented quality system can be developed into an effective company-wide capability to satisfy all their customer requirements.

Developing a Tailor-made Organizational Route Map

A variation on the four approaches and their various combinations is to absorb the 'received wisdom' and the experiences of other companies and extract the ideas, methods and tactics which are appropriate to the particular circumstances, business situation, and environmental culture of the organization. In our experience, organizations starting with any of the four approaches will eventually use this method. A feature of organizations following this approach is that senior management will have visited other companies with a reputation for being 'centres of excellence' to see at first hand the lessons learned from TQM, and have become involved in meetings relating to TQM with executives of like minds from different companies; they are also frequent attendees at conferences and are generally well-read on the subject.

We believe that when getting started on the quality improvement process it is always beneficial for organizations to establish contacts with others that have a reputation for excellence in systems and products. There is much to be said for learning by association and competitive benchmarking agreed performance measures and practices both within the group of companies to which the organization may belong, with domestic and foreign competitors, and also with the non-competing best practices from other industries. In our experience, companies working with or competing directly against companies with advanced management processes, develop their knowledge of TQM and quality improvement at a fast rate.

Summary

Total quality management is a form of organizational change. The process of quality improvement is caused by the intervention of change agents perceived as relevant and influential to the organization. Five forces which may trigger the process have been identified and described in this chapter: the chief executive officer, competition, demanding customers, a greenfield venture, and a restart situation.

The influence of competitors, demanding customers and the chief executive officer are links in the chain of events which will lead to change. The interaction between competitors and demanding customers in changing market perceptions of quality has resulted in a structural shift in the market paradigm, which in turn has influenced the perceptions and actions of chief executives.

The chapter has also focused on the main means of getting started on quality improvement – quality management tools and techniques, the teachings of the quality management gurus, TQM consultancy, quality system development and certification, and customizing an approach based on all four methods in conjunction with the received wisdom on the subject. In our view, the means of starting quality improvement and the approach taken matters little. However, the leadership of members of the senior management team and their commitment and conviction to continuous improvement is of considerable importance.

The means and details of starting quality improvement is usually skipped over lightly by many writers on the subject of TQM and this is frustrating to those organizations wishing to consider all the available options. It is hoped that the material contained in the chapter will help to fill this gap.

References

1   Lascelles D. M. and Dale B. G., 1988, A study of the quality management methods employed by U.K. automotive suppliers, *Quality and Reliability Engineering International*, **4** (4), 301–309.

2   Lascelles D. M. and Dale B. G., 1990, Quality management: the chief executive's perceptions and role, *European Management Journal*, **8** (1), 67–75.

3   Dale B. G., 1990, *TQM2: Views, Analysis and State-of-the-Art*. IFS Publications, Bedfordshire.

4   Crosby P. B., 1979, *Quality is Free*. McGraw-Hill, New York.

5   Deming W. E., 1982, Quality, Productivity and Competition Position. Massachusetts Institute of Technology, Center for Advanced Engineering Study, Cambridge, MA.

6   Feigenbaum A. V., 1983, *Total Quality Control*. McGraw-Hill, New York.

7   Ishikawa K., 1985, *What is Total Quality Control? The Japanese Way* (translated by D. J. Lu). Prentice-Hall, Englewood Cliffs, N.J.

8   Juran J. M., 1988, (Editor-in-Chief), *Quality Control Handbook*. McGraw-Hill, New York.

9   Department of Trade and Industry, The Case for Quality, 1989, Quality, Design and Education Division, Department of Trade and Industry, London.

10 Ford Motor Company. 1990, *Worldwide Quality System Standard, Q-101*. Ford Motor Company, Plymouth, Michigan.

11 Nissan Motor Manufacturing, 1987, *Quality Presentation to Suppliers*. Nissan Motor Manufacturing (UK) Limited, Sunderland, Tyne and Wear.

12 BS.5750/ISO 9000, 1987, *Quality Systems*. British Standards Institution, London.

13   Lascelles D. M. and Dale B. G., 1989, Quality improvement: what is the motivation?, *Proceedings of the Institution of Mechanical Engineers*, **201** (B1), 43–50.
14   French W. L. and Bell C. H., 1978, *Organisational Development*. Prentice-Hall, Englewood Cliffs, N.J.
15   Smith S., 1986, *How to Take Part in the Quality Revolution: A Management Guide*. PA Management Consultants, London.
16   Rohan T. M., 1986, Selling quality to the troops, *Industry Week*, **23 June**, 54–60.
17   Dale B. G. and Shaw P., 1990, Failure mode and effects analysis in the motor industry: a state-of-the-art study, *Quality and Reliability Engineering International*, **6** (37), 179–188.
18   Goldsmith W. and Clutterbuck D., 1984, *The Winning Streak*. Weidenfeld and Nicolson, London.
19   Peters T. J. and Austin N., 1985, *A Passion for Excellence*. Collins, London.
20   Ishikawa K., 1979, *Guide to Quality Control*. Asian Productivity Organisation, Tokyo.
21   Juran J. M., 1979, *Quality Management Workbook*. Juran Enterprises, New York.
22   Fine C. H., 1985, *Managing Quality: a Comparative Assessment*. Booz Allen and Hamilton Inc., New York.
23   Main J., 1986, Under the spell of the quality guru's, *Fortune*, **18 August**, 24–27.
24   Geeruliet V., 1984, *Three of a Kind: A Reflection on the Approach to Quality*. Corporate Quality Bureau, Philips Group NV, Eindhoven.
25   Bendall T., 1989, *The Quality Gurus*. Department of Trade and Industry, London.
26   McBryde V. E., 1986, In today's market, quality is best focal point for upper management, *Industrial Engineering*, **18** (7), 51–55.
27   Imai M., 1986, *Kaizen: The Key to Japanese Competitive Success*. Random House, New York.
28   Mizuno S., *Managing for Quality Improvement – the Seven New QC Tools*. Productivity Press, Cambridge, MA.
29   Nemoto M., 1987, *Total Quality Control for Management*. Prentice Hall. Englewood Cliffs, New Jersey.
30   Shingo S., 1986, *Zero Quality Control: Source Inspection and the Poka-Yoke System*. Productivity Press, Cambridge, MA.
31   Suzaki K., 1987, *The New Manufacturing Challenge: Techniques for Continuous Improvement*. Collier Macmillan, London.
32   Taguchi G., 1986, *Introduction to Quality Engineering*. Asian Productivity Organisation, Tokyo.
33   Snowdon M., 1986, The Japanese approach to productivity and quality: a European's view, *International Journal of Technology Management*, **1** (3/4), 411–424.
34   Dorsky L. R., 1984, Management commitment to Japanese apple pie, *Quality Progress*, **17** (2), 14–18.

35 Lee S. M. and Ebrahimpour M., 1985, An analysis of Japanese quality control systems, *Advanced Management Journal*, **50** (2), 24–31.
36 McMillan C. J., 1982, From quality control to quality management: lessons from Japan, *Business Quarterly*, **47** (1), 31–40.
37 Schonberger R. J., 1982, *Japanese Manufacturing Techniques*. Free Press.
38 Trevor M., 1986, Quality control: learning from the Japanese, *Long Range Planning*, **19** (6), 46–53.

Material Used In Preparation Of This Chapter

Lascelles D. M. and Dale B. G., 1989, Quality improvement: what is the motivation?, *Proceedings of the Institution of Mechanical Engineers*, **201**, (B1), 43–50.

Lascelles D. M. and Dale B. G., 1990, The use of quality management techniques, *Quality Forum*, **16** (4), (to be published).

Dale B. G. and Plunkett J. J. (Eds), 1990, *Managing Quality*, Chapter 1 by Dale B. G., Lascelles D. M. and Plunkett J. J., The Process of Total Quality Management. Philip Allan, Hertfordshire.

Lascelles D. M. and Dale B. G., 1992, *Managing Total Quality Improvement*. IFS (Publications) Ltd.

2

Total quality management – one God
but many prophets

Max Hand

Traditionally, definitions of total quality management (TQM) have emphasized *conformance to specification* or sentiments such as *meeting customer needs consistently at lowest cost*. As companies improve, simply meeting (or conforming to) customer needs may not be enough – several competitors may be able to achieve that level of performance. Even if a customer is satisfied with a supplier, he may still switch to an alternative on the basis that he has little to lose and could conceivably gain. We prefer the definition of quality as *delighting the customer by consistently meeting and continuously improving on his requirements*.

This chapter describes our view of the basic principles of TQM. It does not draw exclusively on the thoughts of any single TQM guru – they all have unique insights to offer.

Basic concepts of Total Quality Management

Total quality management (TQM) is a strategic approach to producing the best products and services through a process of continuous improvement of every aspect of a company's operation. Contrary to some managers' perceptions, it is not solely concerned with manufacturing. The concepts are equally valid and effective in sales, finance or anywhere else. Nor is total quality synonymous with quality frameworks such as BS5750 or ISO9000. There are many companies with BS5750 accreditation who are nowhere near to being total quality companies. Equally, there are total quality companies who have felt no need to apply for the standard.

Some companies have applied the concepts very successfully to manufacturing processes. But what is the point of producing products with zero defects if the company cannot deliver the products on time, or cannot get the customer's invoice right first time?

Equally, some service companies have developed customer care programmes to improve front office dealings with customers. But the full benefits will not be obtained if the back office service fails to live up to the customers' expectations.

So, TQM is really an umbrella for a variety of improvement processes from BS5750 through to customer care, from quality control to quality function deployment, from SPC to Taguchi, and so on.

Everyone has a customer

Total quality embraces more than the external customer. It recognizes that everyone in a business provides a service. Some services happen to be provided to external customers, some to an internal customer. If the needs of an external customer are not met, he is likely to take his business elsewhere. If the needs of an internal customer are not met, he has to spend time putting things right. Either way, the business loses. In a total quality company, everyone strives to meet the needs of their customers (internal and external), and then to improve continuously the efficiency and effectiveness of the service provided.

Build partnerships with suppliers

Many businesses persist in dealing with suppliers on the basis of price tag. Indeed much of the purchasing policy of the UK public sector is based on this criteria. By now, much of manufacturing industry has learned that this leads to a proliferation of poor quality suppliers with consequential high costs of quality. The need is to move to few suppliers, or even single suppliers, based on a long-term relationship of mutual understanding of needs and loyalty and trust. This will have the effect of *reducing* total costs, not increasing them. This lesson has not yet been learned by the majority of service companies.

TQM is a strategy for competitive edge

TQM is not another name for cost reduction. The elimination of waste in all forms is a major objective of any company's TQM process. But the aim should be to redeploy resources away from wasteful activities into value added activities. This will improve customer service, flexibility and responsiveness, reduce product development lead times, and so forth. So TQM is directed at enhancing competitive edge and thereby increasing job security. Improving quality is the most cost-effective and least capital intensive way of improving efficiency.

Everyone is responsible for quality

TQM involves everyone making a commitment to getting things right first time, every time. It does this not by exhorting people to do better or to work harder, but by providing them with the tools and techniques to analyse and drive out problems. So right first time is achieved by a careful process of gradually eliminating the root causes of quality problems. This process requires a substantial commitment from any business to education and training, and a degree of patience.

Prevent problems rather than fix them

Management's attitudes to problems has traditionally been to firefight and fix problems. This is a random strategy. Sometimes management's intuition will correctly identify a root cause and find the best solution. But in the majority of cases, the problem will only be resolved temporarily, or will arise in a different form somewhere else, or get even worse. In TQM, the objective is to find root causes, select the best solution, and so prevent the problem from occurring again.

Scientific approach

Permanent solutions to persistent problems require a process of data collection to identify the problem, to quantify its effects and identify the root causes; and a process of evaluating all potential solutions to the problem; and further data collection after implementation to ensure that the problem has truly been eradicated. This involves the use of mostly simple statistics and data collection tools and techniques, although more complex tools are available for those who need them.

Teamwork

The problems with the highest returns are invariably the most difficult to resolve. These are often problems that cross organization boundaries. In one Research and Development department, we found that over ten per cent of time was spent in dealing with problems relating to purchasing of materials. This included activities like expediting urgently needed material, resolving queries on suppliers invoices, and so forth. Staff within the function had no control over these non-value adding activities. They arose because the purchasing department was not preventing such problems by carrying out their tasks right first time. The key to such problems is teamwork – working together across functional boundaries to understand each other's needs.

Processes fail not people

Hardly anyone goes to work to make mistakes. Yet every day in most companies between 20 and 40 per cent of all activity is wasted in resolving problems or fixing their effects, firefighting and crisis management, checking for errors, and redoing work. While people will occasionally make mistakes, the majority occur because the process has failed. For example because:

- staff are working under constant pressure with little time to think about the quality of what they are doing;
- people don't understand the effects their poor quality work has on other people;
- people are not encouraged or even allowed to co-operate across functional boundaries;
- people haven't been trained, or no documentation exists to help them to do their tasks right;
- the procedure being used is unnecessarily complex, or inconsistently adhered to.

The objective in TQM is to design robust processes that make it more difficult for people to make a mistake. This involves understanding how processes operate; what systems are used, who does what, where decisions are made. It also involves data collection to quantify present problems, and anticipation of where things could go wrong in the future. So, contingency planning is as important as preventive actions.

The truth about quality problems is that they go straight to the top of the organization. If any company produces products or services that fail to meet customers' expectations consistently, the fault lies with top management, not employees. It is top managements' style and policies, their failure to set the standard for quality personally, their failure to invest in and develop people, and their vision of the type of business they are running that ultimately determines the quality of goods and services produced by employees.

Top management must lead the process

Total quality is not simply a framework for improving business performance. It represents a fundamentally different way of operating a business, one that challenges management's traditional role and demands commitment from management at all levels. With that commitment, evidenced by the changed behaviour of management, the commitment of employees can also be sought.

But virtually every management concept proposed has demanded top management commitment as a prerequisite for success. Many academics and consultants recommend that without commitment from the top, it is not worth starting. But even recalcitrant management may be moved by a few bushfires started further down the organization. The secret is to do the basic things well and to get some good results early on. Success breeds commitment, not academic theory. Ultimately however top management must demonstrate leadership and commitment if the process of continuous improvement is to be both successful and sustained.

Middle management's role

Traditionally, middle management's role has been perceived to be that of supervision: to ensure quality, to set priorities and to develop staff. In a total quality company, that role is broadened to include responsibility for the continuous improvement of every aspect of the process under their control. This involves drawing employees into the improvement process, and this is only possible if people:

- understand what services they provide to an internal or external customer;

- understand how well they have to provide those services;
- believe that they are empowered and actively encouraged by the business to alter the way in which they work;
- the business is free from inter-functional conflicts and parochialism;
- feel that their manager is open to new ideas.

While there are many criteria for the success of quality improvement, these are almost wholly determined by the behaviour of middle management.

A key feature of business processes is that they invariably travel across the organization, involving people from several departments. For a process to operate efficiently and effectively, each process must function without weak links. But this will require close co-operation and co-ordination of all the departments involved in the process. Thus a key role for management is to co-operate and break down functional boundaries.

Whilst on a recent business trip to Japan, a colleague asked how Japanese companies organize to break down functional boundaries. His Japanese contact was puzzled: he did not understand the question. Such functional boundaries and the walls they create or the fortress mentality they may engender are virtually unheard of in Japan. And yet, competition amongst managers in Japan for promotion is intense.

The key to continuous improvement is understanding processes: their strengths and weaknesses; and using mostly simple data collection, statistical and participative techniques to identify ways in which the *quality of processes* can be improved.

Quality is typically narrowly defined: the quality of a product or service delivered to a customer as measured by a specification. With this definition, quality is easy to measure by conformance to the specification of the product as measured by: absence of faults, reliability, whole-life costs, dimensions, tensile strength, and so forth; or by quantification of the service provided: delivery on time, order fill, delivery to budget, development lead times, and similar factors.

But quality should be much more broadly defined. It should also include the efficiency and effectiveness of the way in which activities are carried out. This requires a detailed understanding of processes and systems.

A *process* is the means by which a service or product is delivered to an internal or external customer. A *system* is the way a process is designed: the way activities are done and who does them, how decisions are made and who makes them, where computer systems are used, what sequence activities are performed.

Processes and systems

Everyone provides a service or contributes to a product. People work in chains of activities that collectively form a business process. A process consists of a chain of internal and external supplier and customer relationships. A failure to meet the needs of an external customer results in disappointment, and perhaps, the loss of future business. A failure to meet the needs of an internal customer results in wasted time, which itself may ultimately affect the external customer. So, a process is as strong as its weakest link.

System failures are often seen as the normal way of working because management has never tried, or has tried and failed, to find a solution. System failures are plainly visible to the people involved: they live with the problems and do their best to work around them. But these people have not been empowered to improve the system. Managers, who do have that authority, are at least one step, and frequently many more steps, removed from the understanding of what is going wrong.

The dichotomy is that the greater a manager's authority to change a system, the further he usually is from a detailed understanding of what is going wrong. The problems are compounded when one considers that processes are invariably cross-functional. So the root cause of a problem in one function may lie in another function several steps further back in the process. The barriers that exist between staff who have detailed knowledge of system failures and managers who have the authority to improve the system is a recipe for minimal process improvement.

Organizations are fortunate. People want to do a good job. They become demotivated if they are forced to do a poor job: making excuses to customers, chasing other people for information, correcting other people's mistakes. People are motivated by doing tasks that they know are important to the business: providing a service to an internal or external customer.

People respond to management initiatives when the reason for the initiative is made clear to them and when the prevailing culture of the organization is free from fear and uncertainty. People working within a business process have detailed knowledge of exactly what goes wrong. They also have enormous capability to innovate and improve those processes. However, few businesses have a process by which employees are encouraged or even enabled to apply their knowledge to improve continually the way in which they work.

Proof of employee's capability to innovate inevitably comes from Japan. A survey comparing the results of Japanese and American suggestion schemes shows radical differences. In Japan, employers concentrate on participation and implementation, rather than the quality and value of ideas. The Japanese system, known as Kaizen Teian, involves all employees individually in making improvements. Their ideas tend to be small-scale, inexpensive to implement and concern the workers own area of work. The results however amount to vast savings as seen in Table 2.1.

Table 2.1   *Comparison of Japanese and American suggestion schemes*

	USA	Japan (Private organizations only)
Number of eligible employees	8,364,865	1,685,412
Total number of suggestions received	1,010,889	52,989,345
Number of suggestions per 100 eligible	13	3,145
Percentage of employees participating	9	80
Adoption rate	29.0%	82.5%
Average award payment per adoption	$545.68	$2.7
Average net savings per adoption	$7,663	$43
Net savings per 100 eligible	$26,870	$356,531

Source: 1988 NASS/JHRA report

Quality improvement can only be achieved by people, mainly management. In a total quality company, everyone is committed to quality and understands what is expected of them. Every department tries to meet the needs of their customer – the next link in the chain. Data is collected regularly to establish how well the processes and systems are operating and to identify problems and opportunities. Management has the role of involving everyone in improving processes, and everyone is empowered to participate in quality improvement.

The transition to TQM

What the total quality management gurus tell us is largely practical common sense, requiring a process of education and training and management development in total quality principles and straightforward tools and techniques. Why is it then that so many organizations are disappointed by their total quality initiatives?

A frequent problem is that management perceive that TQM is a process that can simply be implemented like any other system, such as BS5750. Where this view is held and a set standard is achieved, managements' behaviour does not change significantly and the organization will quickly revert to business as usual. TQM is a different way of behaving, not a management system. It involves everyone in evaluating how effectively and efficiently they are working in an atmosphere that is free from parochialism, criticism, blame, and fear of the consequences of change. If management does not accept leadership of that process, short-term gains may be won, but no long-term transformation of performance will be achieved.

The other key stumbling blocks are timing and changing management behaviour. Lasting improvement takes time. A process of education and training may provide management with the right tools and techniques, but if they finish their training and return to full in-trays and pressing problems, quality improvement will always take second priority. If the total quality process is structured as a series of improvement projects, the opportunity to be involved will only be extended gradually across the business. Either way will not create the momentum required to carry total quality across the whole organization, particularly in a medium-sized or large company.

Without a company-wide structure and organization for quality and process improvement, committed management will be frustrated in their attempts to improve processes overall by the parochialism of less-committed colleagues.

Managers are motivated by results. Success in improving a process creates the momentum to find further improvements. In this way, the improvement process becomes self-perpetuating.

'Eliminating waste' and 'continuous improvement' are typically understood to be the key themes of total quality. The words are fine, but trite and often lead management to believe that total quality is all about establishing a few 'quality improvement project teams' to tackle pressing problems.

The reality is different. In total quality, large projects are the exception. The real benefits come from implementing a very large number of simple (and usually inexpensive) ideas to improve processes. Simple ideas can only come from the people with the intimate knowledge of the nuts-and-bolts of what happens in a process – the people who work in the process. So total quality is really about the involvement of people and ownership of the benefits of change by those who will be responsible for implementation.

Getting started

There is no single right way to approach total quality management. All companies are different: they have different business needs, different priorities and problems, different cultures and management styles, and different degrees of management commitment to the concepts of quality improvement.

A proper start to total quality is vital. Early problems or a lack of focus will slow the process down and affect the credibility of later stages. Whatever approach is taken, it is essential to get some good results early on to establish credibility. In some companies, this is done by establishing a limited number of corrective action teams to focus on specific problems. In this approach it is important not to tackle elephants. Elephants are large and complex problems. They rarely have a single root cause. Elephants are better tackled piecemeal, a bit at a time. So it is important to choose problems that have a reasonable chance of success, but are sufficiently high-profile to create interest.

Cascaded education and training can be very effective in starting to win hearts and minds, but unless it is coupled with a structure that draws people together across functional boundaries to resolve problems, it will invariably inspire more cynicism than progress.

A company-wide process that involves everyone in identifying improvements may win sufficient short-term benefits. But unless it includes a strong element of education and training, it will not fundamentally alter behaviour, and will not result in sustained continuous improvement.

The right approach may be any one of these, or a combination. What may be right for one company may not be appropriate for a similar company. For example, in one company, different approaches have been used in each factory location. The company is decentralized and does not have a strong corporate culture. Each site has developed its own management culture and striking differences exist between sites. So an approach that would be successful at one site might not be appropriate at another.

There are however some prerequisites for a successful start to TQM.

Mission statements

Mission statements have an unfortunate name. Many managers see them as a waste of time, others as a necessary evil. Few put much time and thought into their definition. Even academics cannot agree on what a mission statement is intended to achieve.

All businesses have a unique culture. Culture is the way things get done, and is function of the values and beliefs of an organization. Successful companies have a strong set of values and beliefs. They are not always explicitly laid out, but nonetheless they exist. At British Airways, the priority of improving front-line service was coupled with the theme of 'putting people first'. With the help of extensive training, that emphasized strong values about the importance of people. This process was only a part of a much broader process of cultural change that had started some years before 'putting people first'. It was not until some other operational priorities were achieved that the process of communicating strong values could be started.

'Putting people first' achieved remarkable success for British Airways because the people trained were highly responsive to the attractive message underpinning the process. It provided a rationale for the process of change and gave a vision of what the company was striving to achieve. For many staff, 'putting people first' became an inspiration, and frequent flyers cannot help but have noticed the dramatic improvement in the company's services.

Within British Airways, the values and beliefs communicated to all staff were totally appropriate to an organization's business needs. But this is not always the case. For example, it is commonly believed that the British motorcycle industry was simply eclipsed by cheap and reliable Japanese imports. What really eclipsed BSA, Triumph and other proud names was their failure to modify their strong beliefs and values in traditional craftsmanship and engineering skills when the market wanted cheap, reliable, mass-produced and well-designed products.

Culture differentiates the total quality organization from others. The business you are in, the markets you serve or the products you manufacture make almost no difference at all. The key is motivation: the sense of doing something of value and feeling valued by belonging to the business. The mission statement is key to the set of beliefs and values the business is able to inculcate in its staff. Their beliefs and values are key to their behaviour. When people believe that they can make a difference to the business, when they know that they are being given the opportunity to develop, when they identify with the company's values and beliefs, then work will mean more than just eight hours a day and money in their pocket.

Texas Instruments' operating philosophy sums it all up.

> There is probably no greater waste in industry today than that of willing employees prevented by insensitive management from applying their energies and ambitions in the interest of the companies for which they work (Management philosophies and practices of Texas Instruments incorporated by Pat Haggerty, 1965).

A successful mission statement should provide people with a sense of purpose and unity and should establish the organization's attitudes towards its staff, customers and suppliers. A mission statement has three components:

- Purpose – explaining explicitly why the company exists
- Strategy – explaining where the company positions itself in relation to competitors and what it is good at doing
- Culture – describing the policies towards customers, suppliers and staff that underpin the beliefs and values of the business

Mission statements provide no instant beliefs. It can take years for the benefits to appear. However strong values and beliefs will provide people with a sense of unity with each other and the firm. Shared values will make a difference to organization and individual vitality by helping people to identify more with internal corporate goals. A greater sense of identity with the business will lead to greater loyalty and commitment, and a more positive and co-operative work environment.

All these things may already exist within an organization. Some well-known companies clearly exhibit strong corporate values and beliefs but do not have a mission statement as such.

Understand the present organization culture

Somebody once remarked that companies were full of people who ran scout packs, or did voluntary work, had interesting and worthwhile hobbies, or were devoted to their families. In other words, companies are full of devoted and loyal people – except for the eight hours a day that they go to work. What is that fails to provide the inspiration to motivate people at work to the extent that their other interests can do?

All organizations have a distinct culture – the way in which things get done. Many things will have contributed to the present culture of an organization: history and tradition; reward systems; industrial relations; past and present management styles; and so on.

Changing the culture is difficult and at times painful. Challenging well-established ways of doing things can provoke conflict and demotivate. Examination of a company's corporate culture is intended to identify aspects that may be out-dated or a barrier to TQM.

Take for example, one manufacturing company I visited. After a presentation to the directors at which the principles of commitment, breaking down barriers and teamwork were discussed, a series of interviews with managment found the following barriers to improving teamwork.

There was a gulf in the way shopfloor workers were treated:

- Office staff parked their cars in a tarmac car park at the front of the building. The shopfloor parked in a field at the back.
- The shopfloor paid for their coffee while office staff got theirs free.
- The shopfloor canteen was dilapidated. The office staff canteen was newly refurbished. Directors had their own dining room.

Sales and manufacturing had declared war on each other:

- Manufacturing's performance was assessed on throughput. In other words, they needed large batch sizes to meet the throughput targets set by the parent company.
- Salesmen's bonuses were based on order value. But the highest value products were invariably ordered in small batch sizes. So if salesmen tried to meet manufacturing's need for large batch sizes, their pockets suffered. If manufacturing did not meet their performance standards, head office wanted to know why not, and they suffered at performance appraisal time.

Strong fortress mentalities existed:

- The company had a 'strong' management culture. For example, one group, working in the basement of the building, had a manager whose office was on the fourth floor. He only came down to the basement to admonish his staff when something went wrong. Outside the basement office there was a marble floor. The manager wore shoes with steel-reinforced heels, and caused a sense of mounting fear each time he was heard walking down the corridor.

This was followed by a sense of relief when he went past a door, because it meant that someone else was going to be on the receiving end that day. This was just one example of the prevailing culture: fear of making a mistake and fear of management, both of which led to the building up of walls between different groups and between managers and employees.

In this company, something had to be done to eliminate the barriers before even beginning to think about TQM. This meant reducing the artificial barriers between shopfloor and office staff, eliminating management by arbitrary numbers in sales and manufacturing, and persuading management to change their behaviour. All of this had to happen before TQM.

Understand customer requirements

External customers

Total quality is not being as good as the rest. It is about excellence and leadership – 'delighting the customer' as Deming describes it. This means that companies must sometimes make extraordinary efforts to explore their customers' needs and their perceptions of the quality of products and services provided by a company. This can often be a most uncomfortable process because it involves listening to criticism, even inviting criticism because it is the only way to learn how and where to improve.

The process also has risks. The results are sometimes so uncomfortable that management reacts too quickly, and TQM is diverted into a form of customer care programme. The other risk is that giving customers the opportunity to complain about poor quality can raise their expectations that the company will do something to improve. If it subsequently fails to improve, the result can be disaffected customers and loss of business.

Internal customers

People often find the concept of having internal suppliers and customers difficult to grasp. A customer is anyone who is dependent on you for a product or service. Payroll are a customer of personnel, because they usually have to rely on personnel to maintain accurate records of leavers and joiners. If an internal supplier does not meet the needs of his internal customer, the internal customer usually has to spend time chasing information or putting things right. So, just like the external customer, the internal customer needs specific standards of service to avoid wasted effort.

Measuring service quality

Many companies measure the quality of service they provide to external customers in some way, but very few measure *internal* service levels. External customer service can be measured in many ways, including:

- Order fill
- Delivery on-time
- Stock availability

Similar principles can be applied internally:

- How frequently a task should be done
- How accurately
- How quickly something should be turned round
- What level of detail is needed
- When something should be done by

Some of these service levels will be implicitly understood within the business. For example, no business will tolerate anything other than very rare mistakes in the payroll, so 100 per cent accuracy and consistent payment on time are the understood service levels. Within purchasing, service levels can also be devised. 'Turn round purchase requisitions within 72 hours', 'Carry out 12 vendor quality assessments per month'. Similar service levels can be devised for virtually any group of people in any business.

The benefits of clear service levels are that they allow an internal supplier to measure how well service is presently being provided, to set goals for improvement, and then to measure performance against those goals.

Measure the cost of quality

The cost of quality is a misnomer. Cost of quality is what it costs a company to get things wrong. It includes wasted time, scrap and rework in a manufacturing process, and costs of lost opportunities.

Management are invariably shocked to discover that the cost of quality is typically 15 to 25 per cent of turnover and usually higher in service companies. Some companies have estimated cost of quality in excess of 40 per cent of turnover. Measuring the cost of quality provides the thrust necessary to drive TQM through the organization.

Basic rules for quality costing are described by BS6143. The starting point is to divide quality costs into four categories:

- Prevention
- Appraisal
- Internal failure
- External failure

Prevention costs are the amount spent to ensure that things are done right first time. It includes, for example costs of ensuring that new products or services meet customer needs, costs of analysing failures and devising improvements, and costs of running a quality assurance system.

Appraisal costs are amounts spent on inspection, testing and other checking of products and services at any stage. It also includes supplier quality assurance activities.

Internal failure costs are the amounts spent putting things right while a product or service is still in the company's possession. These costs include scrap and rectification, the cost of correcting mistakes in administrative processes, and the like.

External failure costs are amounts spent after a product or service has passed into the customer's hands. This includes the costs of warranty and field service, costs of administering customers' complaints, product recalls, and so forth. Perhaps more importantly, external failure costs include lost opportunity costs associated with loss of future business arising from poor service or poor quality products.

Table 2.2 provides a classification of some typical quality costs.

By collecting quality costs, management attention is focused on a major business opportunity. But how does a company approach the opportunity of reducing its quality costs? Figure 2.1 illustrates what has to happen.

Spending more money on prevention will inevitably reduce failure costs. In the short-term, however, it may be necessary to spend more in appraisal in order to drive out failure costs.

However, the change from firefighting to prevention is hard. People and organizations become accustomed to firefighting. There are even people who take pride in being good at such activities. Changing behaviour is difficult and takes time and patience; and no small amount of education and training.

But where do you start? What approach will be most suitable?

Table 2.2   *Classification of typical quality costs*

Costs of prevention	*Costs of appraisal*
Quality engineering	Laboratory acceptance tests
	Inspection/test and related setup,
Quality planning (but not QA)	and materials
Design and development of quality	
measurement/control equipment	
or techniques	Operator inspection
Calibration	Product quality audits
Training	Review of inspection/test results
Quality system administration	
(E.g. BS5750 etc.)	Evaluation at customer sites
System audits	Processing/analysis of test reports

Costs of internal failure	*Costs of external failure*
Scrap and rework:	Administering customer
Reinspection/retest	complaints
Troubleshooting/fire fighting,	
correcting errors, chasing others	
for information, clarifying internal	Recalls, warranty claims,
requests	replacements
	Loss of future business from
Analysis of failures/defects	dissatisfied customers
Manufacturing variances	
Lost production due to supplier or	
own materials	

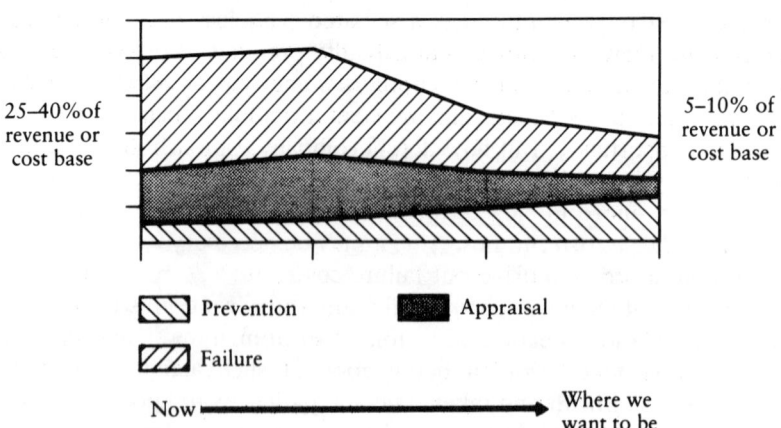

25–40% of
revenue or
cost base

5–10% of
revenue or
cost base

[ ] Prevention   [ ] Appraisal

[ ] Failure

Now ⟶ Where we
want to be

Figure 2.1   *Reducing quality costs*

Strategies for implementation

There are three common strategies for total quality implementation:

- A training cascade
- A project-based approach
- The company-wide approach

Most consultants and academics preach one or other approach. This is both dangerous and short-sighted because each has strengths and weaknesses. When selecting an approach within your business it is important to select the approach that has the greatest chance of success.

The training cascade

David Procter's excellent chapter describes how this approach was applied at a British Steel site. Simply, this approach starts with a top management workshop or seminar. Facilitators are then trained from middle managers, who then train the next layer down from top management. From this layer, further facilitators are selected or volunteer, and they train the next layer down.

While education and training are critical elements of any total quality management process, it is not sufficient in itself to start a process of cultural change and continuous improvement. The experience of a leading finance company is typical.

In this company, first class training was provided by an external consultant. The training was well received by the majority of managers attending. However, managers left the training sessions and were expected to start to improve processes, but no structure had been established to facilitate inter-unit co-operation. Thus managers improved what they could within their own sphere of influence, but their ability to improve processes overall was limited. As a result, little benefit was seen, the prevailing culture was little changed, and the process lost credibility.

In another communication services company, top management had become frustrated by an apparent lack of bottom line benefits. This over two years after education and training had commenced. An initial cost of quality exercise had arrived at a figure of 33 per cent, and when the process was repeated two years later, this had risen to 37 per cent. Again, the education and training process was not at fault. This had been thorough and comprehensive. In this organization, management needed to see some tangible benefits in order to strengthen their commitment to total quality. Without benefits, they had failed to demonstrate leadership and commitment.

This company needed a company-wide structure approach to draw a large number of people into process improvement, and to get some tangible benefits quickly. This created credibility, and enabled top management to commit themselves to a process that they could now believe in.

Another important point is that the education and training in TQM is greatly enhanced if it can be made relevant to the business. Any consultant can pull a standard education and training package off the shelf. But case studies based on problems within the company are much more effective.

A training cascade is a vital part of education and training in TQM. But is not sufficient on its own to create a momentum. To be effective, a structure has to be added to the process.

A project-based approach

At least one TQM guru insists that quality improvement can only be achieved on a project-by-project basis. Since many consultants align themselves with one guru or another, they may also tell their clients that this is the only way to go. In some cases, they have a point. In manufacturing processes, for example, problems are best tackled in this way. The problem with project approaches lies outside of manufacturing. Office processes are usually very complex, involving many functions and a large number of tasks where the quality of service provided is rarely measured.

In a manufacturing company, the recently appointed sales director had decided to tackle the problem of errors on orders made by tele-sales operators. She set up a project to identify the root causes of the problem and involved a number of sales staff in the team. It quickly became apparent that there were many contributory factors to the problem. Some originated within sales, but others involved other functions, such as finance and production. The team worked hard to eliminate the problems originating within sales, and were pleased by their success. But other functions varied in their commitment. Production were eager to become involved because they could see some benefits for themselves. Finance and marketing were much less enthusiastic, and the team ground to an eventual halt.

A finance company set up a number of process improvement teams to review the efficiency and effectiveness of all business processes. But the teams involved less than 5 per cent of the staff. While education and training was provided for all staff, 95 per cent were not involved in the improvement process. Their perception was that the training has been an exhortation by management to improve efficiency.

In another manufacturing company, 80 per cent of sales volumes were generated by less than 20 customers. The remaining 20 per cent was generated by over 600 customers all ordering in small infrequent batches. The disruption caused across the business by these small customers was enormous: frequent rescheduling of production, a high volume of administration (invoices, credit notes, etc.), wildly fluctuating sales forecasts, and so forth. The key problem was that the company did not know whether it was making or losing money on its small customers. In this company, a project approach was the only way to start, at least initially. A company-wide approach would have failed because one issue caused so much disruption.

Other organizations have used this approach very successfully in pilot projects, particularly where top management have been uncommitted to TQM. Success in a few pilot projects can breed commitment at top management level and create interest in areas not involved.

Company-wide approach

This approach involves everyone working together to improve processes, and so harnesses the commitment of the whole workforce to quality in all its forms. Approaches like this are high-risk and high-return. They are intended to capture a very large number of mostly minor ideas from employees, which add up to a substantial benefit. Because the ideas are mostly easy to implement, employees see improvements happening very quickly. They also see that the organization is truly committed to improving quality in all forms, and this creates credibility and builds a momentum.

However, approaches like this require very careful project management. Because the process involves everyone, the effects of failure are visible to all. There is also a risk of reverting to business as usual at the end of the first stage. It is important that the company-wide approach be followed by another initiative. This could be further training, or the establishment of quality improvement teams or even quality circles.

So the approach that is right for one business can be inappropriate for another. The right approach for your business may be a combination of all three. A number of projects to tackle specific high profile problems areas first. Followed by education and training for all. Finally a company-wide process to sustain the momentum.

Summary

For many businesses, survival in the 1990s will require a transformation of performance. A small but growing number of companies have proved that total quality can achieve that.

Over the years, there has been a series of 'new' management techniques. Many of these have promised much and delivered little. Management has turned to each of these fads looking for the easy answer. Some see TQM as the latest of these fads. One that has a single god, but many prophets.

TQM is not a substitute for good management. TQM is a radically new way of managing a business. A way that challenges management's traditional role, and demands leadership and commitment. For many managers, that challenge will be too steep, and they will continue to look for the easy way out.

3

Delighting the customer

David Baines

Rule 1: The customer is always right
Rule 2: If the customer is ever wrong, reread rule 1

Introduction

After decimating British manufacturing industry in the last 20 years, the Japanese are turning their sights on service industries. Is British management, still dogged by poor service, inattention to detail and short-term cost-cutting at the customers' expense, up to the challenge?

All companies compete to at least some extent on the basis of service. Manufactured product quality no longer provides competitive edge because there is little to choose between suppliers. Service is the key to getting ahead. In manufacturing, product quality no longer provides competitive edge because there is often little discernible difference between suppliers. The competitive edge is now determined by service.

Japan's success in manufacturing is well understood. Less well-known is the inexorable growth of its service industry, which grew by 30 per cent between 1986 and 1989, compared to a 22 per cent growth in manufacturing. Services now account for 63 per cent of Japanese Gross National Product, placing Japan second only to the US. Much of this growth has been in the domestic market. Having cut their teeth at home, Japanese service companies are now looking further afield to export their services to the world market, emulating the success of their manufacturing sector.

The message for UK service companies is bleak. To survive in the future, a transformation in service quality will be needed. A small but growing number of UK companies, mostly in manufacturing, have shown that the level of improvement needed is possible to achieve.

Good enough or excellent?

It is not good enough simply to be as good as the rest. Even a satisfied customer may switch to an alternative supplier on the basis that he has nothing to lose, and could conceivably gain. The key to service leadership is 'delighting the customer'.

A number of companies have already demonstrated that a strategy of service leadership is a winning strategy. The common thread among the most successful companies is quality. These leading firms use service to differentiate themselves from the rest. They provide superior service to maintain customer loyalty and they rely on customer recommendations to win further market share. Delighting the customer will win a higher proportion of that customers' business.

Many managers and most quality consultants still take a narrow view of quality as a product or service that conforms to a predetermined specification. This is an internal view, not the view of the customer, who probably knows or cares little about whether the product conforms. Customers have a sharper focus, measuring quality against competing products or services.

Many new products have been launched only to fail in the marketplace because of a lack of understanding of what customers want from a product.

Perceived and actual quality

A customer's perception of quality is as important as the actual quality, which can be measured against the specification for the product or service. Perceived quality is more difficult to measure. Customers respond to companies with high actual and perceived quality because they stand out from the competition. There is often a huge difference between what the customer expects and what he perceives of the quality of service he is getting. The following company is a supplier of office machinery. A survey established customers' expectations for lead time from order to delivery as 16 days. Their perceptions of actual lead times were significantly longer – 23 days – and actual measured performance varied from 10 to 38 days. The variation in lead times was the prime contributing factor to the customers' perception that actual service was significantly worse than their expectations.

Superior quality leads to increased profitability

A company that can produce products or services to a higher level of quality will enjoy a number of benefits:

- Its *cost of quality* will be lower than its competitors, and thus its overall costs will be lower.
- Its consistency of quality will be better, usually a key factor influencing suppliers' purchasing decisions.

Superior quality has other benefits too:

- Some companies are able to charge a premium, which they use to the bottom line, or to increase investment in R & D, which helps the business maintain its leadership. The company may charge the same price as competitors, but its position of quality leadership will give it greater market share.

These are not the only benefits. 'Delighting the customer' will also increase customer loyalty, which in turn will lead to more repeat business. Delighted customers are a company's best salesmen. Happy customers tell other potential customers.

Inferior quality

But what about the unhappy customers? A survey of European companies provides a disturbing insight into the perceptions and future intentions of dissatisfied customers. The research concluded that customers were more likely to switch suppliers because of poor service than poor product quality, and that of every 100 dissatisfied customers:

- only 4 complain;
- 91 say that they will never buy from that supplier again;
- 87 would remain loyal if only the supplier tried to solve the problem;
- each one tells 12 others.

The effects of poor service are not confined to customers' perceptions of quality. All the firefighting, checking, clarifying instructions, making corrections, dealing with customer complaints, rectification, warranty work, and so on adds up to a major cost penalty. These activities, generally known as the cost of quality, can represent as much as 40 per cent of sales. Gradual and continuous quality improvement is crucial in cutting out these wasteful costs.

Getting started – researching expectations and perceptions

The starting point for any company looking to improve quality is a 'customer needs' survey. This establishes what the company must get right if its customers' requirements are to be met consistently, and in which areas excellence will be rewarded by delighted customers. Properly executed, it will establish how well the company is presently meeting those needs, and will guide the company into a process of considering alternatives to the present levels of service.

Case study: a UK electronics company

This company was failing to satisfy the most important needs of its customers: ease of upgrade of equipment, compatibility and maintainability. It was exceeding their expectations in less important areas: service response and delivery. There are few benefits from exceeding these expectations which customers do not think are that important. They are certainly greatly outweighed by the poor perception of service quality in aspects more important to the customer.

Understanding the relative importance of different aspects of customer service is critical to winning a competitive edge through superior service.

A customer needs survey will highlight gaps and deficiencies in service. It will also indicate what level of improvement is required to bridge the gap between customers' expectations and perceptions. It may also identify areas where service levels can be reduced at no risk in order to re-deploy resources into more important areas.

Some root causes of gaps and deficiencies in service

Gap between customer expectations and management's perceptions

Customers' expectations and management's perceptions of customers' expectations often differ, sometimes very substantially. The following case study, from an office equipment supplier, illustrates the point.

The company was failing badly to meet customers delivery and stock availability requirements. It was, however, excellent in terms of quality and brand image where it had invested heavily. Unfortunately, these were not particularly important to customers.

An analysis of customers' and management's ranked service factors highlights the differences in perception, and suggests the company had invested heavily in aspects of service that were not especially important. Note also that management's top ranked service factor does not even figure in the customer's top 12.

Failure to measure actual service performance

Companies frequently fail to measure actual service performance. Without hard facts management is ruled by intuition and emotion, and often gets it wrong.

Even when information is collected, it has to be used carefully. In the office equipment company, the computer systems told management that over 90 per cent of orders were delivered within the company's two week target. But the computer gave this statistic on the first delivery to the customer, which was frequently a part order. A different analysis, based on order completion showed that only 53 per cent of orders were completely filled within the target of two weeks from order to delivery.

Senior management distant from customers

Senior management is very remote from customers. An excessively tall organization structure puts many layers between manager and customer.

Organization structures work like filters. Each layer filters the messages coming from those personnel in contact with customers. This inhibits communication and understanding, and, like Chinese Whispers, information about customers' expectations either does not reach managers, or it is distorted on the way.

In small companies, senior managers are usually in regular contact with customers, with first-hand knowledge of their expectations and perceptions. In larger companies, contact is often restricted to reading reports and summaries which is no substitute for dealing direct with the customer.

It is also important that management should not be too remote from staff who deal directly with customers. They should be a prime source of information on service delivery problems, and changes in customers' perceptions.

Top managers must experience customers' expectations and perceptions first-hand, preferably through a formal programme of visits to the production line, experiencing service delivery, customer visits, and other forms of 'doing the job'. For example, ICL's Quality Director made over 100 visits to customers in one year to maintain his customer contact.

Inadequate market research

Market research is the starting point to understanding customers' expectations. Problems arise when research is either not carried out, is ignored, or is not up-dated.

Market research should show which product and service features are important to customers, what they expect from those features, and how well they think the company will meet their expectations.

But there are other forms of research that may pay substantial dividends. For example, how many companies use customers' complaints to analyse where their service processes are failing? Properly used, complaints can be a valuable contributor to the process of continuously improving service delivery. They can also indicate the effectiveness of a solution to a service problem.

Lack of management commitment to quality

Most senior managers will claim to be committed to quality. But who defines quality? Often it is defined by internal measures, such as productivity standards or absence of defects. This is not management commitment to quality. Management commitment means providing products or services that the customer perceives as high in quality. The customer's perception of quality may be very different to those internal measures.

Woody Allen wrote that '80 per cent of success is showing up'. The same is true of management commitment to quality. A manager must make a commitment to quality a personal priority. He can do this by implying consistent quality in the questions he asks, by the way he communicates and behaves with staff, and by the targets and goals he sets for the business.

Where senior managers consistently emphasize other goals: sales, productivity or market share, they have failed to understand that quality is the key to these other goals.

Middle managers have to continue the process of commitment to quality, driving the message home through the organizations layers.

Another aspect of top management's commitment is its willingness to recognize and reward those involved in delivering quality service. Quality newsletters and awards to individuals and groups can help here. Reward may mean tailoring management compensation packages to include a personal or team element of reward for quality behaviour and performance.

Service promises

A TV rental company promised that any customer who telephoned the company's repair centre before 10 am would receive a same day call from an engineer. But the repair centres were unable to handle the volume of calls, and customers became frustrated either waiting for calls to be answered or by constantly engaged lines.

Customers' expectations of service had been raised by the service promise made at the point of sale. Their subsequent frustration affected their perception of actual service quality, and the company acquired a reputation for poor service.

If a company makes a service promise, customers expect the company to consistently meet the stated standard. So the company must ensure it has invested in the right technology, has trained people and has devised procedures capable of meeting the required performance standard (day in, day out).

A different problem with service promises is that line managers might think they are not feasible. Why is this perception so common?

Most line managers have very limited authority to change the way they and their staff work and they are forced to 'think small'. Managers need to have the power to be able to 'think big' and to challenge the way things are done. They need to be allowed to experiment and be given the authority to modify the way business is done, if that flexibility is what is needed to meet the customers' needs.

Lack of goals

Service leaders are noted for setting goals to guide their employees in providing quality service. To be successful, the goals have to be based on customers' expectations rather than arbitrary internal standards. They also have to be specific and accepted by employees. Goals should set challenges, but be realistic. They should be revised periodically to reflect improving service quality and to set new challenges.

Goals need to be specific because actual performance needs to be measured. Hence a goal of 'turning round a customer order as quickly as possible' is too vague. 'Turn round all customer orders within 24 hours' is both specific, measurable, service oriented and easy for all employees to understand. Further, a quantified goal can become something to beat, so that a new target can be set. In this way, goal setting can complement a process of continuous improvement.

The absence of such goals means that employees cannot be sure what management expects of them, and how they should act to satisfy their expectations. They may establish their own goals. These may not meet customers' expectations, and may be in direct conflict with other business objectives.

Poor process design

The way in which the service delivery process is designed may make it impossible for employees to meet customer expectations.

A specialist finance company promised its customers that it would turn round applications for business loans within 24 hours. Its service delivery process was designed as a series of tasks each performed by a different specialist group. The process worked effectively if volumes were constant. But as soon as volume peaked, bottlenecks appeared and the customer's expectation of a 24 hour response was not satisfied. The process was redesigned to consist of several parallel steps carried out by a smaller number of larger work groups. This eliminated the bottlenecks and allowed employees to meet the company's service delivery goal. It also allowed the company to recognize priority clients and give them a superior service.

There are many ways in which poor process design can adversely affect service delivery:

- Lack of standardization of tasks;
- Conflicting objectives;
- Lack of accountability or authority;
- Lack of, or inadequate, documentation;
- Insufficient, or poorly trained, resources;
- Inadequate, or unreliable, tools or equipment.

Another common failing is a low degree of perceived control over the process. Employees must feel that they are able to respond flexibly to customer needs. They must feel they have a high degree of control over the process. Many organizations allow employees only a low degree of control by forcing decision-making upwards or by making a contact person obtain approval from another department. Low control jeopardizes service quality by creating delays and disruptions and inhibiting people's natural enthusiasm and innovation.

Service leaders put time and effort into designing processes and training their people so that the process can meet customer expectations. They also encourage employees to react innovatively to customers' needs.

Lack of teamwork

Teamwork is a key recurring theme of quality improvement. In many businesses, the word 'customer' is used only in the external sense, as a purchaser of products or services. Service leadership involves a broader definition of customer.

The process of getting a product or service to a customer usually starts and ends with contact staff. For example, the salesman who takes the order and the driver who delivers the goods. But in between there is sales administration to process the order; production planning and purchasing to set up the production run; warehousing to pick the order; and so on. These processes involve internal customers and suppliers in a chain of internal service relationships. The process is only as good as its weakest link.

To provide quality service to the external customer, these support functions must also give quality service to their internal customers. The benefits of producing a high-quality product and getting it to the customer exactly when he wanted it, can easily be lost if the sales invoice is incorrect.

This is where teamwork comes in. In order to establish external customers' expectations, it is necessary to carry out a customer needs survey. To establish the internal customers' service needs, functional barriers have to be broken down. Internal customers have to quantify the levels of service quality they need from their suppliers in order to meet the needs of their own customers. This sounds deceptively simple. In practice it requires a culture where internal suppliers actively seek the criticism of their internal customers in order to improve service. In turn, internal customers provide constructive criticism in an atmosphere free from blame and recrimination.

It is easy to fall into the trap of targeting service improvement on contact employees alone. This underestimates the effect that poor quality in support functions can have on the quality of service perceived by the customer.

A number of techniques can be used to improve inter-function teamwork. These include departmental purpose analysis (DPA) and similar techniques; teamwork training; service level agreements; and quality function deployment.

Quality Function Deployment (QFD)

QFD is a cross-functional planning tool. It ensures that the quality characteristics important to the customer are designed into a product or service at inception, and maintained right through to launch.

QFD is founded on the principle that designing and launching a new product or service requires great attention to detail and a constant focus on the customer's needs.

Most companies have painful memories of failures in such processes: last minute engineering changes; late launches; missing point of sale materials; hurried redesign; and even total failures where a new product or service failed in the marketplace. The main problems are:

- Failing to establish exactly what features the customer wants and retaining these features right through to launch
- Failure to use a common 'language' to ensure that the customers' needs are consistently understood by everyone in the process
- Failing to communicate and coordinate across functional boundaries.

The voice of the customer

One of the basic points of QFD is that it represents the voice of the customer at all stages in the design and development of a new product or service. It ensures that his needs are identified in his own terms, and then deployed into the design requirements. The critical technical requirements are in turn deployed into the critical features in component design. These characteristics are then fed into the processes for producing them.

The whole integrated procedure uses a series of matrix charts as the tool for collecting and disseminating information.

The benefits of QFD are many, including:

- Reduced development time;
- Fewer late changes;
- Reduced start-up problems;
- Greater customer satisfaction;
- Reduced start-up costs.

QFD is not an easy tool to use. It requires a sound knowledge base, strong/close cross-functional teamwork and, at least initially, a good facilitator. It also requires patience and keen attention to detail.

Although QFD has mostly been applied by manufacturing companies, it is equally applicable and valuable to service organizations. It cannot however be successful in isolation. QFD will only succeed if teamwork skills have been acquired and inter-function barriers have been broken down.

Summary

In the 1990s, the successful companies will be those with a fierce determination to achieve the highest standards of customer service – a strategy of delighting the customer. The key will be constantly monitoring, even anticipating, customers' expectations and perceptions.
The foundation for service leadership is:

- A willingness to go to extraordinary lengths to ensure that new products and services meet customers' expectations.
- A willingness to be self-critical and to ask other functions and customers to comment on performance.
- An unequivocal commitment to quality by top management.
- A scientific process of continuous improvement of every aspect of service delivery and product/service quality.

But all this cannot happen in isolation. At the most fundamental level, the culture of the organization must be receptive to the principles underlying excellence in service provision. Customer satisfaction is the fundamental motivation behind total quality management, but TQM is crucial to the culture change that is needed to delight customers.

4

The tools and techniques of total quality management

Professor Tony Bendell and Ted Merry

Introduction

Total quality management is a company-wide continuous improvement process that involves everyone, not only in solving problems but also in preventing them. It is not just for the manufacturing departments or the people in the front line.

People in more central roles, and including those with a knowledge of and involvement in financial management, have a dual role to play:

1   *Improving control and effectiveness in their own areas*
    Suitable topics might be:
    - Basic office practices;
    - Accuracy of information;
    - Improved presentation of data:
        - accessibility for people with limited knowledge of standard financial procedures,
        - timeliness,
    - Relevance of information to decision making.
2   *Participating in and providing information for 'external' and interfunctional projects*
    Examples are:
    - Financial implications when choosing between alternative remedies;
    - Cost data for prioritizing actions;
    - Providing data or methods to monitor and control the 'cost of quality';
    - Cost feasibility analyses;
    - Sharing experiences and ideas with colleagues in other departments in tackling problems and opportunities.

Management's key role

Financial managers, with a structured and methodical approach to issues, can contribute a good deal of realism and business-sense to projects being undertaken by people with little financial awareness. Costly errors can be averted. At the same time, it is an opportunity to get more involved with, and increase understanding of, what actually *does* happen in other areas of the business as well as improving the rest of the organization's knowledge of financial processes and constraints. This improved understanding can only be beneficial to all.

The concept of *internal customer* and *internal supplier* should be fully taken on board for both of these roles. The manager should see himself or herself as a provider of timely, relevant information for the prevention, solution or control of problems and at the same time the recipient of whatever support he or she needs to supply that information.

Lastly, managers have the duty of *leadership* for quality management. If they are not leading from the front, who are the troops to follow?

Quality costs

Effective quality management should be of particular interest to all people with financial responsibility within an organization because they, more than most, will be aware of the money that is deployed, usually unnecessarily, on quality issues:

(a)   *Failure*
        Rework
        Seconds
        Scrap/waste   } Internal failure costs
        Allowed/budgeted variances

        Warranty claims
        Customer allowances   } External failure costs
        Loss of customers
(b)   *Appraisal*
        Inspection
        Testing
        Auditing
(c)   *Prevention*
        Training
        Quality assurance system

Alternatively, these can be looked at from a customer requirement point of view when they become:

(a)   Cost of non-conformance
(b)   Cost of conformance

> In businesses with little or no history of successful quality management, these costs can be as high as 25% of turnover for manufacturing companies, and as high as 50% of turnover for service companies!

By taking part and committing time to improvement projects, financially aware managers can play a major proactive role in reducing failure/non-conformance costs within the company and help to create a more secure enterprise. Few activities yield such a high return on investment.

In summary: *don't just count the cost – do something about it!*

Overview of tools and techniques

There is a wide variety of tools and techniques that can be used during the many stages of an operation, from original planning and design, through to manufacture, distribution and after-sales service.

The tools cover the three phases of quality management (the quality trilogy) as defined by Juran:

(a)   Quality planning
(b)   Quality control
(c)   Quality improvement

These can be compared with similar phases in financial management:

(a)   Budgeting
(b)   Cost control
(c)   Cost reduction initiatives

Prevention

A central concept in the overall philosophy of total quality management is the *prevention* of quality problems (and the attendant costs) as opposed to the more traditional approach of *detection and correction*.

It may come as a surprise to people with financial responsibility – who see 'the budget' and adherence to it as something essential to the company's future – that quality planning is the most ignored phase of quality management. The traditional approach has been to 'get the business' and then 'find out how to do it' as the deadline for delivery approaches or, often, passes.

The majority of the 'cost of non-conformance' cited earlier is the result of failing to plan for quality. Planning for quality and learning from the causes of today's improvement projects are the keys to prevention. Fortunately, there are several tools and techniques to aid the process.

Simple tools

Many of the tools are simple and very easy to learn but, nevertheless, still powerful. Some are more detailed and apparently complex, but still easily learned. Some involve statistics, but usually at a fairly basic level.

The apparent simplicity of many of the following tools and techniques should not be taken as an indication that they are not effective or not worth learning and using. It has been the use of these techniques, in a positive teamwork environment, that has created Japan's economic supremacy in the world.

Teamwork

For many of the techniques, the emphasis is on teamwork and participation, each team member contributing his or her own specialist knowledge during meetings, and then carrying out assigned or agreed tasks between the meetings. Teamwork results in improved communication, motivation, analysis, and problem-solving capability and the development of a collective responsibility.

Teams can be either cross-functional *task forces* created by senior management to work on specific designated improvement projects, or teams working autonomously on day-to-day departmental issues (the *quality circle* concept).

The seven (old) tools of quality control

These are the tools and techniques championed by Dr Kaoru Ishikawa and used so effectively by Japanese companies since the early fifties. They are used by everyone in the organization – all levels, all functions. Data are collected and displayed in simple, visual formats; everyone speaks the same language and there are no misunderstandings. Use of the tools is not restricted to 'quality' problems; safety, productivity, cost efficiency, personnel issues, etc., can all be tackled.

'Quality control' is used in the Japanese sense and not in the, often, much more limited Western usage of the phrase. In the West, 'quality control' usually means 'inspection', 'testing', 'evaluation' and then rejection of non-conforming product. In Japan, following the American gurus Juran and Feigenbaum, the phrase means 'quality management' in its widest sense – covering problem prevention and the continuous improvement of both products/services and the processes that give rise to them in all areas of the business, not just manufacturing.

The seven old tools are used to evaluate current performance, make improvements to it, and then control the process at the new level. Then the whole cycle is repeated: continuous improvement. The tools are used in the teamwork environment and *everyone* is trained in the use of the tools – usually by his or her own boss, the team leader.

Cause-and-effect diagram

This is also known as the fishbone diagram (Figure 4.1) or the Ishikawa diagram (after its inventor).

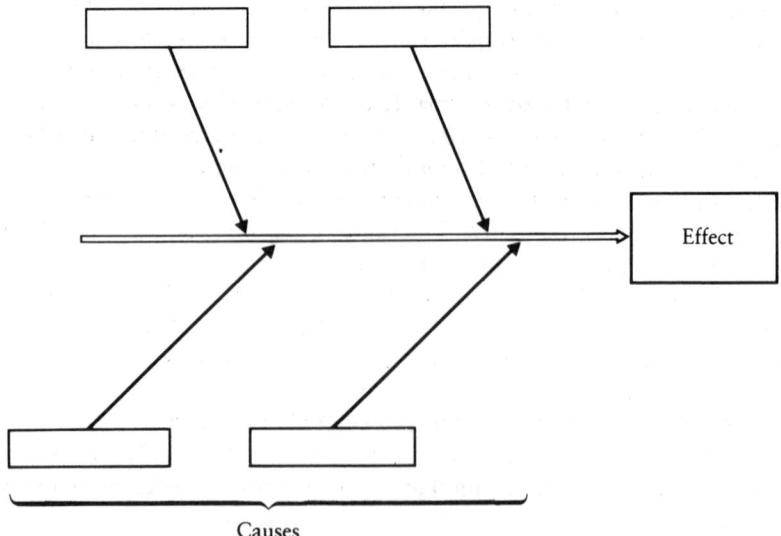

Figure 4.1   *Blank fishbone diagram*

The 'effect' is the quality characteristic that is under investigation; the problem that needs to be solved, the effect that needs to be improved or controlled.

Improvements are made by the removal or prevention of the factors that cause the effect.

The main factors that contribute to the effect are written on the ends of the branches. For manufacturing, 'manpower', 'materials', 'machinery', 'methods' and 'measurements' – the 5 'Ms' – are usually found to be very useful. The words act as a focus for the team's thinking.

Causes for each of these main headings can now be brainstormed onto the diagram. The questions 'Why?' or 'How?' can be asked for each heading, e.g. 'Why does "material" cause the problem?' The answer is written onto the diagram as a branch off the main 'material' branch.

The questioning process is repeated until all of the suspected causes and sub-causes have been recorded. The diagram can be reviewed and the suspected main causes underlined or circled. Plans are then made to investigate these causes further or to implement some remedial action (Figure 4.2).

Check sheets

Cause-and-effect diagrams answer the question 'What do we already know – or think we know – about a problem?' Check sheets are used to collect data to confirm (or deny) this thinking. They are also used to collect data to monitor a process or to monitor the changes that occur as a result of actions taken to remedy a problem. Check sheets can take many different forms and are designed by the team members as they are needed. Data are recorded by tally marks or checks.

In Figure 4.3(a), the frequency distribution of a single process characteristic has been simply recorded and in Figure 4.3(b), the relative frequency of different faults is easily seen.

Data are not collected unless they are to be used, and only the needed data are collected. There is no construction and upkeep of massive databases that are never consulted. Historical data are often treated with suspicion.

A further type of check sheet is the defect location chart (Figure 4.4). Here, the data are collected on a sketch or drawing. Different symbols can be used to record different types of problem. Again, the resultant data are very easy to assess.

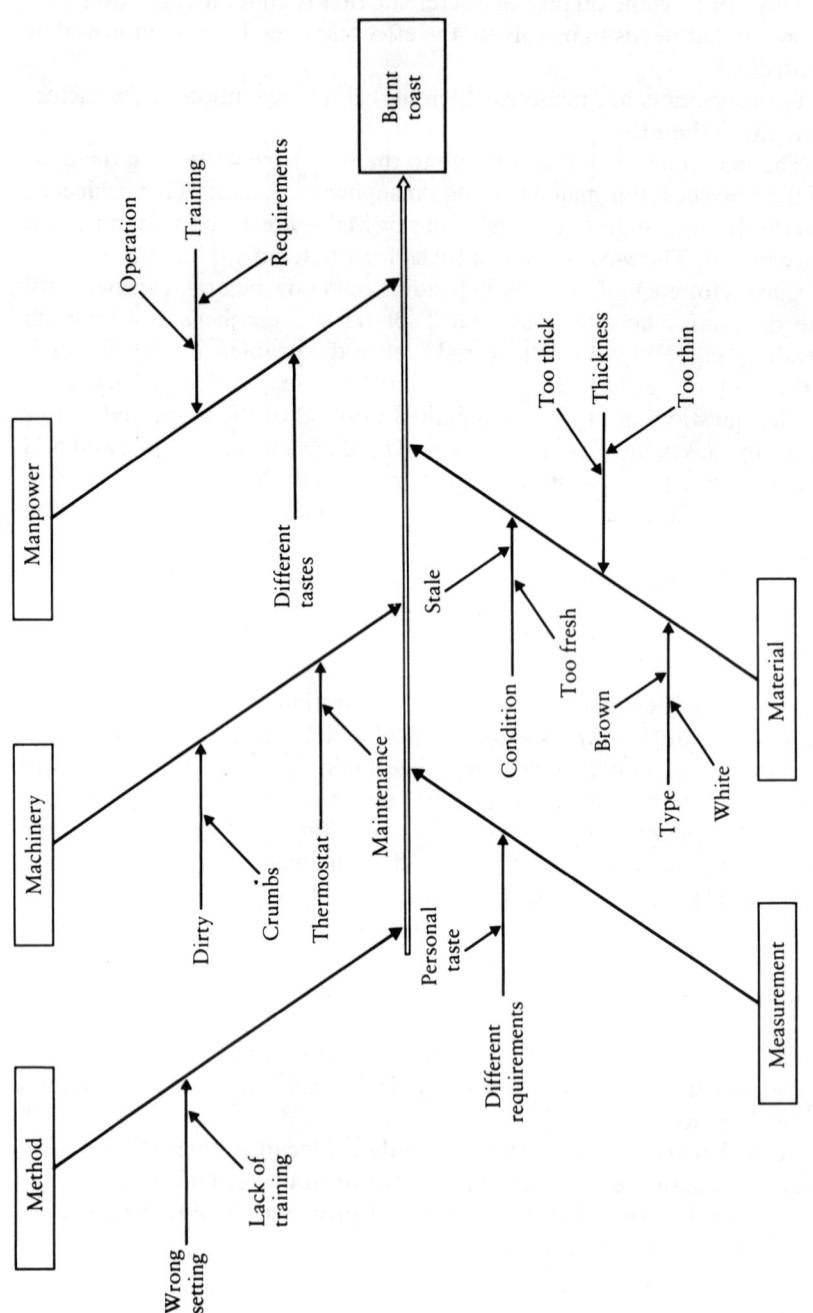

Figure 4.2 Completed fishbone diagram

(a)

Date: _____   Product: _____

Dimensions

	1.4	1.5	1.6	1.7	1.8	1.9	2.0	2.1	2.2	2.3	2.4	2.5	2.6	2.7	2.8	2.9	3.0	3.1	3.2	3.3	3.4
Total	1	2	6	13	10	16	19	17	12	16	20	17	13	8	5	6	2	1			

Frequency axis marked at 5, 10, 15, 20, 25. "Specification" lines at 1.7 and 2.7.

(b)

Product: _____   Date: _____

Fault		Total
Creases	⊞⊞ ‖	7
Stains	⊞⊞ ⊞⊞ ⊞⊞ ⊞⊞ ⊞⊞ ⊞⊞ ⊞⊞ ⊞⊞ ‖‖‖	44
Holes	‖‖	3
Dirt	⊞⊞ ‖‖‖	9
Spots	⊞⊞ ⊞⊞ ⊞⊞ ‖	17
Off-shade	⊞⊞ ⊞⊞ ⊞⊞ ⊞⊞ ⊞⊞ ‖‖	28
Others	⊞⊞ ‖	6
Total		114

Figure 4.3 (a) *Continuous data type* (b) *Defective items type*

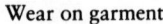

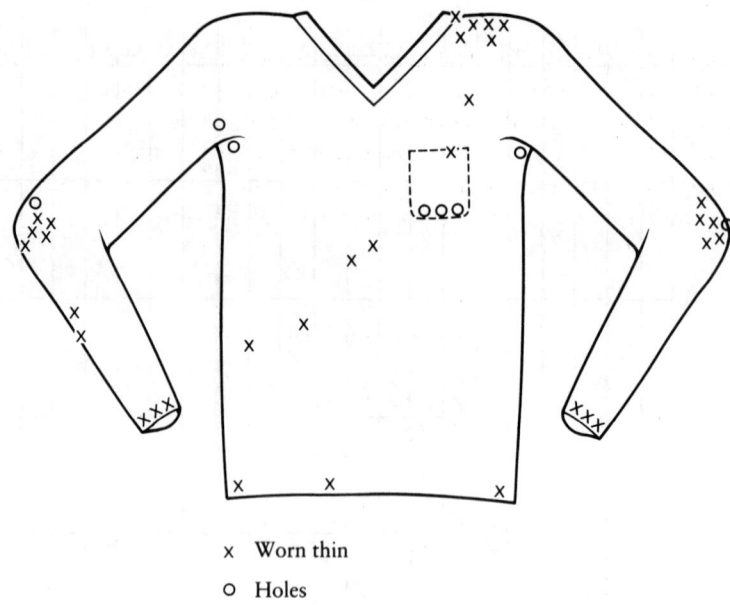

x   Worn thin

o   Holes

Figure 4.4   *Defect location check sheet*

Stratification

Stratification means to separate or classify into distinct layers or levels. For problem analysis, the more subsets used for data collection, the better.

Data from separate sources should be kept separate and discrete. (If there is a need – say for an overall picture, the data can be consolidated later.) The principle of stratification should be borne in mind when collecting and analysing data and also when designing experiments for the purpose of collecting data. Check sheets need to have a matrix design to capture all of the relevant data.

Examples are data from different machines, different operators, different batches of raw material, etc.

For an illustration of the effect of using un-stratified data, see the section on scatter diagrams (Figure 4.7(d)).

Histograms

Histograms are a way of arranging and displaying data so that *variation* can easily be seen (see Figure 4.5). This is exactly the same as the check sheet example shown at Figure 4.3(a), but redrawn with bars instead of tally marks. It shows the frequency of occurrence of one set of values compared with the frequency of another. In this case, the characteristic being compared is the dimension of output from a process.

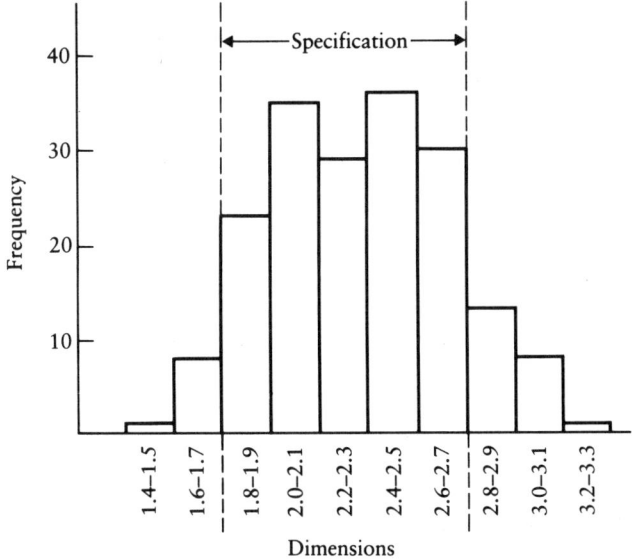

Figure 4.5 *Histogram*

Histograms are used to display numerical data in a form that can more easily be understood than a matrix of figures.

Pareto charts

All of the tools and techniques being discussed are tools for *action* – to make continuous improvements. Pareto charts are a means of prioritizing that action, since all problems cannot be tackled simultaneously. They

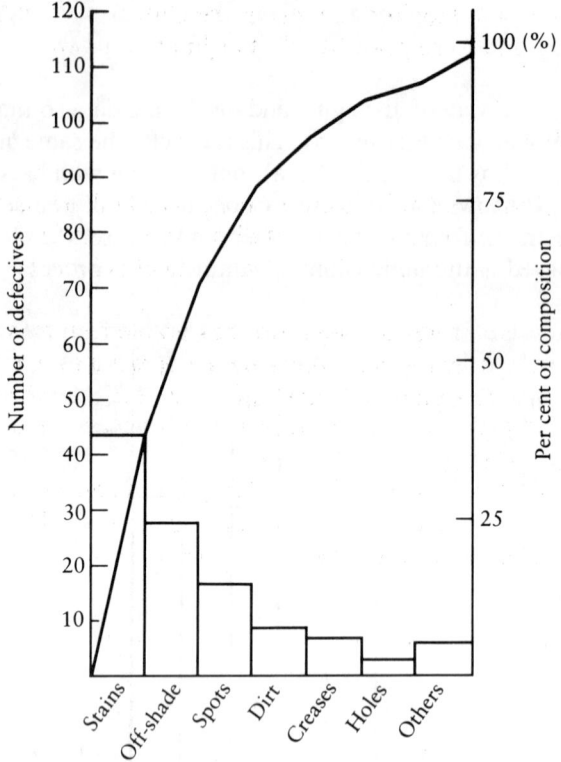

Figure 4.6   *Pareto chart*

are bar charts, redrawn with the item of greatest frequency at the left (Figure 4.6).

The right-hand vertical axis shows the percentage and it is immediately apparent that to make the biggest improvements, the items at the left of the diagram need to be tackled and solved. To prioritize action, it is a good idea, when possible, to put costs onto the various alternatives and then redraw the Pareto chart. Frequently, the problem with the greatest frequency of occurrence is not the same as the problem with the greatest potential for cost-saving.

The law of diminishing returns applies; solving problems on the right of the diagram will only reduce the overall effect by a small percentage and, furthermore, it is often easier to reduce a tall column by half than it is to remove a column completely. By collecting further data and drawing further Pareto charts as the problem-solving process gets under way, it is possible to monitor and review the effectiveness of the actions taken to date, and to re-prioritize if thought appropriate.

Scatter diagrams

When data is collected to confirm or deny the thinking that has gone into constructing the cause-and-effect diagram, scatter diagrams can be used to check for any relationship between the effect and the suspected cause.

If a causal relationship between two measurable factors is suspected, their values should vary in step. A scatter diagram is a simple graph with values for one factor plotted against the values for the other factor.

In Figure 4.7 (a), as factor x increases, factor y increases and so there is positive correlation.

In Figure 4.7 (b), as x increases, y decreases; a negative correlation.

In Figure 4.7 (c), the points are randomly scattered and there appears to be no correlation between the two factors.

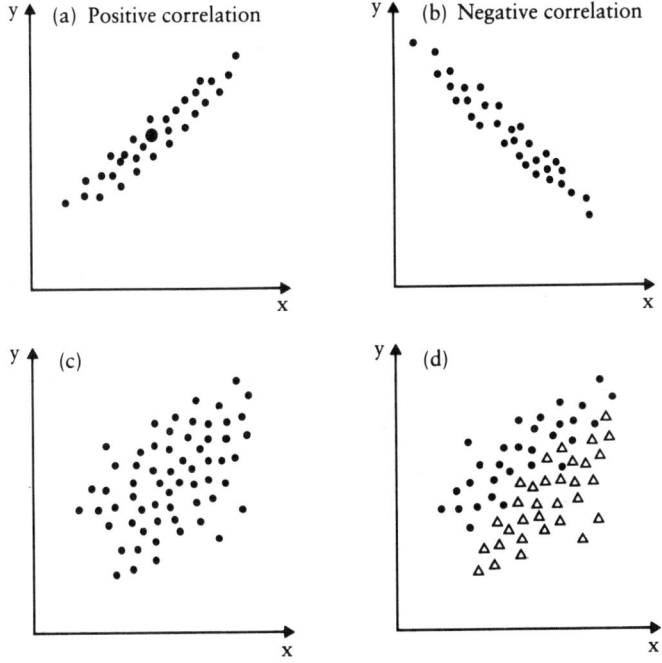

Figure 4.7 *Scatter diagrams*

Figure 4.7 (d) shows the result of not using stratified data. Looking at all of the points together there is no correlation. When the data are stratified, a positive correlation is observed for each of the two components.

Control charts

Control charts are used to monitor a process, to rapidly identify when the process has gone out of control and therefore, to prevent non-conforming outputs from the process (assuming that the process produces conforming outputs when it is in control). This latter condition applies when the desired output parameters are equal to or within the normal capability of the process. The control lines are not specification limits determined by requirements but, instead, reflect the previous stable performance of the process. (See Figure 4.8.)

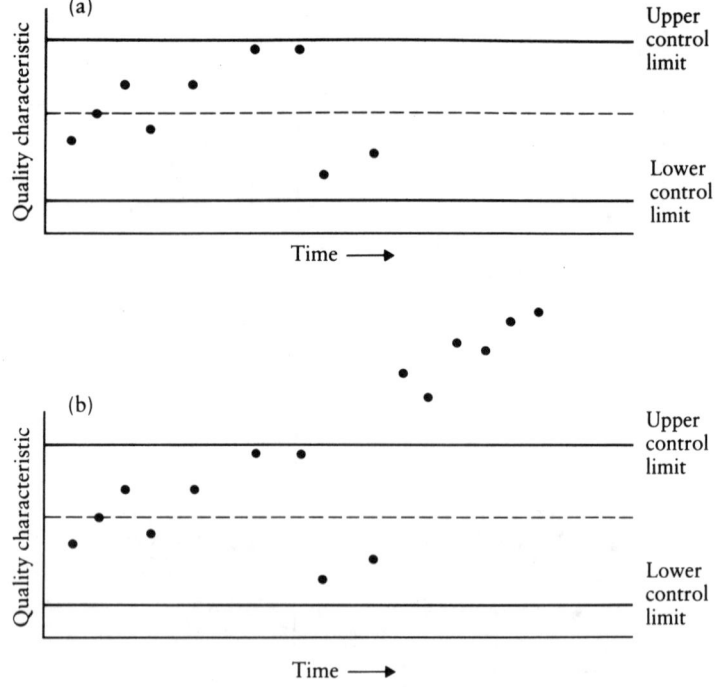

Figure 4.8   (a) *Conforming output* (b) *Non-conforming output*

The process is sampled at regular intervals and the desired characteristic is measured and plotted on a continuous graph. Trends towards non-conformity, or non-conforming outputs, are quickly spotted and corrective action can be taken, if appropriate. (Action should only be taken if the process is capable of producing conforming outputs and if the measurements indicate abnormal variation. For a fuller description of control charts, see a later section on statistical process control.)

The Deming cycle

The Deming (or Shewhart) cycle was introduced to Japan by Dr Edwards Deming in the early 1950s. It is also known as the plan-do-check-action or PDCA cycle and involves a simple feedback loop. It is an ideal technique for linking together the easily-learned problem-solving tools, as a continuous improvement process.

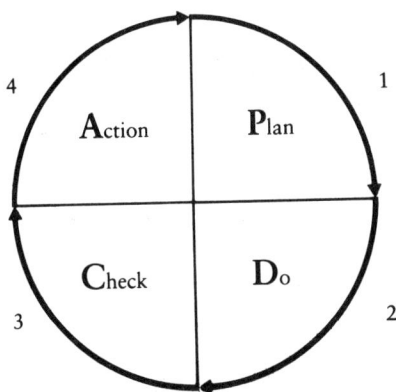

Figure 4.9 *The Deming cycle*

The technique (Figure 4.9) is used to counter the often-used process of leaping before looking or, 'Ready, fire, aim', to quote Juran. The *Plan* stage involves a full investigation of the problem – data collection, analysis and then proposal of solutions (using the above tools). The *Do* stage involves a trial, implementing the proposed change – preferably on a small scale. *Check* means to monitor the trial and observe the results of the change (again, perhaps, using the seven tools). *Action*, the final stage, is the action decided upon as a result of the assessment of the trial.

Statistical process control (SPC)

This technique, mentioned briefly in the section on the seven (old) tools of quality control, has developed from Shewhart's work on statistical variation as taught to the Japanese by Dr Deming in the early 1950s. Its popularity depends on the fact that small samples of data collected on a regular basis from a process can give a statistically determined indication of how the total process is running and whether it is producing conforming outputs or not. This information can then be used to control the process immediately and thus prevent non-conforming output. See Figure 4.8 (a) and (b).

Variation in outputs from a process can be as a result of *common causes* (e.g. weather, atmospheric pressure, small temperature changes, etc.) or as a result of special causes (malfunctioning machine parts, excessive wear, etc.).

Data is collected to help identify any special causes of variation and to establish the *capability* of the process. This is based upon the *range* of values produced and the *mean* (average) value.

In order to set up control charts, it is necessary to eliminate the special causes (by problem-solving) so that the process is capable of running in a statistically controllable way. The control limits are calculated from the data collected using standard statistical formulae and, for processes producing measured data, *Mean and Range charts* are set up.

In use, constant sized samples are taken at regular intervals and the means and ranged calculated and plotted onto the charts. There are various rules for interpreting the plotted data: points outside of the control limits, trends either up or down, too many consecutive points on either side of the central line, points bunching near the control limits. All of these mean that action is needed to investigate the cause of abnormal variation because the process is going out of statistical control and may be producing non-conforming outputs.

As with the other tools, training in the use of SPC is not enough; the benefits only come when it is used and when the information it produces is acted on.

Quality costing

Quality costs were mentioned during the introduction to this article – as a motivator, and perhaps the main reason for pursuing a positive, structured approach to quality management. Costs are also a very useful tool for measuring progress, prioritizing action and communicating success (or lack of it) during the quality management process. The iceberg diagram is a common way of demonstrating the costs of quality (Figure 4.10).

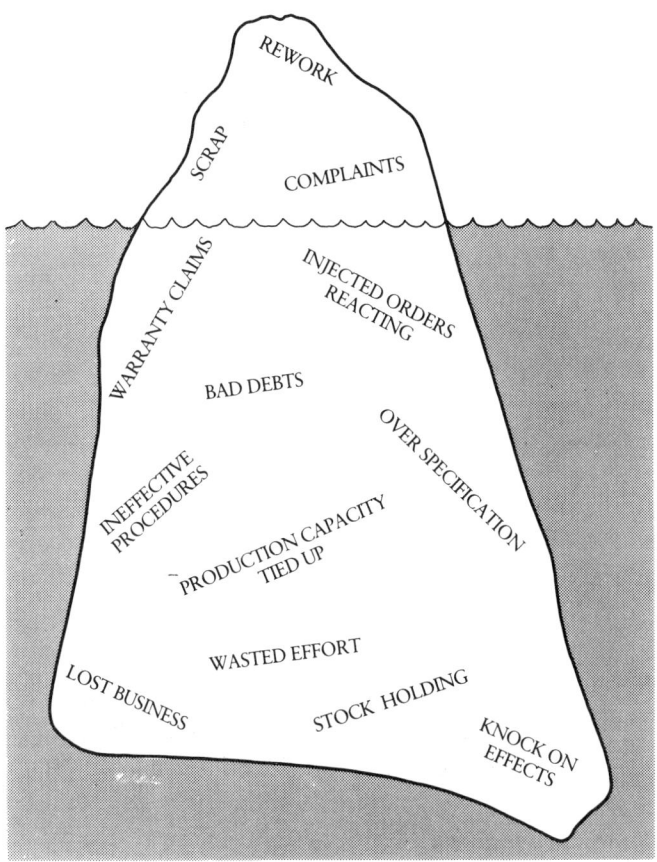

Figure 4.10   *Iceberg diagram of quality costs*

Some quality problems – and their associated costs – are obvious for all to see: those above the water level. However, there are many more quality-associated costs that are normally hidden below the surface. Perhaps you can think of more in each of the two categories that apply to your own particular industry, company or work environment?

A big area is always 'wasted effort' – time that is taken up in trouble-shooting, doing jobs twice, unnecessary checking, dealing with complaints, following inefficient or outdated procedures, etc.; time that could be better employed in looking for opportunities, developing new products, being more productive.

A further consideration concerning quality costs is the relative value that can be put on the stage of detection and correction of a problem. Problems that get as far as the customer may cost ten times as much to put right as those that are stopped before leaving the factory gate. These in turn may cost about ten times as much as those stopped in the area where they are created (see Figure 4.11).

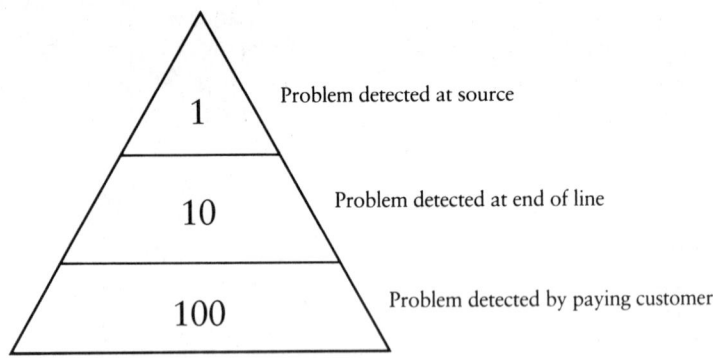

Figure 4.11 *Ratio of costs incurred when problems are detected at different stages*

It is clear that company quality cost information should be communicated to everyone within the organization – not in a blaming way, but as a motivator and as a measure or guide for improvement activities. Moreover, easily-calculated cost information should be made readily available to teams working on improvement projects within the company, no matter at what level. It adds a sense of reality and allows people to use their own judgements, make their own decisions.

One point needs to be made, though, when communicating cost improvement information; the savings are not automatically available for general distribution! The money saved is needed for future investment, reducing or maintaining prices to customers to remain competitive, further training, etc.

Company quality costing should be carried out simply but consistently. It is important to decide what costs to measure and then to continue measuring them; don't change the formula mid-stream. It is not necessary to include everything; timeliness and consistency are more important, and we do not want a whole new expensive department created just to keep track of the costs!

The costs can be split into the areas mentioned earlier – either costs of conformance/non-conformance or appraisal/failure/prevention costs. Some measure of the cost of lost opportunity can also be monitored (e.g. machinery and people being tied up whilst reworking) but care must be taken here; the cost only applies if the opportunity for doing extra work really applies. Part of the quality policy within a company should be to increase spending on prevention initiatives, e.g. quality training and a quality assurance system. The overall quality cost figure is then likely to go up initially but, in time, the benefits will work through and the improvements in failure and appraisal costs will more than offset the extra outlay. Furthermore, if the new levels of achievement are maintained (or improved further), the same saving is made year after year. Quality is *not* free, but good quality is certainly cheaper than bad and the best way to achieve good quality is by investing in prevention.

Departmental purpose analysis (DPA)

Departmental purpose analysis is quite different from any of the other tools that will be discussed. The output from the technique is like a job description for a whole department. The aims are to establish specific measurable targets and objectives for a department, in line with company objectives, and to get rid of wasteful practices. The technique is usually employed as part of a total quality management implementation programme once the board of directors has started to cascade the new company policy down through the organization.

The normal first step is to get the department manager and his immediate subordinates together (preferably for a day), and for them to clarify their own thinking on the department's aims. The process begins with the manager outlining how he views his roles and responsibilities, objectives and targets. These should be in line with the company aims and the requirements of his internal customers. These are discussed and then his subordinates, one by one, outline their contributions to the agreed department goals. Each statement is discussed by the group until agreement is reached. Progressively, understanding is built up on what everyone in the department should be doing to reach the department objectives. At the same time, overlapping activities and omissions are also identified and an improvement plan can be agreed to deal with these.

The agreed desirable activities are then quantified in terms of outputs, and suitable effectiveness measurements are confirmed. The deliberations of the group are documented and submitted to senior management and internal customers for comments, suggested amendments, etc. The process of refinement can then continue.

The seven new tools of quality control

These newer tools for quality management go beyond the original seven tools, both in complexity and in the depth of analysis, but they are still used in a team environment and people from different levels and functions can often contribute. However, the seven new tools are usually looked upon as management tools. With the exception of the matrix data analysis (see later), the seven new tools address verbal rather than numerical data and they are used mainly for improvement projects. Like the seven old tools, the seven new tools are often used in combination to get the best results.

Relations diagrams

Relations diagrams are a more detailed type of cause-and-effect analysis, used when the causes have complex interrelationships. It is a team-based problem-solving technique (see Figure 4.12).

The problem is defined and the potential causes are brainstormed. Often, each cause is recorded on a separate card and then the cards are arranged to build up the diagram, working outwards from the centre. Arrows are used to indicate those items that are related and what leads to what – cause-and-effect relationships. Patterns of arrows indicate key factors or causes.

Affinity diagrams

Like most of the seven new tools, affinity diagrams offer a very visual display of ideas and information, which helps to analyse and clarify issues. The result is *action*, but based on a detailed and well-thought-out structure using creative input from a team of people.

As with relations diagrams, the subject for clarification is defined and then ideas about the subject are collected on separate cards. These are then arranged and grouped so that similar ideas are next to each other.

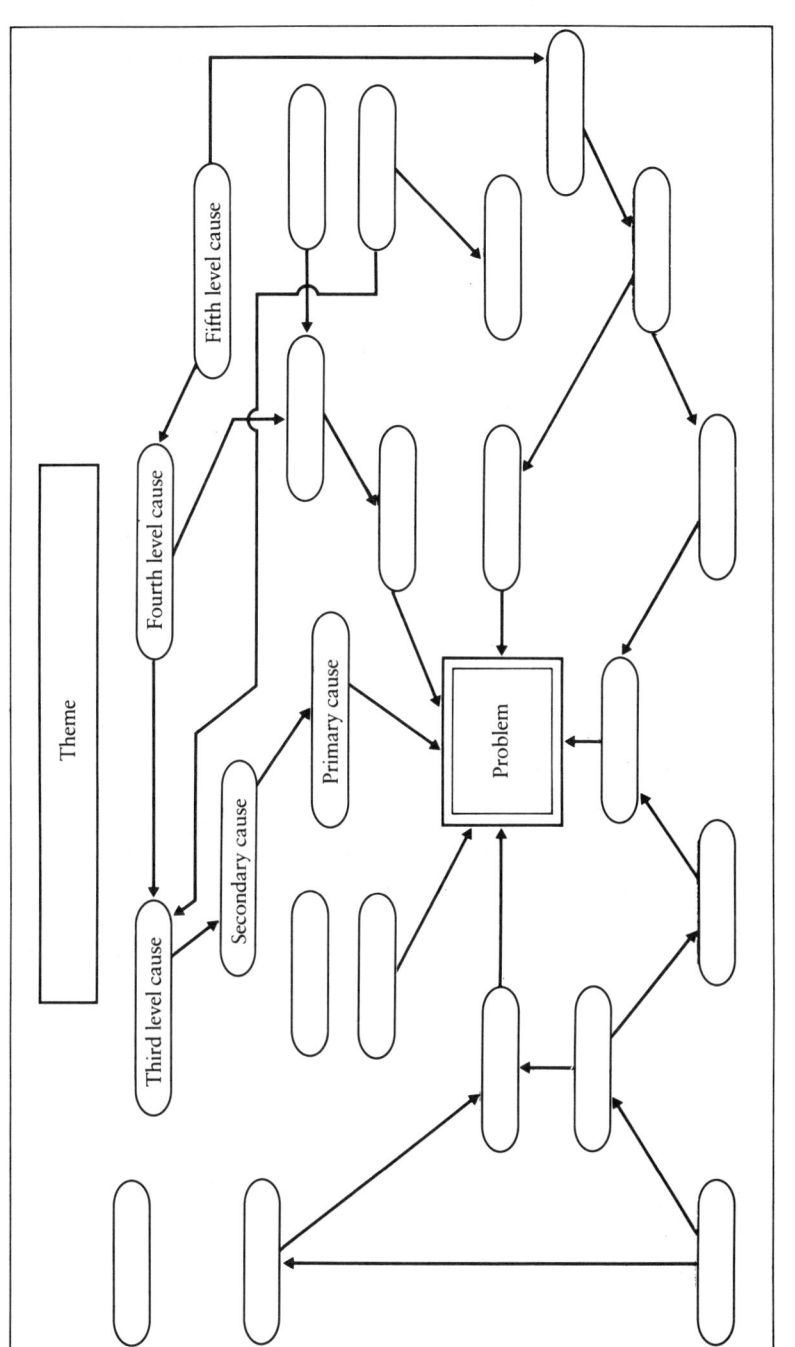

Figure 4.12 *Relations diagram*

The shuffling of cards goes on until all of the cards/ideas are arranged into clear areas or themes which are a subset of the original subject (Figure 4.13).

The subsets and the ideas contained within them can then be used as a basis for action.

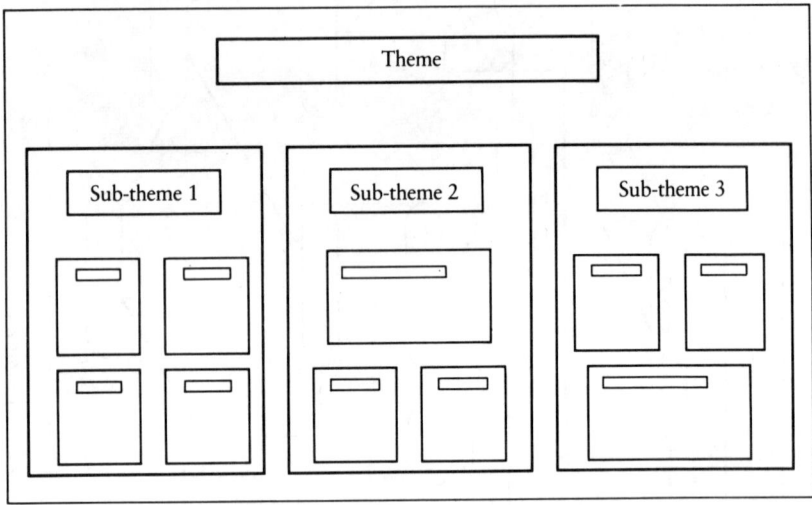

Figure 4.13   *Affinity diagram*

Tree diagrams

These are used to systematically map out the activities that must be accomplished to reach a desired goal, step by step (Figure 4.14). The objective is written at the left of the page and the question 'How?' is asked. The primary means of achieving the objective are identified and recorded. The question is repeated to identify secondary means, etc. Gradually, the tree diagram is built up.

When finished, the diagram is reviewed from the right, asking the question 'If this is completed, will it lead to the accomplishment of the next idea or task?'

The technique is obviously of use for project planning and for identifying the steps along the way to achieve the desired result.

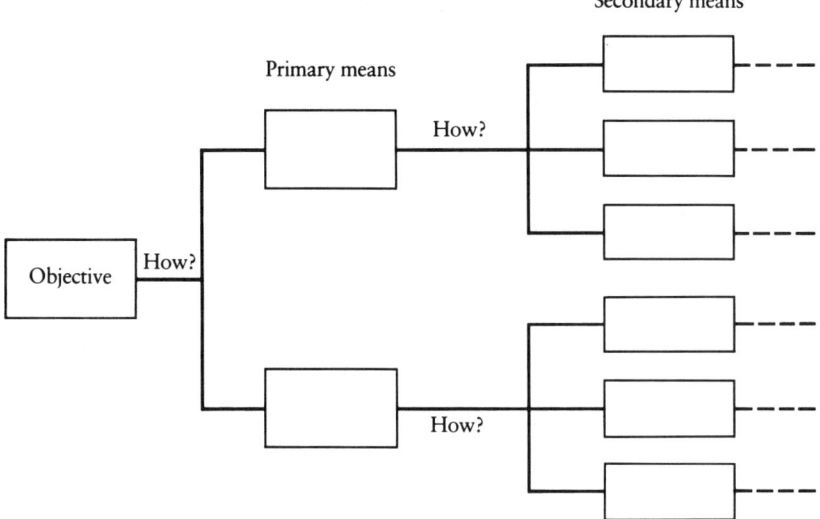

Figure 4.14   *Tree diagram*

Matrix diagrams

Matrix diagrams (Figure 4.15) are used to evaluate for relationships between different characteristics and to establish their relative importance. One set of ideas is listed along the vertical axis of the matrix and the other set is listed along the horizontal axis. The matrix provides the structure for systematically evaluating the relationship between the two sets of ideas.

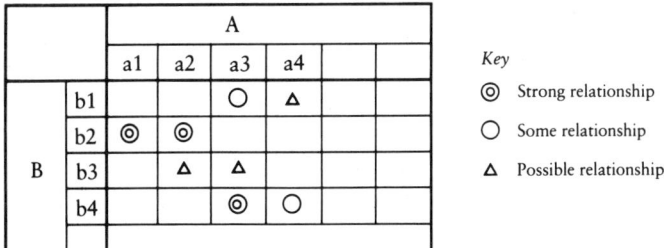

Figure 4.15   *Matrix diagram*

In Figure 4.15, $a1$ . . . could be a series of product features and $b1$ . . . could be a series of customer requirements. Each feature is compared with each requirement and evaluated for relevance and importance, different symbols being used to indicate the strength of the relationship. In this way, a visible picture of exactly what is wanted is gradually built up, and actions can be planned to meet the requirements. Instead of features/requirements, the diagram could be used for causes/effects, objectives/methods, etc.

Matrix data analysis

With large matrix diagrams, a technique is required that provides results in a more visually acceptable manner. The symbols are converted to numbers and the large arrays are usually evaluated and displayed by a computer. The tool, known as matrix data analysis, becomes a specialized method using a technique from statistical multivariate analysis called principle components analysis.

Process decision program chart (PDPC)

PDPC is used for process optimization and error prevention. It uses the tree diagram (mentioned earlier) and evaluates the proposed process, step by step, to anticipate possible problems and make plans to prevent them.

Each major branch is taken in turn and the following questions are asked: 'What could go wrong at each step?' and 'What other path could this step take?' The new direction is drawn onto the diagram. Preventive actions or countermeasures are listed for each step. The process of evaluation is continued until the whole diagram has been picked over and as many probable errors as possible have been identified and planned for.

Arrow diagrams

Arrow diagrams are a flowcharting process used for planning or scheduling tasks and are similar to Gantt charts. The tasks necessary to complete a job are listed and the probable time required for each task is estimated. The tasks are put into chronological order.

Each task is represented by an arrow and the start and end points by a circle (Figure 4.16). Dotted lines represent relationships between tasks but with no time dependency. From the diagram developed, it is

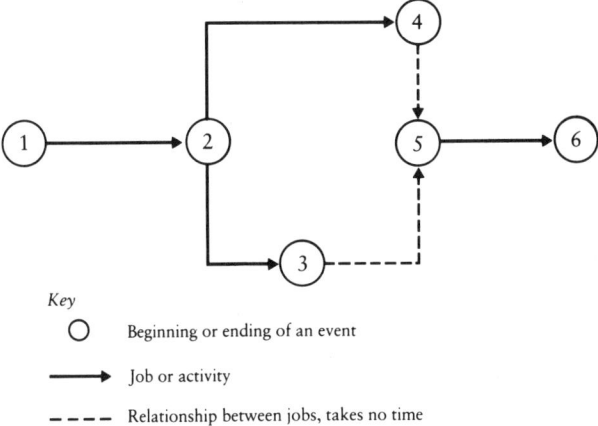

Key

○   Beginning or ending of an event

———▶   Job or activity

– – – –   Relationship between jobs, takes no time

Figure 4.16 *Arrow diagram*

possible to carry out critical path analysis (CPA) to establish the shortest possible time for project completion, and programme evaluation and review (PERT) to consider alternatives ('what if?' simulations). A summary of the seven new tools is shown at Figure 4.17.

Other management tools

Many of the tools discussed previously can be used for planning and problem-prevention in addition to problem-solving, but the following group are used exclusively for the former purpose. The tools described are used by technical people in research, design and development functions.

Figure 4.18 shows a comparison of the number of engineering changes made by Japanese companies and by Western companies when introducing a new product. The areas under the two graphs are an indication of the costs involved.

Our aim should obviously be to adopt the continuous-line graph approach to quality management as opposed to the, more usual, dotted line, i.e. getting the work done up-front instead of the panic just before production commences and the remedial action once production has begun.

Affinity diagram	Provides order to verbal data by organizing it into similar categories
Relations diagram	Logically relates complex cause and effect relationship
Tree diagram	Used to systematically map out the activities that must be accomplished to reach a desired goal
Matrix diagram	Identifies presence or absence of relationship between characteristics and shows their relative importance
Matrix data analysis	Uses data from a matrix diagram and displays it such that it is more easily viewed
Process decision program chart	Helps select best processes by evaluating the progress of events and possible outcome Helps to anticipate the unexpected and thus plan for it
Arrow diagram	Used to plan or schedule tasks

Figure 4.17 *Summary – 7 new tools*

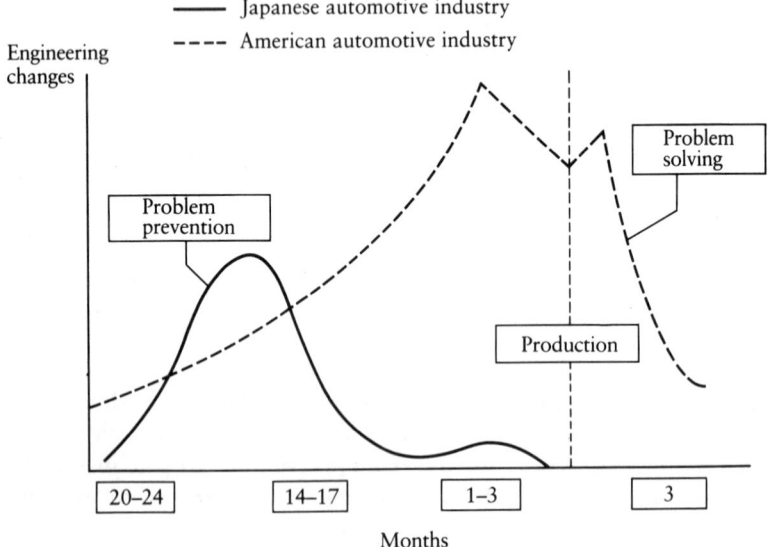

Figure 4.18 *Engineering change comparison*

Failure modes and effects analysis (FMEA)

FMEA is used as a planning and problem-prevention technique and is similar to the process decision program chart (PDPC) and tree analysis discussed earlier. Again, it is a team technique where the team is made up of people who can contribute critical knowledge and ideas for the analysis of a proposed new process or product. The analysis can be carried out for the process itself – *Process* FMEA – or the product – *Design* FMEA. Process FMEA will be described.

The process steps are defined and then critically reviewed asking 'How could this step fail?'; 'Why?'; 'What would be the outcome?'; 'What is the likelihood?'; 'How could we detect it?'; 'What process controls are required to prevent it?', etc. Whenever possible, the potential problems are ranked in order of severity of effect, likelihood of occurrence, likelihood of detection, etc. The risk priority numbers obtained by multiplying together the ratings for occurrence, detection and severity, highlight the criticality of the potential failure modes and offer a means of prioritizing preventive action. This technique is known as FME(C)A – failure mode effects and criticality analysis.

The technique ensures that the process is understood in detail and identifies the need for additional process controls or where elaborate controls are *not* needed. The purpose is to prevent quality problems from arising along with their attendant costs, delays, frustrations, etc.

Quality function deployment (QFD)

'Carrying the voice of the customer through to the factory floor' is the aim of this technique.

QFD is a customer or market-driven planning tool which uses a thorough analysis of customers' requirements or wishes and can then deploy them through all stages – from initial research and product design to distribution and after-sales service. At a basic level, it is a cost-prevention method which minimizes start-up costs and delivery delays. However, the main advantage of quality function deployment is for recognizing and prioritizing the desirable features that *could be* built into a new product or service – and then making sure that they are delivered. It is a competitive-edge marketing tool for producing products and services that exhibit features that are *exciting* and not merely adequate. It is an opportunity-development process rather than one of problem-solving or problem-prevention.

QFD uses a series of matrix diagrams (discussed earlier) to link the needs of external customers to internal processes. The first matrix relates customer requirements to product features, as at Figure 4.15, but also looks at customer priorities, relationships between different product features and comparisons with competitors. The process of filling in the matrix is time-consuming and depends on good teamwork and good team leadership. The resultant diagram is called a house of quality (Figure 4.19).

Once the desired product features have been agreed, the process can be repeated, perhaps with some different team members, to deploy or translate these features into component part characteristics and then further into manufacturing operations and production procedures (Figure 4.20).

At all stages, the questions asked are 'What is the requirement?', 'Which is the most important?' and 'How can we achieve it?'

Taguchi methodology

Two concepts promoted by Dr Genichi Taguchi are of interest to us here: the quality loss function and prototyping techniques using orthogonal arrays.

Taguchi claims that any variation from the specified target causes a loss to society and the extent of the loss can be calculated from a parabola centred on the target (Figure 4.21).

Being within specification limits still incurs a loss. Quality needs to be pushed back to the design stage because quality control and SPC can never fully compensate for a bad design. Design can be split into three stages: system design, parameter design and tolerance design. Parameter design will be discussed here.

The aim is to identify the factors which really effect the overall performance of a system and then to establish those parameters which control the factors. The parameters are identified by carrying out experiments using different levels of the factor; orthogonal arrays are used to drastically reduce the number of trials that need to be carried out.

In Figure 4.22, the subscript to the L in the left-hand column indicates the number of trials that need to be carried out to assess the importance of the variables listed in the second column. The third column indicates the number of experiments that would need to be performed using a conventional (non-statistical) appraisal method.

In Figure 4.23 there are four factors A, B, C, D, each at three levels.

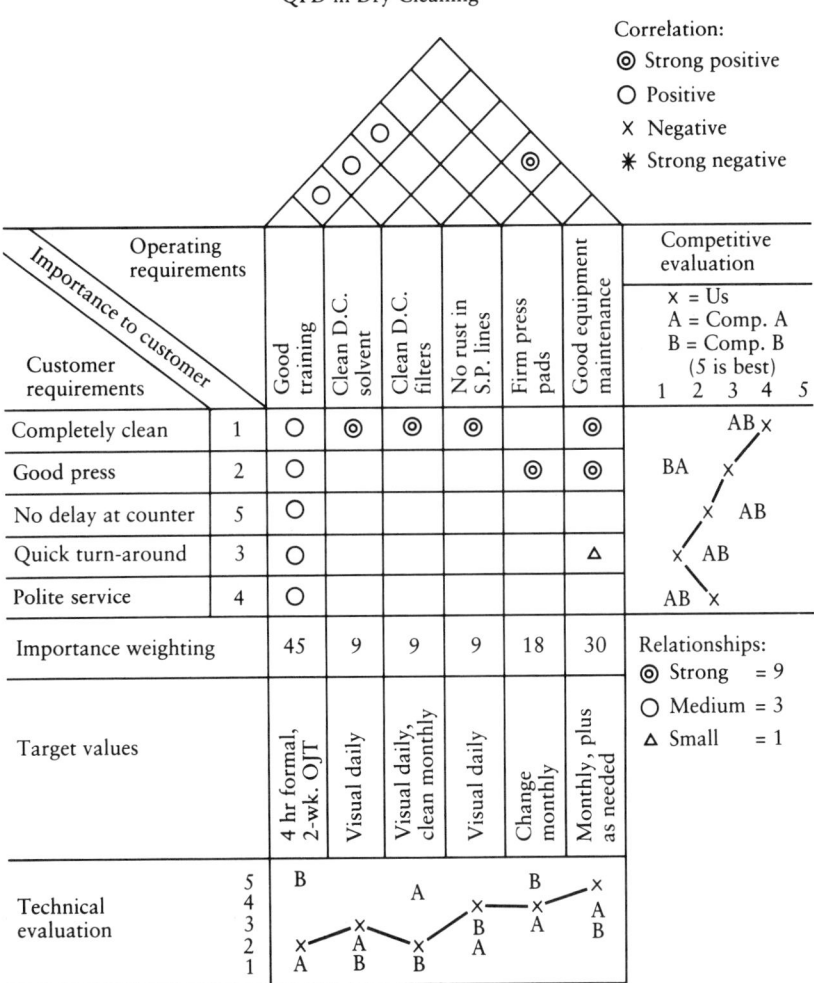

Figure 4.19 *One house of quality*

The factors could be machine speed, temperature, machine pressure and raw material. The 81 possible combinations of variables can be tested in just nine trials using the combinations shown in the rows above. After the trials have been run and the results analysed, further experiments can be carried out (if necessary) to zoom-in more accurately on the ideal parameters.

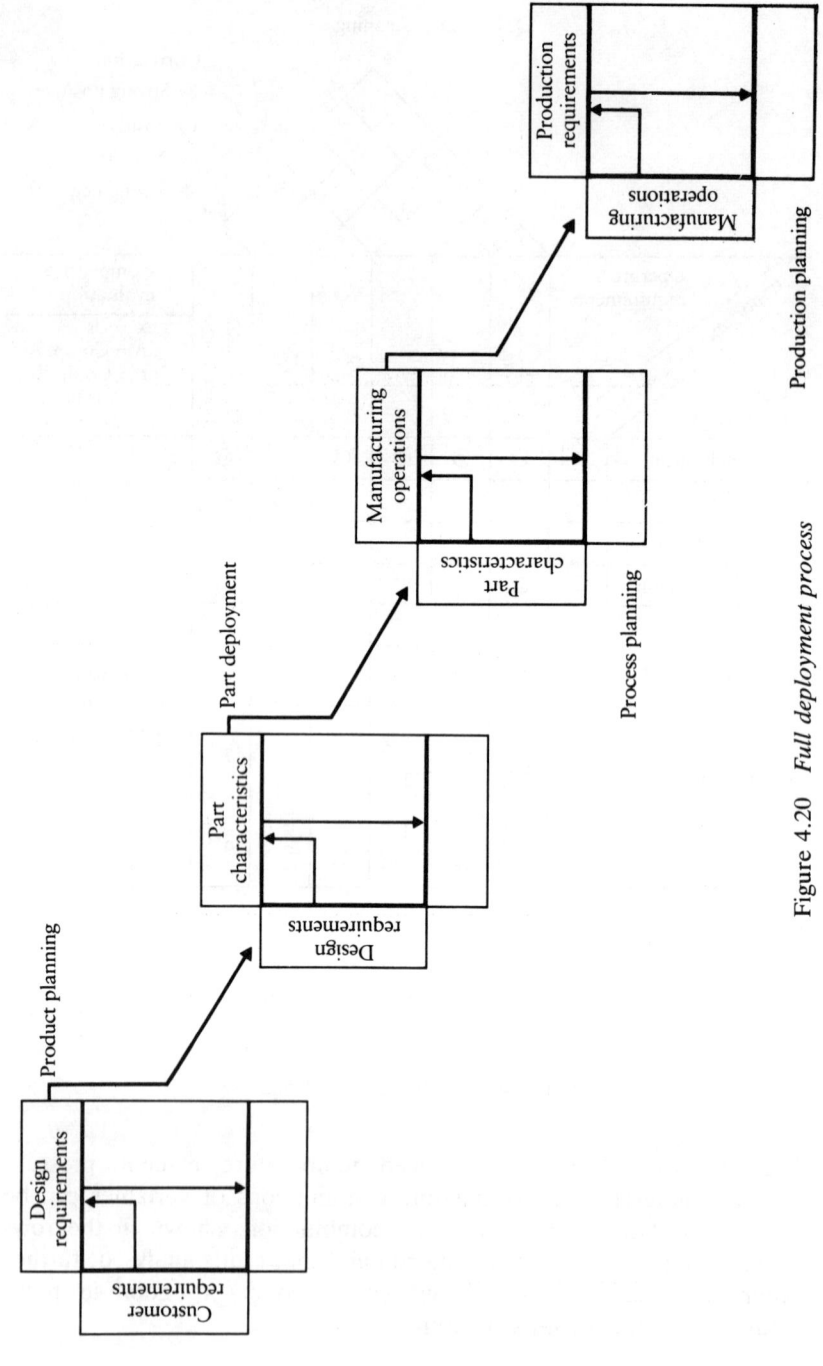

Figure 4.20 *Full deployment process*

Loss in £s

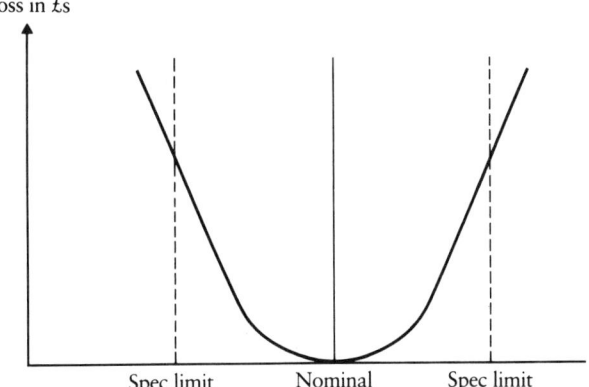

Spec limit   Nominal   Spec limit

Figure 4.21   *Taguchi loss function*

L_4	3 × 2 levels	(8)
L_8	7 × 2 levels	(128)
L_9	4 × 3 levels	(81)
L_{12}	11 × 2 levels	(2048)
L_{16}	15 × 2 levels	(32 768)
L_{18}	$\begin{cases} 1 \times 2 \text{ levels} \\ 7 \times 3 \text{ levels} \end{cases}$	(4374)
L_{25}	6 × 5 levels	(15 625)
L_{27}	13 × 3 levels	(1 594 323)
L_{54}	$\begin{cases} 1 \times 2 \text{ levels} \\ 25 \times 3 \text{ levels} \end{cases}$	(1.7×10^{12})

etc.

Figure 4.22   *Common orthoganol arrays, with number of trials in full factorial experiment*

Trial \ Factor	A	B	C	D	
1	1	1	1	1	
2	1	2	2	2	
3	1	3	3	3	
4	2	1	2	3	
5	2	2	3	1	L_9
6	2	3	1	2	
7	3	1	3	2	
8	3	2	1	3	
9	3	3	2	1	

Figure 4.23   *L_9 orthogonal array*

Summary

We have looked at many tools and techniques in this article; there are several more, and variations on the ones discussed. More important than the tools, however, is the right *management attitude* towards total quality. Continuous improvement should become 'business as usual' for everyone within the organization, where everyone feels ownership for quality and for the company's future. Managements' key role is to develop a participative atmosphere within the organization, where peoples' inputs to the improvement process are valued and encouraged. The aim should be to create a structure and adopt methodologies that develop the full potential of all employees; that allow people to grow.

Facilitation in the use of the tools and techniques of TQM can aid this process of creating a new culture by encouraging teamwork, breaking down barriers, stimulating the learning of new skills and techniques, increasing the understanding of company processes, etc. To allow the TQM process to yield results, time and other resources must be made available for the solution of problems, development of new designs and processes, implementation of new ideas, etc. The expectation of instant results will lead to disappointment.

Training in the tools and techniques is important, but equally important is that the tools get used. There is a danger that people can become tool-collectors, always looking for another tool or technique to add to the list – the perfect tool that will give instant answers for little effort supplied – but using none. Using the wrong tool for the job, or using the right tool in the wrong way are potential pitfalls, leading to lack of progress and frustration. Trying to use tools that are too complex can lead to poor communication, lack of ownership and time-management problems.

Where possible, training should be given in team-leadership skills to get the maximum benefit from the use of the tools and techniques that have been discussed. Some techniques yield very poor results if an open teamworking environment is absent; good leadership is essential to draw the needed information from the other team members and make the team process enjoyable. Finally, the team working on a project need to see their contributions in the light of the overall company effort; they need to be able to relate their efforts to the company strategy and vision. It is important that all projects being worked on are overseen by a steering group and that there is programme cohesion and feedback on progress.

5

Quality – the Sony way
Hiro Nakamura

In 1988, Sony Bridgend Plant won the British Quality Award, the first Welsh-based company to do so. The purpose of this chapter is to provide some insight into the reasons why that award was achieved.

Background to Sony Bridgend

The manufacture of high-quality products has always been a major objective of Sony Corporation. The plant employs about 1,500 people, supplies 30 different countries and has a turnover of £181 million.

In 1973, when Sony Bridgend was set up, the public believed that Japanese-made electronic goods were far superior to those made in the UK. Therefore one of the major tasks of the Bridgend management team was to ensure that the quality of Bridgend-made products was seen by the public to be at least equal to those made in Japan.

For ten years, we ensured that the quality of our finished products was first class by methods based on inspection. However, in the early 1980s we realized we would have to change our ways. Three factors influenced our views:

1 The plant was still growing in size and complexity and we had proposals for it to develop even further.
2 Market competition was intensifying – the quality of our competitors' products was improving and we could no longer justify a big price premium for our products.
3 We needed to increase the volume of our production in order to reduce costs.

Our drive to change our method of operation was triggered by Mr Masaaki Morita, Deputy President, Sony Corporation, who launched a company-wide programme to improve Sony's manufacturing operations worldwide – this was called Innovation '86 – and the aim was to make Sony the strongest, most efficiently productive manufacturer in the world of electronics. The basic theme was to ensure that management tackled not just problems themselves but the real source of those problems, what Mr Morita called *upstream action*.

In fact, when faced with requests to authorize expansion of output at Bridgend, Mr Morita made a very simple point to us. He said 'show me you can improve your performance by actual results and I will support your further development'. It was quite clear to us at Bridgend that our existing methods of achieving quality were not based on the principles of *upstream action* and that much of our management activity on quality was *downstream action*.

We realized that *in-process quality* was the key issue – that *quality must come first* and new means had to be found to produce higher quality the first time. We had to *do it right first time*.

Motivation

We realized from the start that the key issue would be motivation. We knew that we would achieve little without the whole-hearted collaboration and support of our company members. We believed a fundamental point was to establish a company theme. The theme had to be:

● simple;
● common to everyone;
● quantifiable;
● ongoing.

We decided that quality had to be our first priority.

In order to provide a common quality *language* for all company members we decided that the *defect rate at the final assembly lines* would be our universal quality parameter.

It is our belief that most people have a sense of pride in achievement and that this is a great motivating factor. It was our objective to harness this in our drive to improve our company's operations.

The role of top management

Having said that the motivation of company members was basic to the achievement of our goals, it must be said that the drive for improvement came from the top and that Innovation '86 was very much '*top down*' in its approach.

It is clear that unless senior management is fully committed to the idea of a real improvement in quality, exercises leadership and devotes time, energy and resources to this objective, then it is impossible to motivate the rest of the organization.

The plant's quality strategy

The basic principles underpinning our quality strategy were:

1 Upstream action;
2 Quality must come first;
3 Do it right first time.

From those three basic points we developed our 1984 *action plan*. We divided that action plan into two areas:

● *Software* which includes: communication
                                   education and training
                                   management by objectives
● *Hardware* which includes: company re-structuring
                                   equipment
                                   product

Software

Communication

The first priority was to ensure that all company members recognized that the senior management policy was *quality must come first* and that this message was ongoing. Also the progress of the company towards its goals must be known and understood by all company members. All company members need to know that quality is their own individual responsibility.

Regular communication systems and methods which already existed were modified to include regular updates on both overall company quality achievements and individual unit quality achievements. All parts of the business were required to adopt *visual control* methods to indicate quality performance and output. These charts were, and still are, prominently displayed throughout the plant. For example, an overall summary chart of total process quality is displayed outside the main canteen. By updating these charts on an hourly, daily and weekly basis, all company achievements, problems and failures are communicated to all employees.

Education and training

A series of management techniques was identified by senior management as being necessary. These were introduced at all levels of management as company policy by a planned sequence of education and training programmes. The most important of these being:

- *Kepner Tregoe* These are techniques to aid management in problem analysis, decision analysis, potential problem analysis and situation appraisal.
- *CEDAC* CEDAC stands for cause and effect diagram with the addition of cards. This technique comprises the standard Ishikawa cause and effect (fishbone) diagram, but is operated through the use of add-on cards in such a way as to involve any company member who can contribute either towards problem identification or solution, or both. Apart from its direct strength in problem-solving, its power is increased through visibility. Each unit manager was required to display CEDAC diagrams within his section, thus making progress against target achievement clearly visible to everyone, providing added pressure for successful outcomes. Line managers and supervisors found the CEDAC diagrams to be excellent focal points in their continual aim for improved quality communication and involvement of the production workforce. *Such visual displays are a very important basic management tool.*
- *Frequency charts* This is a method of displaying and prioritizing 'one-off' problems together with intermediate actions and 'foolproof solutions'.
- *Quality action groups* These are, in effect, quality circles, but with the important addition of a supervisor. Activity is targeted at improvement by the group itself, not as a vehicle to make suggestions for other people to implement.

Management by objectives

A comprehensive series of meetings and discussion sessions were held which set targets for the company as a whole. These targets were then broken down by each 'unit' into firstly *unit targets*, then *section targets*, and then *individual line targets*. Thus every manager had his/her own set of individual targets which he or she was expected to meet.

In addition, the existing annual personnel appraisal scheme was modified to include an assessment of the ability of an individual to meet his/her targets and how effectively he/she had used the management techniques.

Actual achievement of the target was important but not as important as the method.

Hardware

Company re-structuring

The key elements of the re-structuring were:

- clearly define 'bottom line' responsibilities; and
- ensure that the individual with the 'bottom line' responsibility had the resources under his/her direct control to meet the 'bottom line' objectives.

Therefore a *matrix management system* was introduced with the plant being split into 'units' and each 'unit' having its own 'managing director'.

The production manager of each 'unit' was given the 'bottom line' responsibility and controlled day to day priorities whilst people from the service departments ensured that the correct company standards were maintained.

Equipment

A project was started to re-equip the plant for 'quality manufacturing'. The production equipment, together with total preventative maintenance, had to be capable of producing goods with zero defect. Total capital expenditure on this project was £14 million.

Product design

It was recognized in 1985 that the product must be designed to meet both the customers' specifications and the manufacturing specification.

A TV chassis was therefore designed specifically for the European market – the *Eurochassis* – which was not a derivative of a chassis designed for the Japanese or North American market. The first products designed with the Eurochassis were introduced in July 1987.

What we have managed to achieve at Bridgend is a change in our manufacturing culture. *We have moved to a system where we now manage the process – not the rejects.*

Some major issues

In achieving this fundamental change there are a number of issues that we believe are important. They are:

- The taste of achievement
- The power of the target
- The visual display of information
- Interactive communication
- Management by example
- Design improvements
- Supplier quality

The taste of achievement

If you are going to motivate people they must have confidence they can achieve the targets that have been set. Therefore, we decided that the first target we should set should be on just one product and should be such that our people could see clear and definite progress towards that target. If a target is too hard then people give up; if it is too easy there is no incentive to make a real effort.

Having achieved the first target – a taste of achievement – it is much easier to set a second more difficult target because people then have much more confidence in their own ability – in effect *success breeds success*.

To recognize success we have a '*defect-free zone award*' system in which groups of operators can achieve *bronze/silver/gold* awards depending upon the amount of time they have achieved production without creating any defects.

The power of the target

Having said that it is important to set achievable targets, one should not underestimate how powerful a motivating factor targets actually are. Without a target people have nothing to aim for. Providing the target is clearly understood, it is amazing how quickly and easily people will respond. One simple trick that we have found to be effective is to set an initial target at, let us say, 10 per cent and then to set the next target at half that, 5 per cent. The third target is then 2.5 per cent, etc. From our experience, people who have achieved the 10 per cent target can accept that the achievement of 5 per cent is possible but if we had set 5 per cent as the initial target, I am doubtful if we could have reached it in one step.

The visual display of information

Whilst we have developed many sophisticated computer-controlled systems for displaying schedule achievement, one of the simplest and most effective means we have employed has been a manual system.

Our production supervisors must, on an hourly basis, complete a large white board showing their production targets and achievement throughout the day. The fact that it is a manual and not an automatic operation means two things:

- the supervisor must be aware at all times exactly what is going on in production;
- the fact that it is written down for everyone to see makes it clear to everyone the progress of the lines during the day.

It must be admitted it took many months before this simple system became effective but now is regarded as a normal part of life for our production supervisors.

In addition, wherever you go within the plant you will see visual displays, not just of production achievement, but of every kind of measurable performance factor.

Information in itself is useful but unless it is widely displayed and widely understood it cannot hope to be a means of motivating the entire workforce.

Interactive communication

The Bridgend Plant communication system has been in existence for 15 years. It is an improvement on what is known in the UK as the *'briefing group system'*. Every Monday morning all senior management and a wide group of middle management (about 50 in all) meet for approximately one hour to discuss the business of the plant.

Three topics are always discussed first. These are:

- Production output
- Quality results
- Production efficiency

The rest of the meeting is unstructured and each manager in turn can raise whatever matter he wishes to communicate. These items can range from important safety matters through, for example, to social events and visitors to the plant.

The meeting is then summarized by a senior executive of the company with the responsibility for employee communications. That summary must be prepared by 12 noon and usually comprises 4 A4 doublesided sheets. Approximately 100 copies of the document are circulated to the people who attended the meeting. In the afternoon subordinates are briefed by their managers on the content of the communication meeting. At the start of the following morning, supervisors and managers brief remaining company members on what went on during the previous day's communication meeting. By 12 noon on Tuesday everyone in the plant must have been briefed. This procedure is repeated each week.

What we are concerned about is making sure our people get the information. We are not too concerned about the *style* but we are very concerned about the *content*. The information is immediate, it is regular, it is authoritative and it is true. We believe the problem with the traditional *briefing group system*, which relies on meetings every month or longer, is that by the time the meeting is held the information is out of date and everyone knows it anyway.

As far as Innovation '86 was concerned the key decision was to elevate *quality* to the most important item on the communication sheet – it became headline news each week and thus signified how important quality was to the management team and to the company as a whole. Week after week company members were informed of our progress towards our targets. It gave us the opportunity to highlight success and congratulate groups or departments which had achieved notable results.

It also enabled us to point out our failures and what we needed to do to avoid them in the future.

Management by example

If you are going to convince people that you care about quality you *must be seen to care*. You cannot isolate yourself in your office and rely on statistics. You have to go out and see what is actually going on so that people can see that *you* are really interested.

In our plant the general managers will visit the production lines at least twice a day to talk to management and supervisors, to ask about results, to give advice and to help create good habits. This *hands on* approach is, I believe, an essential requirement. *It is the essence of leadership*.

Management alone cannot create good quality. We cannot manage people on a minute by minute basis. We have to leave them alone and trust them to do the job in the correct way. Therefore, we must encourage them to manage themselves. Talking to people on the shopfloor, understanding what is really going on is, I believe, a vital part of the role of any manager who wishes to improve quality. It cannot be done by simply sitting in an office. *Management by example* is the way to do it.

Design improvement

I have already mentioned that one of the areas we looked at was the design of our products. Good design is vital to the consistent production of high quality products. A good basic design has enabled us not only to improve the quality of our production process but this in turn has led to a situation where we can now really contemplate a *just-in-time* production system.

Just-in-time can only work if the quality of production is first class and therefore the improvement in our process quality has given us enormous gains in terms of lead time and inventory reduction. The result of this is that we can now be much more flexible in our response to the market.

Supplier quality

I must also make reference to the impact that our quality campaign has had on our suppliers. We have moved away from a system based on incoming inspection to a system based very firmly on the belief that suppliers must provide us with components which match our specification. It is *their* responsibility to ensure that we do not receive faulty components.

Therefore the philosophy of our component quality control system now emphasizes control of the process at the supplier. The management group concerned spends the majority of its time assessing the ability of suppliers to produce defect-free components and helping them to improve their production process to match our requirements. We have found in general that suppliers are enthusiastic about our approach and are more than willing to co-operate on developing a long-term relationship. They not only gain a reliable customer for their products but also reap the same kind of rewards that we have in terms of increased efficiency and reduced inventory. Again, it is a case of *success breeding success*.

As we move towards a *just-in-time* production system we see developing around us a larger and larger group of local suppliers who are committed to supplying us with the very highest quality components.

Conclusion

Winning the British Quality Award was a great achievement for us, but it is not the end. The improvement of quality is a continuous process, and we are aiming for *zero defects*.

But even when we have achieved this goal we will not be able to relax. We will have to maintain that achievement and there will always be room for further improvement.

6

In pursuit of customer satisfaction
Peter Pring

There is nothing new about the need to compete vigorously in international markets but now the sheer pace of change is quite staggering. As world markets open up, as all forms of communication become easier and faster, as new technologies shorten product life cycles, customers are making more and more exacting demands. I think it was an engineer who said that insanity is doing the same thing twice and expecting different results. I think a marketing man might say that in today's world it would be insane to do the same thing twice and expect the same result.

Globally, 3M employs 89,000 people with sales in 1990 of over $13 billion. In Europe, we employ about 22,000 people in 19 countries designing, manufacturing, distributing and marketing over 60,000 products, ranging from abrasives to sophisticated medical products, from Scotch videotape to cleaning management systems, from reflective materials used in road signs to the ubiquitous and happily addictive Post-It™ note. We serve many markets through country-based subsidiaries within which we have set up small market-focused business teams whose primary role is to keep us as close as possible to our customers.

3M United Kingdom PLC is just such a subsidiary company, employing over 5,000 people in laboratories, factories, offices and, of course, in the field. The management challenge is to ensure that each of these 5,000 people – no matter what job he or she does – understands that quality improvement is his or her responsibility and that anyone who fails to recognize that becomes part of a problem the rest of us have to solve.

We manage the business with clear financial goals and with strongly defined human resource and business principles. Every manager and supervisor has personal accountability for achieving his or her part of the corporate plan which is clearly identified and regularly reviewed. The sum of the parts has to add up to the desired whole. This means that our planning processes are sophisticated and time-consuming They are, however, an essential basis for a quality programme. We believe that a quality organization has to have clear direction, a clear mission and clear standards of behaviour and business practice.

Like many organizations, we were inspired in the late 1970s by the realization that Japanese companies were proving more effective in designing quality into products and processes than their Western counterparts. So how did we begin to create a total quality culture? Well, the first step was to build awareness of what good quality means.

This involved a recognition that good quality costs less than poor quality; that good quality means high productivity; that quality must be practised in every part of the organization, not just in production; and above all, that quality is customer-driven and leads to growth and increased profitability.

We tackled this awareness issue by inviting all our employees to participate in quality workshops in which we defined the nature of the challenge and sought everybody's active participation in the process of improvement. Meeting customer requirements was the order of the day.

Not everybody was impressed by this type of publicity. The lesson learned was that managers only respond well if quality is seen as an integral part of the management process, not an extra piece of bureaucracy or flavour of the month dogma foisted on them by a keen, newly appointed quality manager who has a job to do. So it was not until some managers – mostly in manufacturing – began to realize the potential of their people by empowering them to identify and solve problems through corrective action teams, or quality circles, that things began to happen.

Initially, the focus was on product quality and internal processes, but it gradually spread to service issues, with a steady switch from improving productivity to customer satisfaction as the driving force. Today, quality is part of every business plan, is aimed at the market and is designed to anticipate customers' future needs, needs of which even they may not be aware.

Our quality process is led by a corporate quality improvement team (see Table 6.1), currently chaired by our managing director, but always chaired by one of our board members. The team exists to provide leadership and drive; to ensure that key corporate quality issues are identified and addressed; and to remove any major 'road blocks'.

Table 6.1 *Total quality management structure and process*

- QIT
- Rotating chair
- Annual plan
- Corporate quality manager
- Awareness
- Visits
- Quality managers

The key elements of our quality improvement plan for 1990 were as follows:

- Demonstrate commitment
- Assess customer expectations and define requirements
- Meet customer requirements
- Involve suppliers
- Add value to product offering
- Maintain new product flow
- Improve business systems
- Involve everybody
- Create publicity – promotion – recognition
- Measure progress

Nothing can happen without commitment. But the word commitment is often over-used. When a manager talks about commitment, sometimes compromise isn't far behind. We demonstrated commitment by doing things rather than saying them. We have all been victims of the boss whose idea of leadership is to wait for somebody to do something well so he or she can claim the credit. That is why each of our directors has identified an area of quality improvement and made it his own. We call these 'Bellwether Projects'. Here are some examples:

- Improve telephone call handling quality
- Increase customer satisfaction with service for non-standard items
- Improve inventory ratios
- Improve new product introduction systems
- Improve receivables systems
- Enhance new product launch disciplines
- Develop a better appraisal system
- Improve delivery reliability

A particular project chosen by our managing director was 'improving telephone call handling quality'. It affects everyone in the company and, despite its simplicity, it has a profound impact on attitudes. We all receive and make telephone calls and know how it feels to get a truly helpful response. We also know how it feels to get the opposite. By highlighting this issue, and investing some of his personal time in it, our managing director has been able to influence attitudes in a very positive way. By agreeing to invest in a new telephone exchange network which provides systems improvements, he has demonstrated commitment in a way nobody can deny.

Another way in which we demonstrate commitment is by giving employees time and travel budgets to participate in problem-solving or corrective action teams. This always involves bringing people together from different disciplines in the company, and often people from different countries. These teams are expected to disband as soon as their job is done. We also encourage ongoing quality circles for which facilities and time are provided when enthusiasm for them is apparent. Our view is that quality circle membership has to be voluntary – you can't legislate enthusiasm; you can't legislate innovation.

One of the most successful of these quality circles is in 3M's Treasury Department where active employee participation has produced dozens of sound ideas and significantly enhanced employee morale. This demonstrates that quality is no longer – and should not be – the preserve of the production manager. It must permeate all functions.

Here is an example from our Treasury Department. Every month, a major retail chain – the 'victim' in this case – queried as many as 90 invoices for goods despatched to its stores by 3M. That was unsatisfactory for them and for us because they didn't pay the bills while they were querying the invoices. Therefore, at the instigation of people in the accounts department we put together a team of people from 3M, their customer and the carriers used to deliver orders. They got to the root of the problem which was related to delivery documentation systems. As a result the team eliminated virtually all of the monthly queries. Moreover, we were able to enhance our reputation with that customer, develop a partnership with him, and create long-term positive relationships for the future.

Another such quality circle is led by a sales manager. It was set up in 1989 and it comprised people from different disciplines, based at our Manchester office. They devised a quality action request system which produced twenty-one significant improvements in its first two meetings. Sixteen of those ideas have now been implemented.

Table 6.2 illustrates one of their achievements. The records filing system at the office consumed valuable space and was time-consuming to manage. It was replaced by a purpose-built document management

Table 6.2

MANCHESTER SALES OFFICE Quality Circle Document Management Project	
	BEFORE
Space Required	90 × 4 − Drawer Filing Cabinets
Space Costs	£70,000 over 7 years
Labour	5 Clerks
	AFTER
Costs	£600 over 7 years
Labour	3 Clerks

system. The employees knew that the old system had outlived its useful time and the quality action request system provided them with the opportunity to get it changed.

The most important benefit was not the cost saving but improved customer service. Previously, it had taken an average of 45 seconds to retrieve a document in response to a customer query. Now this time has been reduced to an average of 15 seconds. The group had identified an issue, found a better way, obtained management support and measured the result.

Measurement of improvement is vital. It provides a guide for the future and, more importantly, it provides encouragement for participants. The danger is that it is easy to get caught in the trap of measuring activities that make our own people feel good, but which reveal little about levels of customer satisfaction.

We have made that mistake on occasions in 3M. Examples of measures of self-gratification include numbers of sales calls per day, sales growth, or percentage distribution costs. All these are necessary, but they do not measure customers' satisfaction. For example, transport costs savings which are achieved at the expense of reliability are counter-productive. We must measure the things the customer experiences, not allow him to be the victim of our own perceived internal success.

Measurement is tough. It is easy to fool oneself and that tends to provide cynicism amongst the staff experiencing a problem but getting no response from management. That is why we have just invested over a million dollars in a survey of our European customers. It involved over

18,000 interviews. The survey was designed to tell us four main things about our customers:

- what customers look for in a supplier;
- what matters most to them;
- how 3M performs against customer expectations;
- how competitors perform.

From this we are developing detailed customer service plans for each of our markets and are setting up corrective action teams to tackle the gaps and deficiencies in our performance.

We have discovered a great deal from the customer service survey. For example, we were surprised that some of our customers were comparing us with companies which we had not previously thought were our competitors. In other words, when customers look at service, they do not just look at the service of your direct competitors. They look at the company which gives the best service. That is where we have had to benchmark. We also gained a keener appreciation of the sheer diversity of customer expectations – and that's a real challenge for large organizations with centrally managed logistics functions such as ours. Not surprisingly, key issues included things like direct contact activities, information flow, order handling, reliability of supply. Even more interestingly, product quality was not a highly ranked issue. That does not mean product quality is unimportant to customers. They take it for granted.

The need to know more about individual customer expectations has caused us to make a very substantial investment in enhanced order management systems and to challenge some of our previous performance criteria.

An example of the way that performance criteria can be highly misleading was found in a business that involved the supply of a large variety of fast-moving goods through an extensive network of third-party distribution in which distributors place orders for up to 100 different line items on a single order.

We thought our service was good. Everybody said they were achieving 98% delivery performance. What nobody recognized was that 98% of 98% of 98% does not actually add up to 98%. Orders were indeed shipped fast, but rarely were they complete. In fact, we found on analysis that only 83% of items, as opposed to orders, were despatched on time, and sometimes it took up to four separate despatches to complete a multi-item order. Something was always out of stock. The result, more paperwork for us and for the customers, and delays in supplying the products the customer wanted.

After the analysis, the business manager set 100% as the target. Nobody really believed that 100% was possible, but nobody was prepared to accept that we build in an element of failure into the target and make it part of our mindset. That was a tough challenge and it required the establishment of a whole new relationship between every function in the supply chain. We started by publishing the goal – 'to achieve a 100% order fill rate by ensuring that every aspect of the service chain from sales forecasting through to the physical receipt of the goods by the customer operates to specific standards'.

A team was put together involving all key disciplines in the supply chain. Each was made aware that his department had to contract to achieve specific performance targets if the goal was to be achieved. Some of the actions taken are shown at Table 6.3.

Table 6.3

INVENTORY MANAGEMENT
Service results achieved with virtually NO
additional investment in inventory

Key Actions

- Detailed Service/Communication Specifications
- Clearly Defined Interface – Key Supply Sources
- Improved Forecast Accuracy: 75–80% → 90% +

- Lead-time Management
- Agreed Safety Stocks

Contrary to the original belief of the sales group, the solution was not a matter of holding more inventory. We had to give better performance specifications to our internal groups, we had to communicate better with each other, we had to improve forecasting skills, we had to plan inventory holding better, we had to measure internal supply performance better and we had to refine safety stock parameters.

The result of all this hard work by that team illustrated the value of this approach (Table 6.4). Stock availability improved dramatically, despatch date reliability improved and paperwork was reduced. In particular invoices were reduced. Fewer shipments meant fewer invoices. Most important, a high order fill rate was achieved. Strangely

Table 6.4

KEY RESULTS

- Stock availability up: 83% $\rightarrow$ 96–99%
- 94–96% of items shipped on time
- Items per customer invoice up: 3.5 $\rightarrow$ 6.8 items per invoice
- Order fill rate up: 80–85% $\rightarrow$ 95–97%

---

enough, but I suppose we should have expected it, the result of all this work was not that the inventories had to go up to give better service, but inventories actually reduced quite significantly.

As we discover how to serve our customers better, we become clearer about what we want from our suppliers. So just as we are now measured and ranked as suppliers by our most sophisticated customers, we now work with our suppliers to define clearer expectations and measurement systems. We measure the performance improvement of some 100 key vendors against delivery quantity and quality indices. Their quality assurance systems are being audited directly or through third party approval to ISO 9002 or equivalent standard. We expect this to result in us having stronger partnerships with a smaller number of suppliers, more tuned in to our business objectives. All our own major plants in the UK are now qualified to ISO 9002 and, where appropriate, other standards such as the Ford Motor Company, Q101.

A key area, that depends on excellent teamwork and mutual understanding at all levels, is lead-time reliability. By this we mean delivery which is neither early nor late. That's one of the most critical issues today when inventory carrying costs are so high. An early delivery used to be regarded as a good one. That is no longer the case. In the period 1984 to 1988, we reduced our inventory ratios by 31 per cent and we aim to achieve a further 30 per cent reduction by 1992. Our customer service survey told us that consistent on-time delivery was a key customer expectation. Indeed, supply chain management, by which I mean efficient management of the flow of goods from raw materials supply through manufacturing and distribution chains to the end user, is a great opportunity area.

The next part of our 1990 plan related to adding value. It's no longer sufficient to provide a good quality product. Today's buyer is looking for quality in every aspect of the business relationship. It is with this in mind that we invested quite heavily in a new technical centre just a stone's throw from our administrative headquarters. We can invite our existing and prospective customers to visit us so we can offer them technical advice and help in applying our technologies to solving their problems. Over 1,700 companies came to visit that technical centre in its first year – we had expected about 200.

I have already emphasized that to remain competitive companies have to pre-empt and manage change by anticipating future market needs, because it's only by having an eye on the future that anyone can hope to meet customer expectations. Customers of 3M expect us to provide new and better products that help them stay ahead of their competition. Our way of stimulating attention to this is expressed in one of our four corporate objectives, which is fairly unique. We set ourselves the target that in any one year at least 25 per cent of our sales should come from new products – that is products which were not in the market five years earlier. This constant spur to innovate, backed up by investment in research and development at twice the level of most large industrial manufacturers is another key element of our quality plan. All of these things are part of our quality approach.

Improving customer satisfaction is only a part of our quality approach. The continuous improvement of our internal processes is also a vital part of the plan. We have to ensure that our cost structures are right. To do this, we have to drive down the cost of quality by eliminating waste and failure.

You can see from Figure 6.1 that over the last four years we have reduced the cost of quality in our manufacturing operation by about 30 per cent, as a result of opportunity analysis and investment in preventative systems, state of the art technology, design, or enhanced work practices. But, to achieve this, we have had to make organizational changes so that responsibility for quality rests with the primary producer of the work, not with an external inspection/audit function.

There's one other key and topical quality strategy. We call it pollution prevention pays. It's a 15 year old programme that seeks to eliminate pollution at source. In other words, not to create pollution, which is another word for waste, in the first place. This 3P programme is a global one which we have implemented to good effect here in the UK with estimated savings of over £10 million. But, just as important, we have prevented hundreds of tons of pollution. When we research customers and their expectations, we find that evidence of caring environmental policies are figuring higher on the list of their priorities than ever before. We saw that in some research we recently carried out in four countries in Europe. One in five of the respondents said that a caring environmental policy was the top attribute they looked for in their suppliers, a quite astonishing finding.

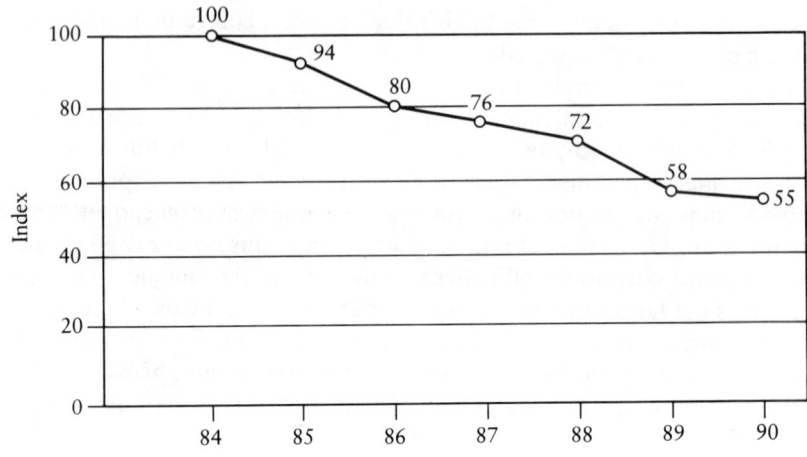

Figure 6.1   *UK manufacturing – cost of quality*

Our quality policy is specific. 'Products and services must be useful, safe, reliable, environmentally acceptable and represented truthfully in advertising, packaging and sales promotions.' Easy to say, but tough to live up to in today's environment.

In our employee opinion surveys, the responses illustrate a healthy intolerance of failures wherever they occur. We are, indeed, fierce critics of ourselves.

In 1989 we were naturally delighted to receive the British Quality Award, especially to be the first company to be recognized for its total corporate programme. Obviously, such an award provides welcome enhancement to a company's reputation. But the real importance lies in the recognition such an award bestows on our people, for it is they who make or break the company. This recognition has helped to provide encouragement and focus.

We also try to convey a quality message through our own internal award schemes. Globally, 3M recognizes the contribution of teams and individuals who bring about significant improvements. 3M in the UK won two of these awards last year. In the UK, exceptional individual performances are rewarded by a Bond of Excellence. It's like a share certificate, equivalent in value to two 3M shares, so it gives people a sense of ownership. And to date over 300 of our employees have now received these bonds. Every year we send 10 randomly selected people who have won these awards to the United States to attend the Annual

Shareholders Meeting. Our view is that if you do not take care of your people, they will not take care of your customers.

It's always encouraging to note that these awards are available and we're delighted that the European Foundation for Quality Management, of which we are regular members, has now decided to launch the European Quality Award. Let's hope that this will again stimulate European companies to strive for competitive excellence through total quality management.

A former Chairman of 3M, Lou Lehr, once said, 'if you look at quality as a fad, then I think you have to look at 3M as a fad'. That is not how we want to be viewed. As we enter the 1990s, we recognize the need for continuous improvement, based on an even deeper understanding of customer requirements and on an increasingly meaningful evaluation of our performance, by which we mean rigorous measurement of customer satisfaction. Whatever we did in the 1980s is now history. It certainly won't be good enough for the 1990s.

7

Training for total quality: British Steel shows the way

David Procter

Introduction

No matter what you read or see with regard to total quality, the message is clear. You must train you workforce in the principles, tools and techniques of quality improvement. To quote Philip Crosby 'If you want people to get it right first time, you must tell them what "it" is'.

In the late 1970s Teesside Works had around 22,000 employees. Less than a decade later this had been reduced to under 7,000. Over the same period, dramatic productivity improvements were achieved that brought the Works towards world best standards. A simplistic view of this change would be to review the number of departments that had closed. Whilst this was certainly a factor, the picture is actually very complex. Retrenchment alone would not have led to the survival of steelmaking in an area with 150 years of tradition. The ability to change year upon year, backed by investment in training and retraining, was the key to success. Training had to be designed to extend the skills and knowledge of individuals and groups to cope with the changing demands of their particular jobs.

British Steel, General Steels, Teesside, therefore adopted the policy of 'telling' the workforce what 'it' was in respect of their changing role within the Works and the General Steels Business.

Total quality performance

In 1988, in order to continue to strive to be a leader of the International Steel Community, the Works launched 'total quality performance'

(TQP) and was faced with the daunting task of training *every employee*. Previous training initiatives had involved only relatively small numbers.

But, whilst gurus, academics and consultants exhort management to train, little practical advice is forthcoming when faced with the question 'How do we handle it?'

In describing the key features and organization of training at Teesside Works, it is hoped that others may benefit and find that training the total workforce can be straightforward if you have committed and dedicated management (see Table 7.1).

Table 7.1   *Teesside works TQP objective*

Teesside Works will be a profitable, efficient and innovative leader in the international volume steel market.
Our aim is to provide all customers, internal and external, with quality products and services and to strive for continuous improvement.
This will be achieved through harnessing the capabilities of safety conscious, high calibre, technically aware and well-trained employees.

The basics of TQP

TQP approaches the problem of long-term survival by focusing on Teesside Works' most important asset – its people. One part of TQP is a training and development strategy that started at the top and is reaching every part of the organization. Its ultimate aim is that everyone will recognize that quality is the most effective route to customer satisfaction and that this is the key to survival and growth.

TQP begins with top management

Total quality performance is not a quick fix. The encouragement and reinforcement of a different emphasis in attitudes and behaviour goes deep into the underlying culture of an organization. To change culture, behavioural change must start at the top. Managers at all levels must have a strong and lasting commitment to the strategy and provide the bedrock on which others can build their own conviction and structure their own activities. Quality companies have a management style and approach that reflects their focus on quality. One of the aims of TQP is to provide the knowledge and the techniques for managers to develop the attitudes and behaviour required to carry commitment through to action.

TQP puts the emphasis on people

TQP is about balancing all resources – people, systems and technology – to optimum effect so as to maximize customer satisfaction. Not just in terms of products but also the kind of company with which the customer would prefer to do business. The human resource drives both the systems and technology used in companies and provides the link between them. It is the human resource that provides the most scope for total quality improvement. TQP promotes improvement through people, using systems and technology to support what they do.

The conventional route to quality in the West has been the systems route – an emphasis on structure and procedures, for example BS5750/ ISO9000, to control quality rather than improve it. This has been inadequate because the systems have been imposed on people, rather than developed with them, and so may fail because inadequate attention is paid to the human element. It's easy to produce scrap faster when automation tackles the symptoms rather than the fundamental problems. The systems and technology routes are both high cost routes.

The low cost route is to start from the assumption that people are assets to be invested in and developed.

TQP aims

As commitment and action towards improvement extends throughout Teesside Works, so a process of bottom-up pressure will be set in motion. The energy and initiative of employees will be released. A climate will grow in which all-round improvement can take place. People are more aware both of what they are supposed to do and what Teesside Works is attempting to do (see Figure 7.1). They recognize that their desire to do a job well and be part of a successful company can be fulfilled.

Duration		Approx. start date	Audience	Group size	Population size
1 × 2 days	Top team workshop	April 88	Works steering committee		12
1 × 2 days	Blue and red card workshops	June/August 88	Blue card/ Red card	18	120
4 × 1 day	Middle management training	November 88/ July 89	Middle management	18	1050
1 × 2 hours	TQP communications presentation	March 89	Everyone below middle management	50	5760
2 × 1 day (min. 1 week apart)	TQP supervisor training	June/July 89	Supervisors/ foremen	18	460
2 × 1 day (min. 1 week apart)	TQP workforce training	September 89 onward	All other employees	18	5300

Figure 7.1 *TQP education/awareness*

Organizing for TQP

TQP is monitored and controlled by a steering committee at Works level and by committees established by each works manager for their area or function.

It is not the role of any committee to take action but to ensure that actions are given priority and that resources are available to take such action. Where actions cannot be taken by individuals there will be a need for a teamwork approach. Teams comprising of individuals in an area under the control of a single manager are called *action teams*. Where the problem crosses department boundaries the team is called a *task force*. Task forces are initiated by the steering committees. Whilst this formal arrangement applies in most companies with a total quality philosophy, once a need is identified the resource to meet the challenge is usually provided without the need of a formal request to the steering committee.

If not handled correctly, the setting up of a new total quality department can undermine many of the principles reviewed earlier. There is a need for co-ordination of the whole programme, and most companies have a small resource to action the plans determined by the chief executive.

The training strategy for Teesside has been to take a *cascade* approach (Figure 7.2). This was felt to be vital to ensure that all areas of the Works progressed simultaneously.

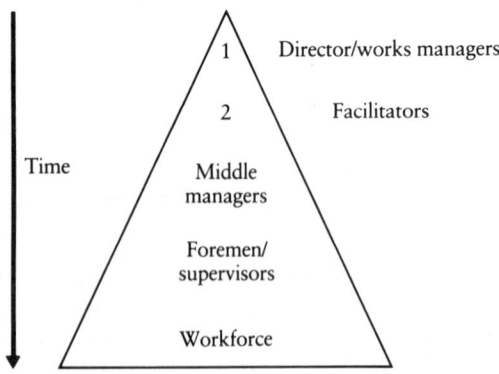

Figure 7.2   *Cascaded training*

The training cascade

The first to be trained were the director and his team of works managers. This was undertaken by external consultants. The works managers and the consultants then trained the departmental managers. At this stage volunteers were sought from the ranks of departmental managers to be trained as 'facilitators' to train the middle managers.

As middle management training progressed a number were selected or volunteered to train as facilitators for the foremen and supervisor and workforce training. The cascading process has thus provided strength at every level in every department. The facilitators have been drawn from all areas of the Works including purchasing, sales, marketing, personnel and finance. There are now 164 facilitators in total but none is full time. Facilitators leave their normal duties for one day per week to guide employees through total quality education and training.

The aim was to train all employees by the end of 1990. Again it is significant that the facilitators have given freely of their time. There has been no reward other than recognition by the works director and the steering committee for a job well done.

To progress the training at the same pace across the works, area training co-ordinators were identified. Again the individuals volunteered for this important role and their managers reorganized around their additional duty. At the peak of training activity in the autumn of 1989 there were seven centres on the works for training, with up to 40 workshops per four week period each with 18 members.

Whilst it is vital to have an efficient training procedure, it is surprising what can be achieved with a dedicated team co-ordinated within the Works.

By the time Teesside Works had completed the training of total quality, over 16,000 man days had been utilized. This investment in the workforce was part of the overall training strategy with a budget of £7m a year – approximately £1,000 per employee (1989/90). Whilst the statistics may be impressive the training is not the end in itself but the means to the end. Everyone leaving the training workshops will be able to identify areas of waste and rework in their areas and to make proposals for improvement.

They will also have first-hand experience of the tools and techniques available to identify problems, gather and analyse data, find root causes, solve and test solutions and assess the effect of implementation. We have given employees a significant insight and 'hands on' experience of this management process.

The response to training has been very encouraging. The biggest problem for management has been channelling this energy into areas for maximum impact on the aims and objectives of the business.

Initial facilitator training

Two training courses were run in parallel each consisting of 14 managers representing every function within the Works.

The courses were organized in such a way that each facilitator presented a part of the proposed workshop. Some guidance on content was given by the external consultants, but much was left to the individual course members to adapt the material to suit the needs of Teesside Works. All examples had to be considered and integrated into a very flexible approach to presentation including use of flipcharts, overhead projector slides and video material. At this stage, few recognized that this integration of all the material would give the workshops a life of their own!

After a month of pre-course preparation the team assembled for their training armed with their own case studies to support the programme. The briefcase that had been given to each member which seemed like a perk at the time, was now bursting at the seams and had become an invaluable aid to facilitation.

The course lasted seven working days, and was led by consultants. Each member made their presentation in turn. After each session team members assessed performance by considering aspects well presented, those needing improvement, and facilitation style. The early performances were well presented as lectures but lacked the involvement of the course members, and so did not take best advantage of all the visual material. This was not surprising as most of the early presentations demonstrated some degree of stage fright. It was quickly recognized that the comments made by the team were constructive. After all, who is going to be less than constructive when their turn is next! During the course the team knitted together very quickly.

The team spirit generated helped everyone to quickly develop their facilitation style, that is to present in an interesting, practical manner and avoid it becoming an academic exercise. Even those with little previous experience of presentations quickly gained confidence and acquired the necessary facilitation skills.

The last two days of the training consisted of customizing the material for use within the Works. By this time confidence was high and most of the debate centred on seeking a sensible balance of the material to be presented.

The facilitators were to work in pairs, and team spirit was such that all agreed readily to be paired with any other team member. The actual pairing was therefore undertaken by the consultants and the total quality performance manager. When considering the pairings they made sure that different areas of the Works were represented, and that the styles of the individuals were such that each pair could handle any of the facilitation methods with ease.

A few days later the pairing list arrived with the recommendation that the two meet quickly to 'share out' the workload over the four days of the course.

On the training course the facilitators had practised only 1/14 of the actual programme, and now had to become proficient on at least another 6/14, although to be on the safe side they had to ensure they were capable of the other 13/14.

To ensure success, the pairs of facilitators prepared (much of it done at home), practised and put into practice total quality in their own areas. The fund of knowledge and practical experience grew daily. One of the team felt confident enough to apply for the British Quality Association Award for 1989 – and went on to win.

By November 1988 the first of 60 workshops commenced. A sleepless night preceded the big day. Eighteen middle managers arrived on cue representing a combined experience of over 200 years in the industry. These were the people who had been through the bitter experience of the early 1980s and helped shape the industry into a profitable world leader in steel. How would they react? Were the facilitators up to it?

Within the first few hours they recognized they were up to it, they could facilitate, lead discussion, take questions and use material to best advantage. And yes, middle managers shared their desire to make further improvements in the business through the adoption of total quality. Any fears were quickly dispelled.

At the end of the first day the facilitators were exhausted but as course members left they said how much they had enjoyed the course, and were looking forward to the other 3 days.

Additional facilitators

Discussions with the consultants resulted in further development of the workshop material, to the stage where the material could be produced 'in house' and still retain the professionalism of the presentation. It was agreed that with some initial guidance the TQP department were capable of training the future facilitators. But how? The consultants were invited to present a further training course. On this course were two middle managers who in addition to undertaking the course were preparing a course manual for future internal use. As part of their post course work they not only prepared for facilitation duties, but produced a comprehensive manual that was to be known in the total quality section as the 'Hitchhikers Guide to Facilitation and all that'.

Armed with the guide and the continuing enthusiasm of managers, the total quality department then proceeded to train the balance of facilitators required for the total training needs.

The Teesside Works Management Committee recognize that the facilitator resource will continue to play a significant role as total quality becomes 'The Teesside Works way of doing things'. The facilitators have skills both in total quality and in communication. With the former they will offer an expertise in their departments for the implementation of quality improvement plans, additional training to problem-solving teams and for other departmental training initiatives. Their communication skills will be used to enhance the already much improved communications with the workforce. This is particularly important where shift systems can result in teams in the same plant rarely meeting unless a positive effort is made.

As each group has been trained and 'sent into the field' the same mixed emotions have been apparent. One thing is sure – everyone who has been on the workshops has recognized the commitment from the facilitators to ensuring that the experience gained in the classroom can be translated into positive action for business improvement in all departments.

During the winter of 1990 and spring of 1991 an additional thirty one employees from all levels were trained as facilitators after volunteering as a result of workshop attendance.

Management training

The first workshop was held at British Steel's Management College in April 1988 and consisted of members of the Teesside Management Committee. Any thoughts that the 'top team' were treating themselves were quickly dispelled when it was realized that the workshop was held over a Bank Holiday weekend. The workshop was organized and run by consultants with assistance from the newly identified TQP manager.

Following this, nine workshops of two days duration were held during the summer of 1988 when all departmental managers received initial training for total quality. The 135 managers involved at this stage were trained off-site to ensure their total involvement and insulation from day-to-day work routine. The training was again delivered by consultants and the TQP manager. A member of the Teesside Management Committee acted as workshop owner. This role was more than a symbolic chairman and involved the owner in presenting some of the material and receiving the feedback from syndicate sessions.

During this period plans were made for the training of over 1,000 middle managers. It was felt that trainers from within the organization would have greater impact with employees, and thus the word 'facilitator' entered the Works' vocabulary.

The newly trained facilitators assessed the available range of training material and determined the content of the training workshop. As a result a four-day training course for each middle manager was established. The programme was based on eight separate modules each with a clearly defined objective and a custom-built package of short lectures, videos, group discussions, syndicate sessions and 'homework' between training days. The eight modules were:

1   What is total quality performance?
2   Customers first
3   Managing for TQP
4   Teamwork
5   Tools/techniques
6   People make quality
7   Barriers to TQP
8   Making TQP a permanent part of our culture

The TQP department had the task of organizing the workshops, but before doing so an analysis of previous failures to achieve efficient training was conducted. The key issue identified was attendance. All training providers are aware of the last-minute withdrawal for 'operational reasons or pressures'. This had to be avoided if the training programme was to be completed as planned. The commitment of all Works managers was sought and readily obtained to ensure that individuals nominated for a workshop would attend under any circumstances. It quickly became accepted that the only acceptable excuse for not attending a workshop was serious illness. As a result less than one per cent of workshop potential members failed to attend.

For each workshop, members were drawn from all areas of Works activity. This gave a unique dimension to interaction during training. Prior notice was given and course materials were provided approximately one month prior to attendance so that members could familiarize themselves with the content. A key element of this stage was a pre-workshop briefing undertaken by each member's line manager.

Full use was made of computerized employee records, and individual invitations to attend were produced via a word processor. Computerized training records recorded the completion of training for monitoring and control.

At this stage basic course materials were purchased from the consultants. Customized handouts and conference folders were provided by the TQP department.

Each workshop was owned by a departmental manager and presented by two facilitators. This method kept the link with the earlier workshops and gave the owner first-hand knowledge and involvement in the training of his staff. Departmental managers not owning courses attended as workshop members to ensure the consistency of training.

Members were requested to complete a workshop appraisal question-naire, the results of which were analysed and used to steer future workshops. All those completing the workshops were awarded an attendance certificate.

Foremen and supervisors

As the middle management training progressed, plans were laid to cascade the training to foremen and supervisors. This group included some blue collar employees who had supervisory responsibilities. The target population was 460, and it was planned to complete the exercise in June/July 1989 prior to plant holiday shutdowns.

Further facilitators were identified (24 in total), this time drawn from newly trained middle managers, and were again trained by the consultants in March/April 1989. They had the benefit of the earlier experience and their own training and quickly produced the workshop materials. A two-day programme was devised on the basis of those aspects of the programme that the supervisors could directly influence. All materials were produced in-house (Table 7.2 shows the workshop content).

This particular phase of training commenced shortly after the end of management training and was completed in approximately 6 weeks. It was more vital than ever that attendance was 100 per cent. In the event, only three were not trained, all due to serious illness. This phase was completed at a rate of 288 per month, double that for middle management.

Table 7.2 *British Steel, General Steels, Teesside – training workshop content*

Module/Techniques	Management	Supervisor	Workforce
1 What is total quality performance?	X	X	X
2 Customers first	X	X	X
3 Managing for TQP	X	X	
• Department purpose analysis	X		
4 Teamwork for TQP	X	X	X
• Brainstorming	X	X	X
• Cause and effect diagrams	X	X	X
5 Tools and techniques	X	X	X
• Graphs/histograms/bar charts	X		
• Scatter and concentration diagrams	X		
• Ranking techniques	X		
• Consensus reaching techniques	X		
• Pareto analysis	X		
• Statistical process control	X	X	X
6 People make quality	X	X	
7 Barriers to TQP	X	X	X
• Solution effect diagrams	X		
8 Making TQP permanent	X	X	X
• Failure prevention analysis	X		

At this time therefore the TQP department was arranging training for middle managers, foremen and supervisors, and also making arrangements to carry out the training of the extra facilitators, who would be necessary to carry out the workforce training commencing September 1989.

Workforce training

A further 90 middle management level facilitators were trained during the summer of 1989 by the TQP department and together with the foremen/supervisor facilitators formed the resource for training of the 5,400 strong workforce.

To administer the workforce training from the centre would have required much additional resource and still have been difficult to arrange due to the many different day and shift systems in use throughout the Works. Arranging a simultaneous Works-wide release at the required rate of over 420 employees each month for 12–15 months in succession would have proved impractical. The TQP department reviewed earlier successful training initiatives and decided to adopt a similar policy.

A steelworks splits naturally into three main production areas: ironmaking, steelmaking and rolling and finishing. In addition there were two areas which made convenient travel to Teesside either difficult or impossible; Hartlepool and Shelton Mills. Teesside Works also have large engineering shops. Finally the offices and any smaller departments were considered together giving a total of seven areas for training.

Each area nominated a co-ordinator to pull together the needs of their particular employees and to plan training on a least-cost basis. Each co-ordinator was provided with sufficient trained facilitators to undertake the training. They were given control of a training room and syndicate rooms equipped to the same standard as for all other training. The co-ordinators were section managers, plant engineers and personnel officers who gave freely of their time to further the aims of the business.

All training materials were produced in-house. Co-ordinators drew their training material from the central store administered by the TQP department on a monthly basis, working with a four-week buffer stock to allow pre-reading of materials by course members as for previous training.

The workforce material included a unique feature – a section on accident prevention under the headings 'Total Quality is No Accident' and 'Zero Defects = Zero Accidents'. Another key element was the 'homework' which was continued and done willingly by the participants.

Resources for TQP and training

It may seem from the above that a large department of total quality administered and controlled the whole training exercise. Nothing could be further from the truth.

At Teesside Works the decision was made very early in the programme to have a full time TQP manager. Recognizing that the Works was about to embark on a significant programme of education and training for total quality, a second manager was identified to organize the training administration. A third member was added to deal with such matters as production of a monthly newspaper, production of videos and other aspects of communication. At the peak of training the team was supplemented by an additional manager and clerk/typist for a three month period.

None of this small team has been permanently appointed to the position. This is not seen as a weakness, but as strength in the organization's ability to move managers around to gain greater experience of different aspects of the steel business.

A large department was not needed because the whole works was committed to assisting with the programme (Figure 7.2 outlines the programme timetable).

Actions from workshops

The workshops themselves provided a platform for quality improvements.

On the management workshops, each manager was asked to prepare a five-point action plan for quality improvement. This yielded about 5,500 individual or group actions. During workshop debriefing these actions were incorporated into departmental plans wherever possible.

The same format on the foremen and supervisor workshops produced another 2,600 action points.

On the other workshops the 'homework' question was to identify areas of waste and rework in the individual's department. Such was the response that the facilitators and course owners were able to highlight numerous areas for improvement. All workshop members were debriefed on return to their workplace by their managers. The areas of waste and rework identified were used as the basis for discussions on the training workshop, to facilitate early involvement in the department's plans if possible. Analysis of all improvement proposals was carried out on an ongoing basis by teams to ensure no points were missed which may have had potential benefits.

Clearly with such a large number of proposals there was a need to identify priorities and action plans were produced and communicated so that each workshop member could recognize that his proposals had at least received consideration.

Where next?

Such was the enthusiasm at all levels in the organization, that requests have been made for workshops to reconvene with original members to discuss quality improvements made as a result of the initial training. This has already commenced and eventually all employees will be invited to a review to give details of their contribution to business improvement.

Such is the commitment to making 'Total Quality Performance – the Teesside Works Way of Doing Business'.

8

Total quality culture – an endless journey

Ken Sanders

The most important judgement, though, is the opinion of our ultimate customers – the ones who pay our salaries.

Introduction

I don't claim to be an expert on total quality management. What I do claim, is to be an expert in one company's practical implementation of the process. Based on my experience as managing director of Texas Instruments Limited (TIL), I hope I can give a little insight into some of the practical aspects of implementing a total quality management programme – the pitfalls, the things to avoid, the things to emphasize.

TIL has always been in the vanguard of quality programmes. We started on our journey towards a total quality culture – TQC as we generally refer to it in TIL – in the early 1980s when we took a corporate decision to measure our managers on a set of parameters which encompassed quality as well as profit (see Figure 8.1).

We have always prided ourselves that good profit management is a philosophy deeply embedded in our company. To this end, departments keep a 'bluebook' which requires managers to forecast the way their businesses are heading and measures their success against a number of specific indices – turnover, profit, overheads, people, inventory, and so forth.

With this in mind, we introduced a quality bluebook so that we could measure ourselves as effectively on quality parameters as we did on the profit line. We had been quite proud of our profit ethic, and its central position in our management priorities, but the quality bluebook soon

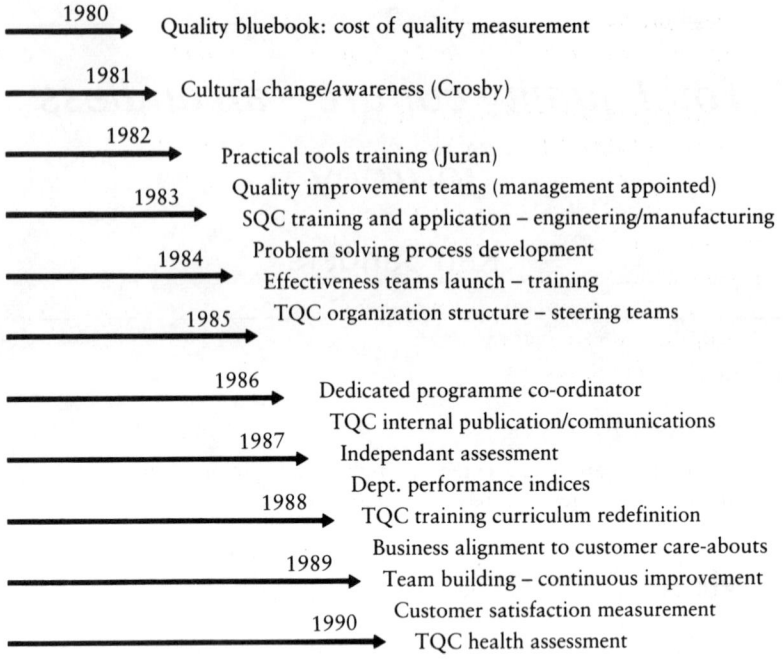

1980 → Quality bluebook: cost of quality measurement

1981 → Cultural change/awareness (Crosby)

1982 → Practical tools training (Juran)

1983 → Quality improvement teams (management appointed)
SQC training and application – engineering/manufacturing

1984 → Problem solving process development
Effectiveness teams launch – training

1985 → TQC organization structure – steering teams

1986 → Dedicated programme co-ordinator
TQC internal publication/communications

1987 → Independant assessment
Dept. performance indices

1988 → TQC training curriculum redefinition
Business alignment to customer care-abouts

1989 → Team building – continuous improvement
Customer satisfaction measurement

1990 → TQC health assessment

Figure 8.1 *The journey*

told us we needed to make some fundamental cultural changes if we were to have equal success in terms of quality.

We therefore embarked on a whole series of training schemes. Initially we sent our management team to listen at firsthand to gurus such as Crosby and Juran. Then we asked the team to go out and train their managers who, in turn, would train the people reporting to them, and so on down the line. At the end of each training session we finished with a practical problem-solving exercise for each team to work on and, from this, we rapidly learned that we must set up more effective training, specifically in the development of team-building skills.

We then started to assemble a TQC structure: a site quality steering team (QST) and, under it, a number of divisional QSTs which are responsible for a whole range of TQC activities, quality improvement teams and effectiveness teams. Having a structure is one thing, but making it work requires that it has the understanding and commitment of all the people involved.

Twenty-five years ago, TI's then chairman, Pat Haggerty, said '*There is probably no greater waste in industry today than that of willing employees prevented, by insensitive management, from applying their energies and ambitions in the interest of the companies for which they work'*.

That statement was incorporated into TIL's management philosophy and practice (Table 8.1). From the outset, our company has applied the principles of single-status employment, the use of first names, open communication channels and an annual, results-based performance review for every employee. These principles give an essential foundation for good communications and are prerequisites for a quality improvement programme. I am convinced that, if a company does not have such a base firmly established, then it is too early to start talking to people such as Juran and Crosby.

Table 8.1   *Management principles*

- Single status terms
- First name terms
- Open communication channels, employee involvement
- Results based performance review system for all employees
  - *Emphasis on continuous improvement*
- Individual accountability and strong teamwork
- Competitive pay & benefits structure
- Recruit & develop essential skills, promote from within
- Positive response to 'change'

At TI, we already had that base on which to build. Now, with a decade's hindsight, I can identify four major building blocks which we put onto the base and which led to the structured programme we have today. I say 'hindsight' because I would be the last to claim that we built in a totally logical manner. We made plenty of mistakes and had to go back and correct them as we went along.

The four blocks

The first of the four blocks was *training*. Kaoru Ishikawa, another leading proponent of total quality, said that TQC starts and ends with training; and TQC training never ends. We started off in the way I would always recommend to others – by consulting outside experts and organizations. They gave us a training philosophy which, we realized, we could easily adapt with examples tailored to our own organizations, and which we could propagate through people with whom our own employees could readily identify. We are now carrying out some 39,000 man hours of training a year for our total staff in Bedford of about 1,000 employees.

The second building block is one I have already referred to – the *quality organization*, which runs in parallel with our functional organization. Due to the way TI is structured worldwide, some divisions report directly to managers in other countries, rather than through the site managing director. But we are adamant that the site quality steering team is, indeed, a *site* function. The managers of all divisions in Bedford participate in this team whose charter is to steer the development, communications and team recognition elements of the quality improvement process. It manages the cultural transition in the organization and oversees the activities of the next level of quality steering teams, the departmental QSTs. The main elements of training are illustrated in Figure 8.2.

Team problem-solving is our third building block, and for this we have two approaches (Table 8.2). The first is the effectiveness team (ET) – similar in function to the groups that, elsewhere, are often called quality circles. The ET usually relies on the voluntary participation of people from a single work-group who can concentrate on a shared problem

Table 8.2   *Team problem-solving*

Effectiveness teams	*Quality improvement teams*
● Voluntary participation	● Management appointed
● Team selects problem	● Problem assigned by manager
● Usually local problem	● Usually cross functional
● Permanent	● Team reassigned on completion
● Team presentation on project completion	● Milestone feedback to quality steering team
● Training in problem solving and interpersonal techniques	● Trained in problem solving techniques
● Participation and development emphasis	● Problem solving process emphasis
● 26 teams active	● 38 teams active
● *Creates an environment of participation*	● *Obtain maximum benefit from human resources*
● *Establish broad based problem solving ability*	● *Standardize team activity*
● *Encourage synergy*	● *Overlay team activity on organizational structure*
● *Provide recognition for quality project activity*	

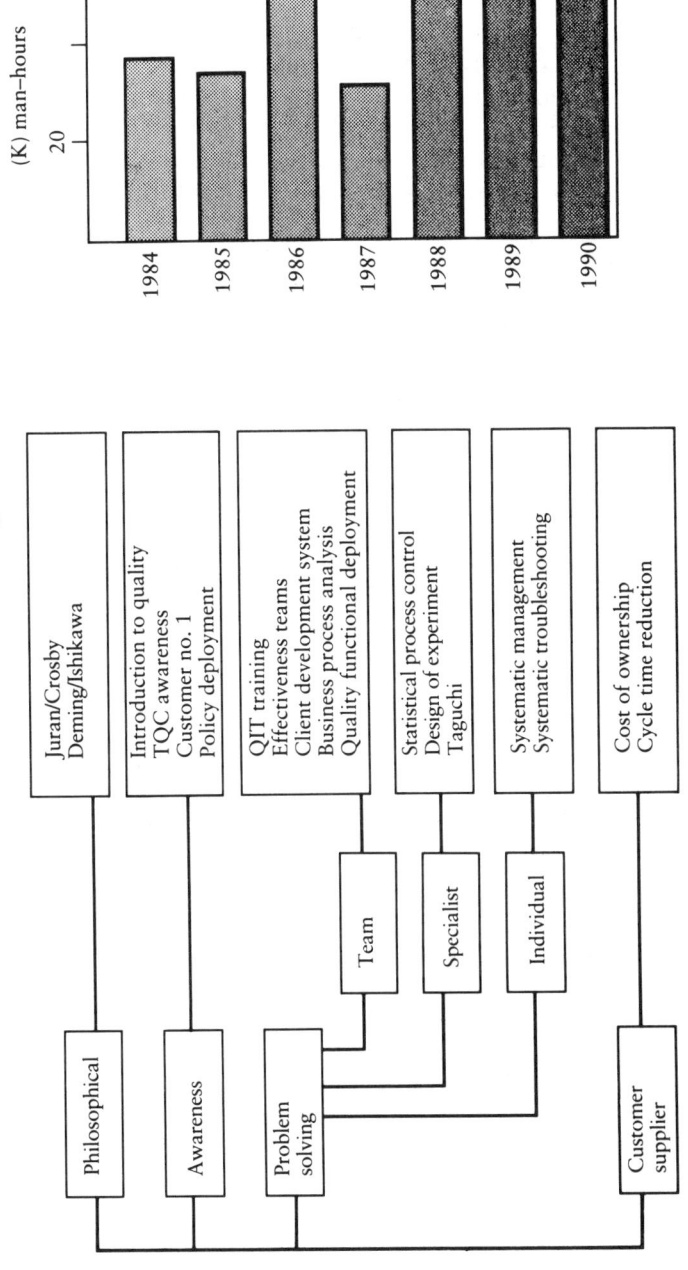

Figure 8.2 *Training*

which they themselves select. The minimum entrance qualification for an effectiveness team is a 4-day training course and we have found that they really do work, both at supervisory and shop-floor levels – and not just in manufacturing but also in administrative (what we call 'indirect') areas. They give the first broad base of recognition that problems are there to be solved – and that they can be solved.

The second approach is the quality improvement team (QIT). It has much in common with ET – in its approach and in the half-dozen problem-solving steps it takes – but these teams work on problems which span departmental or functional boundaries. Here, it would be unrealistic to expect the team to form voluntarily so it is appointed by management. Management also defines the problems and monitors progress to ensure that the solution process is rigorously followed.

Our final building block was the *calibration* of our peoples' understanding of the TQC process. We approached an external consultant to sample about 10 per cent of our site population, taking particular care to cover all levels and functions. We found out what TIers liked about TQC and what they thought should be improved, and we used the results to estimate our chances of success and to give guidance for the future. In summary the feedback was: *'It's a great concept'; 'We can believe it'; 'We like being involved and we get satisfaction from making our customers satisfied'.* The 'wants' can be summarized as: more communications; more resources; and more commitment from managers.

TQC in the UK

A question we continually asked ourselves about TQC is 'Will it work in the UK?' Personally, I believe that cultural adaptation is very important but not difficult. Some of the recommendations I would make, based on 5 to 10 years' experience, are: train continuously; involve everyone; be totally open; discuss the good news with the bad news; and discuss the failures with the successes – but be very clear that the failures are going to be addressed by the whole organization from the top down (see Table 8.3). Look for participation, and for a cultural change in the organization, a change whereby people really begin to understand what the challenges are, and are keen to assist management in meeting them. Lastly, be very, very patient.

What we found did not work well were exhortations. For example, badges which say 'Do it right' or 'Did you deliver today'. Someone told me he brought back from the US a badge which said 'Don't tell me what sort of day to have!' So maybe the reactions are similar there! We

Table 8.3   *How the UK version works*

Do	Don't
● Train continuously	● Use exhortations
● Involve everyone	● Have zero defects days
● Be honest (good & bad)	● 'Sign the pledge'
● Actively participate	● Delegate TQM
● Establish teamwork	● Focus on results
● Review the process	● 'Change your mind'
● Focus on customers	● Look for short cuts
● Recognize success	
● Structured decision making	
● Be patient	

Measure the benefit not the expense

found exhortations entirely counter-productive, particularly in the early stages when people needed more convincing that management was serious about the task. We also steered away from events such as *zero defect* days, although they may have a role later in the process.

If asked to give advice to other managers, I would say '*Don't delegate responsibility for the programme: don't focus on results too soon, don't try to take short cuts – and keep the accountants at bay, for a while, at least*'.

Philip Crosby, in one of his books, wrote 'Quality is free'. At TI we add the words' . . . but the cash flow is non-zero'. It does require investment in the early stages and it is better to measure the benefit rather than the expense.

Results achieved

First, to achieve a culture change we need participation (Figure 8.3). It's not the overriding parameter, but if you can achieve it in the right way, then you are gaining ground. Currently, we can show that about half our people at any one time are forming part of the problem-solving structure through effectiveness teams or quality improvement teams. We have achieved this in spite of the fact that, at TIL, direct manufacturing forms a very small part of our total activities. We really have had to push very hard for team problem-solving processes to work in 'indirect' areas such as purchasing, control, payables and customer service, where it is much more difficult to get started.

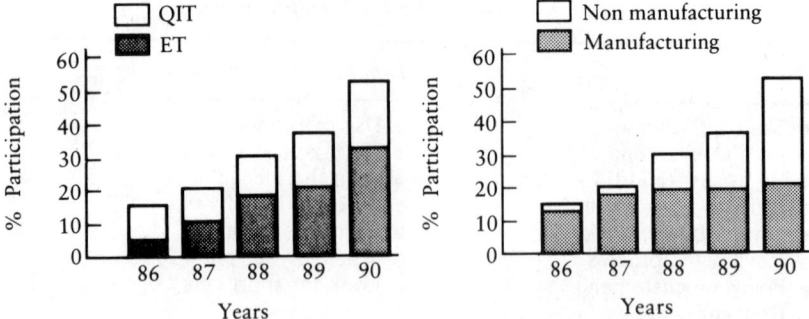

Figure 8.3   *Participation*

We are also seeing that the process helps to develop people: we have found that around seven to eight per cent of participants in our manufacturing effectiveness teams have moved on and up.

We carry out regular surveys of people's understanding of TQC and, in the last two to three years, we have seen a 20 per cent improvement in responses to the question '*Do you understand what TQC is?*' We can also demonstrate a cost-saving benefit, from effectiveness teams alone, of some £150,000 per annum.

There is another series of questions we keep asking ourselves: '*Are we winning? Are we getting better? Are we satisfying more of our customers?*' Our quality steering team spent a long time trying to figure out how to find the answers to those questions.

Recognizing that *satisfying customers* is the route to the business objective of stable and profitable growth, we set about trying to measure customer satisfaction for our product groups and marketing ideas. We also included those of functions which have an impact on satisfying customers' objectives – such as our personnel, QA, control and systems departments. We asked each of these groups to conduct a poll of their customers – who could be inside or outside TI. We asked what were the four or five things that mattered most to the customers in terms of overall satisfaction and determined the customer-satisfaction measurements that should become the priorities of each department manager.

For the product groups they were very predictable: delivery on time, quality, cost of quality; and so forth. The service groups also identified a number of criteria. The personnel department's, for example, were: effectiveness of recruitment, cycle time, training coverage; employee retention, and so forth. Then we asked each group to set goals looking one or two years ahead, and we normalized the results and goals so that we could represent progress on simple graphs which we display in our cafeteria for all employees to see. We also discuss them at our regular plant meetings. It is not essential for everyone to understand the measurement process in detail: merely that if the graph is going up, it's good; if down, it's bad.

Sometimes I am asked whose problem it is if a graph starts pointing downwards. I reply that it is certainly not the problem of any one individual. It may not even reflect the trend of a single department. This is because we choose to assign some key customer-satisfaction indices to the department most likely to champion the problem-solving process, even though they do not totally own the problem. No, a downward graph is an indication that the management team and the whole organization needs to increase, or re-prioritize, resources to focus on that particular facet of customer-satisfaction.

The most important judgement, though, is the opinion of our ultimate customers – the ones who pay our salaries. For this, we have developed a measurement programme called *cost of ownership* in which we try to recognize that in a customer/supplier relationship there are many more factors that add to the cost of a transaction than the basic price of the product. In fact, the total of other costs such as inventory, cycle time and systems plus, perhaps, retest and quality assurance, warranty and field repairs may be 10 to 15 times the original unit price of the product.

To address this fact we are now working with a number of customers in *joint* quality improvement teams. We look at reducing the cost of ownership through improved delivery programmes, the use of bar-coding, electronic communication to cut out paperwork, and a host of similar ideas.

The future of TQC

Of course, TI is a global company; it operates on a worldwide scale. Many of our customers do the same and they expect to see a uniform approach throughout TI. There is a comment about the US – made by an American – to the effect that '*You can always rely on the Americans to make the right decisions and do the right thing, but only after they have tried everything else*'. So it was with our TQC process in its early stages.

Table 8.4   *Vision and quality policy*

SEMICONDUCTOR GROUP VISION

- To become the preferred supplier of semiconductor solutions and be recognized as such by customers and competitors worldwide

- QUALITY POLICY

- To achieve this vision, we must dedicate ourselves to the Customer #1 philosophy which means:

  For every product and service we offer we will understand the requirements that meet the customers' needs, and we will conform to these requirements without exception.

Finally, however, we have a worldwide policy which has customer-satisfaction, usually shortened to 'CUSTOMER #1', at its core.

I started by saying we look on TQC as a journey. Our journey has many staging posts. One of the next ones for us is Quality Policy Deployment – a technique which should allow a large, diverse company such as TI to focus on just a very small number of worldwide priorities which we believe are essential to our success. Some of these are listed in Figure 8.4. One which we have identified is the cycle time for the introduction of new products. Another is statistical quality control, with its ability to manage a process – be it manufacturing or administrative – so that its output is within predictable and acceptable limits. Thirdly, we are looking at consistent, systematic ways of comprehending customer

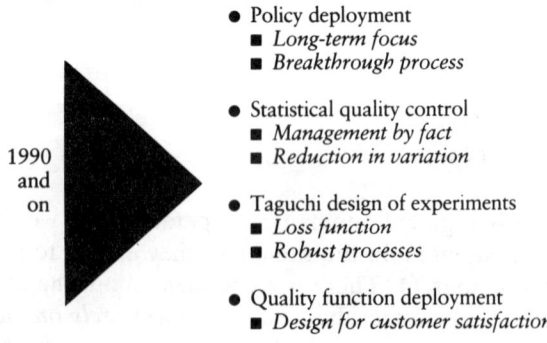

Figure 8.4   *The journey continues*

'care-abouts', of researching them, weighting them and using them as the basis of future product design.

Within Texas Instruments Limited, we still have a way to go in merging quality management with functional management. We also have to find a better way of recognizing and rewarding the contributions that individual employees make through the quality team activities. Team participation is key – making it the way we do our business, and seeing the quality tools and techniques used much more in the day-to-day running of the business. This means that we need to find a better way of rewarding teams. We do it now primarily by recognition and awareness, and by bonus schemes in certain areas, although these do not form a key element of any individual's total performance related remuneration. I believe this has to change if team activity is to be the prime vehicle for changing the culture of our people. Organizational flux is another problem we must solve, particularly in effectiveness teams where, as a team moves on to deal with its second or third problem, we find that some of the team members have also moved on, to other roles within the company. More organizational stability is the only solution to the problem.

To provide solutions to some of these problems will require the total commitment of our top management. However, I shall know that we have achieved a measure of success when I can move out of the driving seat, and feel confident that the vehicle will continue its journey towards our goal of complete customer-satisfaction, without slowing down and without changing direction.

9

Deming – a new dimension in quality

Dr Henry Neave

Why Deming?

About three years ago the well-known writer and speaker on quality, Tom Peters, said in an article for the London *Sunday Times* (14 February 1988):

> Which system? There's a lot of controversy here. Should you follow W Edwards Deming, father of the Japanese quality revolution via statistical process control? Or Phil Crosby, author of *Quality Is Free* . . .? Or Armand Feigenbaum's Total Quality Control? Or Joseph Juran? Or invent a system of your own?

The list could have been extended. It could have included Taguchi; it could have included Bill Conway's *Right Way to Manage*; and, of course, it could have included the Great British contribution of BS5750, now becoming known the world over as ISO9000. In addition, there's a whole host of tools and techniques supposed to be helpful in quality improvement efforts: a list too long for me to try to construct here.

It's a complicated and confusing picture, and I have sympathy for the many people who peer into this morass and wonder where, if anywhere, they should turn.

Reactions vary. Some decide they should take bits and pieces that they like the look of out of all the approaches. Unfortunately, that's rather like putting cornflakes, fillet steak and chocolate ice cream all together on the same plate. Others take refuge in the belief that it doesn't matter: regrettably, that is precisely what Tom Peters' article implied:

> Frankly, it makes little difference which you choose, among the top half-dozen or so, as long as it is thorough and followed rigorously.

I submit that it makes a great deal of difference.

Finally, there are those who fondly think (or, at least, hope) that it really has nothing to do with *them* – people in finance, for example. Dr Deming had a few words for them in 1988 when addressing an audience of some 450 delegates in Nottingham – 450 delegates with probably not a finance director nor even an accountant among them:

> I'd like to ask you a question. Where are the financial wizards of the company? You hear of some companies run by the financial people. They have a very important part to play, they sure do. What have they been doing? Allowing the company to go to ruin, that's what. Because they don't know their job. Permitting expenditures for the wrong things at the wrong time.

Incidentally, lest this be interpreted just as an excuse for another round of ill-thought-out cost-cutting, let me anticipate the very first of Deming's 14 Points (summarized later in this article):

> Create constancy of purpose for continual improvement of products and service, *allocating resources to provide for long-range needs rather than only short-term profitability*, with a plan to become competitive, to stay in business, *and to provide jobs.*

Out of proliferation of approaches to quality, this article is about Deming. Why? Moreover, why should I have bothered in 1987 to bring about the formation of an educational and research organization dedicated to spreading awareness of the Deming approach and deepening understanding of it?

I guess my reasons are pretty personal. It took me some four or five years between first learning of Dr Deming's work and eventually reaching some level of appreciation of its great importance. And I figured it would be good for British industry, and society in general, if that process could get speeded up for others! But why *Deming* in particular? In a single (if long!) sentence: because his work is based on both scientific and human principles that I subscribe to; it develops through impeccable logic concerning the way processes and systems work – processes and systems of *all* types (manufacturing, non-manufacturing, service, administration, financial, managerial, human); and it results in an approach and an overall philosophy which accentuates and encourages valuable and good things of life and of human nature rather than always dragging things down to lowest common denominators.

Maybe that paragraph provided rather surprising answers to the questions. You might have instead expected a list of success stories. I could have tried that, but I hesitate to do so. I'm mindful of Deming's own warning that

> Experience and examples are of *no help in management* unless studied with the aid of theory. To copy an example of success, without understanding it with the aid of theory, may lead to disaster.

We are involved here with a *philosophy* of management, not a list of instructions and illustrations. Deming certainly guides us as to what needs to be done but, far more important, he helps us to understand *why* it needs to be done. Further, a philosophy is not a programme. It's not a case of 'doing Deming' for a few months, and then judging whether it works or not. Also, he talks of the need for no less than 'total transformation of Western style of management' – hardly a short-term consideration! Deming began working with the Japanese in 1950. When might we have judged the results of his influence on that country? 1951? 1955? 1960? 1970? Or longer still? And *how* might we have judged? Hardly by short-term financial figures.

But, if looking for examples, one can hardly avoid citing the Japanese. For they *did* begin paying serious attention to him that long ago – 30 years before the Americans started listening and even longer before we in Britain did. Actually, that's an oversimplification. Deming's influence was quite strongly felt in various areas in America during the 1930s and 1940s: in the United States Department of Agriculture, where he worked for some ten years after receiving his Doctorate at Yale in 1928; in the National Bureau of the Census, which he joined in 1939 (efficiency and productivity of several of the operations of the 1940 American Census saw up to six-fold improvements compared with previously); and during World War II, during which his eight-day courses on the statistical control of quality were taken by thousands of people involved in the war effort and had a strongly beneficial effect on both the quality and volume of production, spectacularly reducing scrap and rework.

As regards what has been happening since Deming's Western 'rebirth' around 1980, I won't mention names: there are very many companies and other organizations that have been influenced by Deming, and I (like anybody else) have detailed knowledge of only a few. For them all, the day is still young and there is, of course, no guarantee that they will stay the course – though I have to say that, in the cases I know of where the Deming-interest is now less than it was, it has virtually always been because of a takeover or other type of substantial change at the top. (Deming points out as early as the preface to his 1986 book *Out of the Crisis* that 'unfriendly takeover and leveraged buyout are a cancer in the American system': I fear he could easily have broadened the geographical range of that statement.) One could talk to the companies (there are many in the States, and even one or two in Britain now) that have sent dozens of their managers through his celebrated four-day seminars. How are they doing?

However, the 'search for examples' is referred to by Deming (*Out of the Crisis*, chapter 3) as one of the 'obstacles' to the needed transformation; so the best advice has to be for you to take time to learn what Deming is saying and why he is saying it: then you'll be able to judge for yourself. I want people to get interested in Deming's work *because of what it is*, not because of what some results and examples indicate it might be (in any case, we all know we can find figures to support *any* argument). This article is a small contribution which I hope may enable a few more people to begin that learning process.

Open minds

Nobody will get far into studying Deming's work unless he/she approaches it with a very open mind. I think that everybody will find issues in his teaching which contradict long-held beliefs about 'facts of life', 'human nature' and 'the way things are, and will ever be'. Come to think of it, if such were not the case, I suppose there wouldn't be much for us to learn. But there is.

An article in the *San Jose Mercury News* of 20 November 1988 listed numerous quotations which combined humour with a deep, penetrating message which was well-summarized in the article's title: 'It's Not Creativity We Lack But Receptivity'. Here are a few of my favourites:

> This 'telephone' has too many shortcomings to be seriously considered as a means of communication. The device is inherently of no value to us.
> *Western Union internal memo of 1876*

> The wireless music box has no imaginable commercial value. Who would pay for a message sent to nobody in particular?
> *David Sarnoff's associates in response to his urgings for investment in the radio in the 1920s*

> Who the hell wants to hear actors talk?
> *H M Warner, Warner Brothers, 1927*

> Heavier-than-air flying machines are impossible.
> *Lord Kelvin, President of the Royal Society, 1895*

Drill for oil? You mean drill into the ground to try and find oil? You're crazy.
Drillers whom Edwin L Drake tried to enlist to his project to drill for oil in 1859

Clearly common to all these reactions was a short-term view, and an attempt to judge matters for tomorrow using the tools of today. What better way to miss opportunity and kill innovation! In the view of the speakers, all of the opportunities alluded to were, at worst, incomprehensible or, at best, not worth the risk. They couldn't do cost-benefit analyses on these ideas. They couldn't predict the return on investment. In the presentation at Nottingham mentioned earlier, Deming referred to common reaction to Harvey Firestone's invention of the pneumatic tyre: 'How silly! Riding on air. Nonsense!'

The fact is that if we always restrict ourselves to what we know – standard tools, techniques, strategies – then obviously we're going to stay stuck in that mould, 'bound up in the tangled knot of the problems of today' as Deming puts it in his discussion of the first of his 14 Points (*Out of the Crisis*, page 24). Obviously, we can't ignore the problems of today, but shouldn't we shift the balance to think a little more of the problems – and opportunities – of tomorrow also? The difficulty with Deming is that he has always had great ability to look and think well into the future – I guess some people would refer to that as being 'visionary'. He had vision when he spoke in Japan in 1950 – when he told meetings of chief executives of that country's biggest companies that they would be able to take over world markets in pretty much any areas that they set their minds to. Yes, he was saying that in *1950*. Think of what the Japanese situation was at that time. They were still suffering massively from the devastation of the war, Japanese industry had a well-deserved reputation for cheap and shoddy product, and they had essentially no natural resources (except people!) – as is obviously still the case and will ever be. But that was Deming's vision for Japan in 1950. Of course, many people in recent years have come up with all sorts of explanations for Japanese success. But who was explaining Japanese success in 1950? Only one man that I know of. Fortunately for them, the Japanese executives were not restricted by short-term thinking – else they could also have thrown away their opportunity just as other short-term thinkers do.

Short-term thinkers generally have very different ideas from Deming on how quality can be achieved: in particular, there is the idea that quality can simply be *bought* – bought by investment in state-of-the-art technology and by financial incentives for people. Returning one more time to the Nottingham event, now to part of an interview which he gave during that same day:

> Everybody thinks he knows what quality means. The answer that so many people give is hard work. Well – hard work will not ensure quality. Best efforts will not ensure quality. Gadgets, automation, computers are not the answer. Not at all. Investment in machinery is not the answer. There's a little ingredient that I call *profound knowledge*.

We might refer to 'profound knowledge' as *state-of-the-art thinking about quality* – and that most certainly *is* needed. It is that which Dr Deming is researching and developing right now – well into his 91st year of age.

History

I believe it is important that we learn something of the history of the development of the Deming philosophy, from its origins in the 1920s until the present day. It is not just that it is a good story (which it surely is): to wade into Deming's work without knowledge of its background has some similarity to steaming into the Arctic only looking at the tips of icebergs. What we see and hear from Deming today is not a collection of bright (or you might think not-so-bright) ideas thrown together in recent years when his countrymen eventually exercised the courtesy of listening to him. It is instead the product of more than 65 years of active thought, development and practice on the part of this brilliant and far-sighted individual, aided by the creativity of countless others in industry, education, statistics, physics, psychology, etc., whose work he has diligently studied, sifted, and selectively adopted.

This historical account is relatively brief, bearing in mind that it covers most of the century! More substantial accounts are easily found elsewhere. In particular, I recommend Nancy Mann's *The Keys to Excellence* and Cecilia Kilian's *The World of W Edwards Deming*; I also have a relevant chapter (Chapter 2) in *The Deming Dimension*.

The story is compactly summarized by the 'tree-ring' diagram (first suggested to me by my good friend John S Dowd, a consultant in California) in Figure 9.1. This diagram is particularly effective in that (1) each new period – each new ring – is wider-ranging than the one inside, and also (2) each such new development contains and builds upon what was there previously.

The story begins with some work carried out, beginning in 1924, for the Western Electric company by the respected physicist and statistician

Dr Walter A Shewhart. We shall present the relevant details a little later. For now, we shall content ourselves with pointing out that the context was manufacturing operations – specifically the manufacture of telephones and telephone systems (despite our earlier extract from the *San Jose Mercury News*!). Shewhart's work provided important theory and practice for the improvement of such manufacturing processes and systems. That this initial work was in such a context is made clear by the title of Shewhart's 1931 book: *Economic Control of Quality of Manufactured Product.*

It was a happy coincidence that led to Deming's early awareness of Shewhart's work. During the time that he was studying for his PhD at Yale, Deming took vacation jobs at Western Electric's Hawthorne Plant in the summers of 1925 and 1926. He recalls those days in Mrs Kilian's book:

> What I learned at the Hawthorne Plant made an impression for the rest of my life. The men were talking about uniformity of the telephone apparatus, and about Dr Walter A Shewhart, saying that they did not understand what he was doing, but that it was important.

Deming was not introduced to Shewhart until the autumn of 1927, but the two spent much time working together thereafter. Together they realized that Shewhart's great work on statistical control was not only appropriate to manufacturing processes and systems, but to processes and systems of all kinds: service, administration, the census, and human (as mentioned earlier). That realization eventually led to some of the most controversial of Deming's 14 Points, as we shall see a few pages on.

But Deming did not rest there. Some try to say that, when he began lecturing to and working with the Japanese in 1950, he was teaching them just statistics. Certainly, statistical methods were substantial and important components of that teaching. But by then there was more, much more. On my tree-ring diagram I have referred to the 1950s and 1960s as being the time of 'systems for improvement'. Three such 'systems' are particularly well known, and each one deserves at least a whole chapter in this book rather than just brief mentions in this one. There was the *Deming chain reaction* (Figure 9.2) – the realization that quality and productivity should be positively rather than negatively correlated, and that the generation of this positive correlation is the key to lower cost, increased value, increased business – and the creation of employment, not unemployment (which obviously is the connotation that most people still have, 40 years later, of 'lower cost'). Then there was the portrayal of *production viewed as a system* (Figure 9.3):

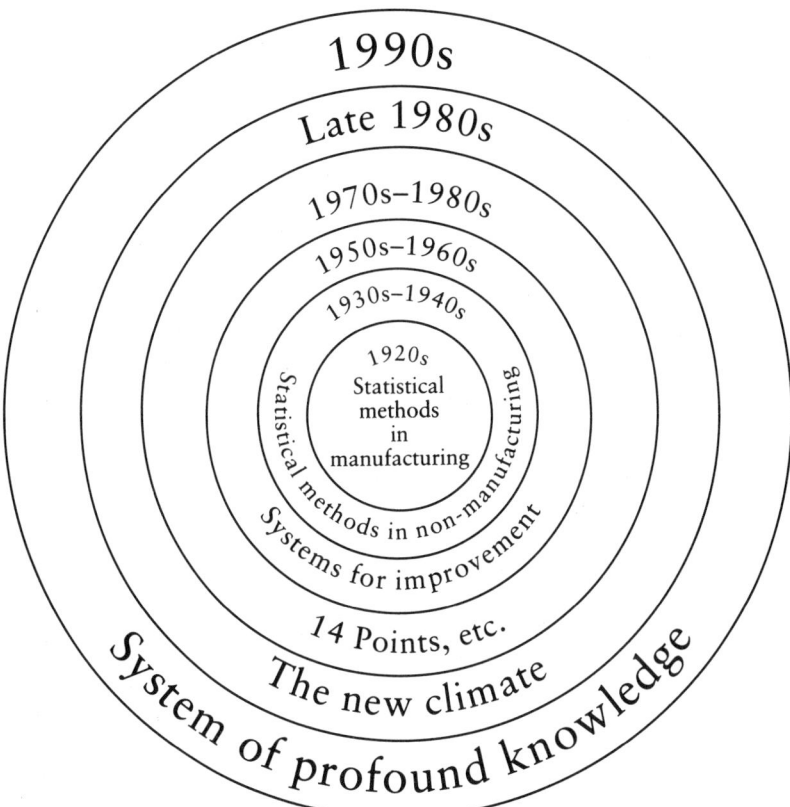

Figure 9.1   *Tree-ring diagram*

regarding work in terms of horizontal flow, internal and external customer–supplier relationships, and feedback for improvement, rather than treating work as compartmentalized and shackled by the hierarchical organization chart (Figure 9.4). Nearly half a century later, the Western world is just beginning to struggle to recognize the necessity for these concepts: yet Deming regards them as so obviously fundamental that they appear as early as the third and fourth pages respectively in his 500-page *Out of the Crisis* – and he takes pains to remind us there that these were 'on the blackboard of every meeting with top management in Japan from July 1950 onward'. So simple, but so different. And there was the *Deming Cycle* (plan-do-check-act or, as he now prefers it, plan-do-study-act) – see Figure 9.5. Agreed, that was not fully developed in 1950; but a more rudimentary version, based on a concept which

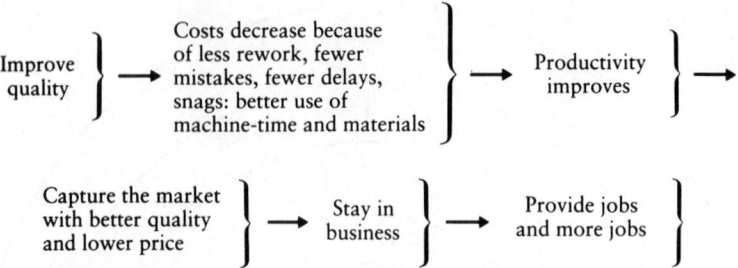

Figure 9.2 *Deming's 'chain reaction'*

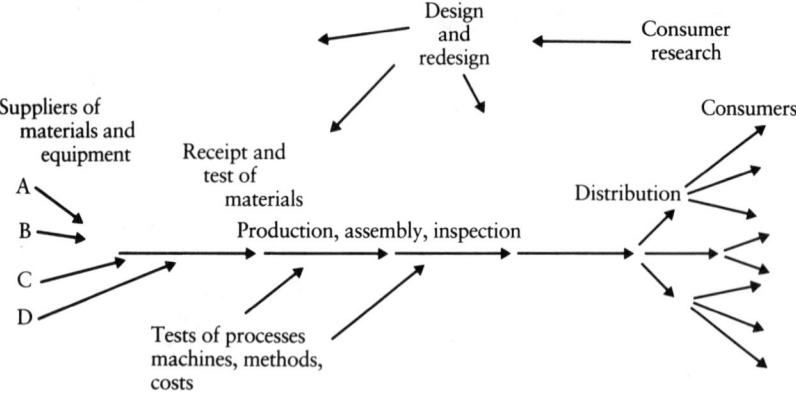

Figure 9.3 *Production viewed as a system*

appeared in Shewhart's 1939 book, certainly figured in his teaching from the beginning. Does all this really sound like mere statistics?

In December 1950, the Board of Directors of JUSE (the Union of Japanese Scientists and Engineers, founded in 1946 to aid the industrial reconstruction of Japan after the war) created the famous Deming Prizes 'in commemoration of Dr Deming's contribution to Japanese industry and for encouragement of quality control development in Japan'. Deming returned often to Japan to lecture and to work with their leading industrialists. In 1960 he was honoured by the Emperor of Japan with the award of the Second Order Medal of the Sacred Treasure – the first American to ever receive such an award from the Japanese.

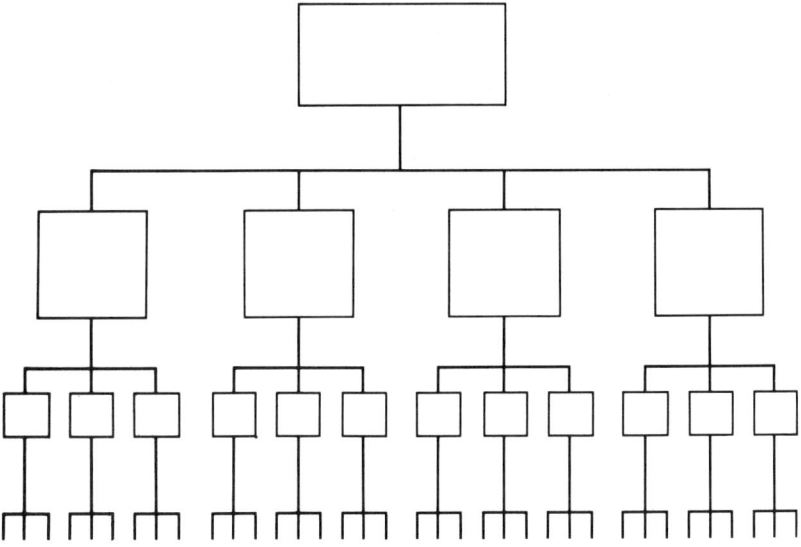

Figure 9.4   *Hierarchical structure of an organization*

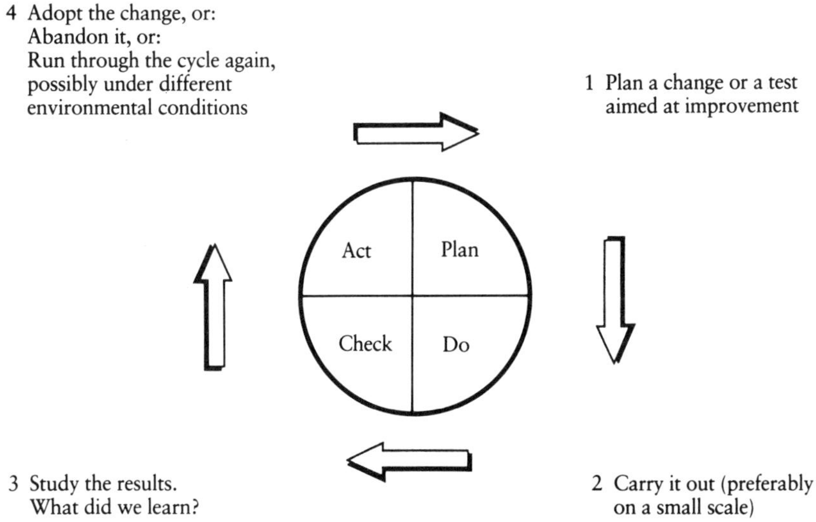

4 Adopt the change, or:
Abandon it, or:
Run through the cycle again,
possibly under different
environmental conditions

1 Plan a change or a test
aimed at improvement

Act   Plan

Check   Do

3 Study the results.
What did we learn?

2 Carry it out (preferably
on a small scale)

Figure 9.5   *The Deming cycle*

The years rolled by. During the 1970s, Western industrialists and others started to realize that something remarkable was happening to Japan. 'Cheap and shoddy' was getting replaced by 'reliable, dependable, great value for money'. We were no longer buying Japanese for the sake of cheapness, but for quality. Many people, having bought their first Japanese car, or radio, or hi-fi subsequently deliberately sought out Japanese products. They told their friends how good the stuff was. What could it all mean? The world was changing. The world had already changed.

Amazingly, it was almost by accident that the name of Dr W Edwards Deming began to get associated in some Western minds with the Japanese transformation. I have told the story elsewhere (*The Deming Dimension*, Chapter 2), so there is no need to repeat many details. In brief, in 1979 Bill Conway, Chief Executive Officer of the Nashua Corporation, engaged Deming as consultant. Nashua were selling copying machines manufactured by Ricoh. During the mid-1970s, Ricoh had won the Deming Prize, and that is how Conway first heard the name. Also in 1979, Clare Crawford-Mason was invited to produce a documentary for NBC on the 'Japanese secret'. After some slow progress in collecting material for the documentary, somebody eventually pointed her toward Deming. What happened then is well-related in *The Deming Management Method* by Mary Walton, a staff writer for the *Philadelphia Enquirer* magazine:

> Crawford-Mason contacted Dr Deming, who invited her out to talk. He spoke of his work in Japan, and showed her yellowed clippings of stories the Japanese had written. Crawford-Mason didn't know what to think. He was nice, if eccentric; he reminded her of her father; but what he said, if true, was astonishing. 'He kept going on and on and on that nobody would listen to him.' Their first conversation led to five interviews, consuming 25 hours. The more they talked, the more impressed she was, and the more suspicious she became. It was simply incredible. 'Here is a man who has the answer, and he's five miles from the White House, and nobody will speak to him'. She contacted a high-ranking economics official from the Carter Administration and asked if he knew Dr W Edwards Deming. He didn't.

The final 20 minutes of her documentary *If Japan Can, Why Can't We?*, first screened on 24 June 1980, featured Deming and Conway at Nashua. And at last America's industrialists started to seek out the man who Bill Conway was already referring to as 'The Father of the Third Wave of the Industrial Revolution'.

With Conway's encouragement, Deming had already started to present his four-day introductory seminars. Attendance quickly grew from dozens to hundreds. Deming constructed the famous 14 Points as a teaching and learning aid for those seminars. Even they, along with the rest of his teaching, have developed and improved during the subsequent decade as Deming has continued to work, to learn, to think, and to further develop his teaching.

Some think that the 14 Points somehow encompass the Deming philosophy – some think they *are* his philosophy. That is quite wrong. They are results, outcomes, manifestations of the philosophy – carefully-thought-out consequences of his fundamental thinking. There are plenty of other such manifestations – the Seven Deadly Diseases of Western world management, the 16 Obstacles to the Transformation, the 4 Prongs of Quality, and much more. The 14 Points are crucially important, but they are not everything. Maybe that, in part, has influenced him in very recent times to work further on the fundamentals – the core of his thinking from which all else has flowed – which since the autumn of 1989 he has referred to in no less terms than a 'System of Profound Knowledge'. Since that is still in course of active development, we shall not attempt any comprehensive coverage here. But we shall now say more on some of the other main issues to which we have so far just briefly referred.

Variation

> If I had to reduce my message for management to just a few words, I'd say
> it all had to do with reducing variation.

So said Dr Deming in response to a question at a recent four-day seminar. And a good answer it was. For quality surely includes concepts such as dependability, reliability, consistency, uniformity, predictability. What all these words imply is *low* variation. *High* variation is the antithesis of quality. Don't confuse variation with *variety*, which is both desirable and necessary. By 'variation' we mean that which is undesirable and unnecessary.

There is an important lesson to learn from the very circumstances which led to Shewhart carrying out his early studies on variation. As we have seen, the Western Electric company was at the time heavily involved in the development and manufacture of telephone systems. They were keen to improve the quality of their product, and were pouring considerable resources into the task. But all was not well. The people involved found themselves becoming increasingly frustrated and perplexed. Quite simply, irrespective of the amounts of time, money and effort expended, it began to seem as if it were just a matter of chance whether any real improvement was seen: sometimes things got better, sometimes they got worse.

Shewhart, who was then working at the Bell Laboratories, answered Western Electric's call to investigate their problems. The work which transpired led to his discovering the foundations of what we now refer to as *statistical process control* and to his invention of the associated essential tool known as the *process control chart*. The first control charts were drawn in 1924.

The essence of Shewhart's work was disarmingly simple. It was that, although all processes exhibit variation, in some processes that variation is *controlled* or *stable*, while in others it is *uncontrolled* or *unstable*. In other words, a process is either *in* or *out of* (statistical) control. The incalculable value of this elementary observation is that appropriate action for improvement of the process depends very much on which of the two situations we have; the wrong choice of action is not only likely to fail to bring about improvement: it is highly likely to *make things worse*. And this is what Western Electric had already discovered – not by understanding but through bitter experience!

Let us summarize some of the main issues stemming from Shewhart's work. First, examine the graphs in Figure 9.6. They represent typical measurements taken regularly over time of some characteristics of interest from the processes and systems we may be studying. Figures 9.6a and 9.6b come from processes (or parts of processes) which are in statistical control; in Figures 9.6c and 9.6d the processes are out of control. In the first two cases, although there is some variation (as there always is), the *behaviour* of that variation is, as far as we can see, staying pretty much unchanged as time progresses; in the second two cases, clearly that is not the case. In the first two cases, we can predict what the future may hold in store, with some reasonable chance of being right. Such prediction could of course not be in any sense *exact*: but we could produce a reasonable guess at the range within which the measurement is likely to continue varying and, maybe, given rather more data, some further guidance on how the measurement is distributed over that range. The reader may not be overly impressed by this level of predictability, but it is the best that can be done. However, in the second two cases, we can't even go that far. While the general behaviour in Figures 9.6a and 9.6b seems unchanging over time, the underlying behaviour in Figures 9.6c and 9.6d is seen to be subject to change, sometimes quite drastic change. As regards prediction, we might hazard some very short-term guesses, though without great confidence; medium-term and long-term prediction is just impossible.

Figure 9.6e lies between the two extremes. If the cause of the trend

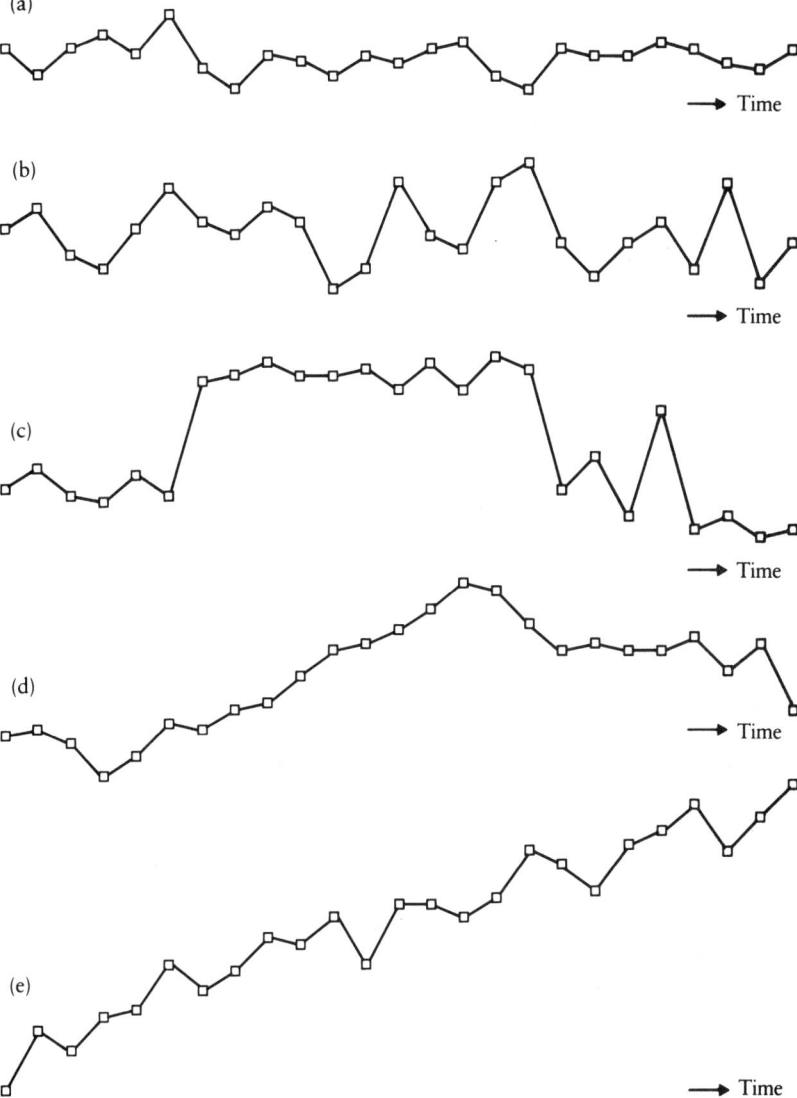

Figure 9.6

which is seen there is known and understood, in particular regarding whether or not it will continue, the process is effectively in control once that trend is taken into account. If we lack such knowledge, the process is effectively out of control. We shall not discuss this any further here:

space will not permit and, in any event, we can clearly not make progress with such 'in-between' cases before developing good understanding of the two main situations above.

Realizing, as we now do, the necessity to reduce variation in order to improve quality, we need to discuss what *causes* variation – since variation will not be reduced unless we can identify and act upon its causes. As one might expect, having now recognized the existence of two very different types of *variation*, we find that there are correspondingly two very different types of *causes* of variation. Deming's terminology is simpler than Shewhart's, so that is what we shall use: stable (in control) variation is due to *common* causes, while unstable (out of control) variation is due to *special* causes. In practice, the choice as to which of the two situations we are in is the job of Shewhart's control chart.

What can we deduce about these two types of causes of variation? Fortunately, quite a lot. We have only to think of the types of variation which they produce. Common causes produce variation which is a permanent feature of the process: while the process itself stays unchanged, the nature of that variation stays unchanged. Therefore common causes are inherently part of the process itself – to do with the way the process has been designed, built, set up, the way people are trained to work with and within it, etc. Special causes are quite the opposite: special causes unpredictably *change* the behaviour of the process, altering the nature of the variation which it produces – sometimes increasing it, sometimes decreasing it, sometimes raising the level of the output, sometimes lowering it. Thus whereas common causes are, in effect, inherent or internal to the process, special causes have influence upon it 'from the outside'; they are external to the process, but move it around, varying the behaviour of the variation! The effect of special causes over time is therefore to make measurements from the process far more widely spread than would be the case if those special causes didn't exist, in which case of course the process would have been left to produce the smaller variability of which it is actually capable if only it were given the chance.

Although this analysis sounds relatively straightforward, the implications are huge – particularly for management. Let's look at a few of the things which follow as natural consequences of the above analysis.

First, when a process is out of control, attention must surely be directed on trying to get it into control, i.e. to identify and tackle the special causes which are making it unstable. Why? Well, suppose you tackle common causes instead, i.e. try to improve the process itself (by some change of policy, training, design, etc.). At some later stage, you may see some change in behaviour of measurements from the process.

But how then can you know whether this change is due to your attempted improvements to the process, or whether it is just due to some old special cause disappearing or a new one exerting its influence? You just 'can't see the wood for the trees'.

Second, suppose special causes have been tackled effectively, and the process is now in control. What next? An unarguable consequence of this analysis is that further improvement has to be the *responsibility of management*. The reason is that we are now needing to tackle common causes – and common causes, as we have seen, are part and parcel of the process or system itself. And where do the processes and systems come from? They come from management. It is management that create, design and update them, not the people who work within them. As Myron Tribus, Director of the American Quality and Productivity Institute, has often said:

> The people work in a system. The job of the manager is to work on the system to improve it, continuously, with their help.

Note that we are not saying that management have to, or indeed can, produce such improvement by themselves. They surely need guidance and information from those that spend their working lives suffering from the current system! But the 'workers' *cannot* do it all themselves. They need the permission, encouragement, resource and willingness from responsible management.

Having introduced this division of variation into the types caused by common and special causes, it is obviously of interest to learn where the bulk of the problems, i.e. undesirable and unnecessary variation, lies. The answer to that has been known for decades. At least 30 years ago Dr Joseph Juran, one of the other big names in quality, was talking in terms of 85 per cent common and 15 per cent special. Deming went along with these figures for a long while, but in the mid-1980s he changed them – to 94 per cent and 6 per cent respectively! The specific figures do not matter, but the general order of magnitude does. The message is clear. The vast majority of what needs to be done in pursuit of improvement is the responsibility of management, not the responsibility of the 'workers'.

A further natural consequence of Shewhart's work provides the explanation of Western Electric's original problem: by tackling the less appropriate type of cause, things really can be *made worse* rather than better.

Bill Scherkenbach, for several years Director of Statistical Methods at Ford Motor Company, and now holding a similar position in the Buick-

Oldsmobile-Cadillac section of General Motors, provides an example which has become widely-known. We summarize it as follows:

> Input shafts for a transmission were turned in a machine equipped with an automatic compensation device. If the diameter of a shaft was measured as being too large, the compensation device reduced the machine setting by an amount equal to the discrepancy; similarly, if the diameter was too small, the machine setting was increased by that amount. Sounds sensible? Of course.
>
> Figure 9.7a shows a frequency distribution (histogram) of 50 shafts consecutively manufactured by this process. As the story goes, the statistician (presumably either Scherkenbach or Deming himself) suggested that the compensation device be turned off in order to see what the process itself was actually producing. Somewhat unwillingly, the Ford people agreed. Figure 9.7b was the result: *less* variation, i.e. *better* quality. How could this be?
>
> The answer is that the production process was already in statistical control. Without the compensation device operating, the process was exhibiting the lowest variability of which it was capable: only common causes were present. Reduction of that variation could therefore only be achieved by improvement of the process itself. The compensation device was not improvement of the process. It was simply *tampering* (Dr Deming's own term for the effect) with a process which was already stable. Since the variability was already down to its minimum possible level *without* the compensation device, the tampering by the device constituted an external influence on the process, 'moving it around, varying the behaviour of the variation', as we referred to it earlier. So the only possible effect of such an external influence is to *increase* the variation – exactly the opposite effect from that desired. Of course, had there been special causes present, the compensation device might well have helped smooth out their effect. But, in the absence of special causes, it could only *harm* the output. It can be proved that, in such a case, the compensation device increases the variability by just over 40%. Further study (in particular, through Dr Lloyd Nelson's 'Funnel Experiment' – see Chapter 5 of *The Deming Dimension*) shows that there are actually much worse forms of tampering in common practice, ones which increase variation even more seriously. What becomes apparent is that management who lack understanding of Shewhart's theory of variation have no protection against such hazards.

The example we have just seen, like Shewhart's initial work itself, comes from the relatively simple context of a manufacturing process. But, as we have seen, and will continue to see, its applicability is far wider. Many non-manufacturing applications are, for example, detailed in *Out of the Crisis*: illustrations there include typing, cost of service to

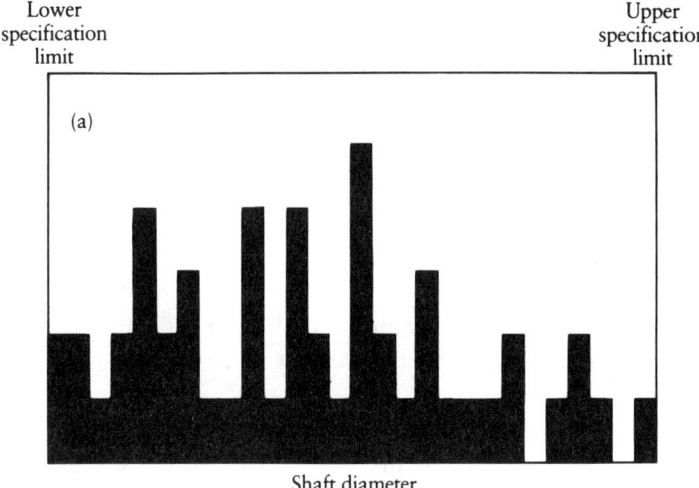

Figure 9.7 *Histogram of data: automatic tool compensation* (a) *turned on*
(b) *turned off*

customers, effects of hospital therapy after operations, petrol consumption in cars, fires, sales, the filling of orders, and even learning to play golf!

But however important and/or interesting such illustrations may be, the major value of this theory is that it underlies the Deming philosophy itself – including the 14 Points. Indeed, Shewhart's breakthrough on the understanding of variation affects every facet of management. With this new perspective, so much of what management at any level are currently doing is so clearly seen to be wrong. Thus for managers – in every area – to spend time learning and understanding Shewhart's and Deming's teaching on variation surely seems to be no longer a luxury but an absolute necessity.

The Joiner Triangle

We can have no doubt of Deming's admiration for Shewhart's work, and his judgment of its crucial importance. Quoting again from Mrs Kilian's book:

> Even if only ten per cent of the listeners absorb part of Dr Shewhart's teachings, the number may in time bring about change in the style of Western management.

However, to most ordinary mortals, the ramifications of Shewhart's teaching on variation, and the emphasis which Deming lays on reducing variation, may not be immediately apparent. So we need some help.

Of particular help, I believe, is the Joiner Triangle (Figure 9.8), an eight-word construction formed by Brian Joiner, who leads one of the most learned American consulting organizations devoted to helping companies understand the Deming philosophy and apply Deming's approach to their own situations.

The words on the three vertices of the Joiner Triangle all follow from realization of the need to reduce variation. But they give us some particular clear guidelines as to the type of principles which are

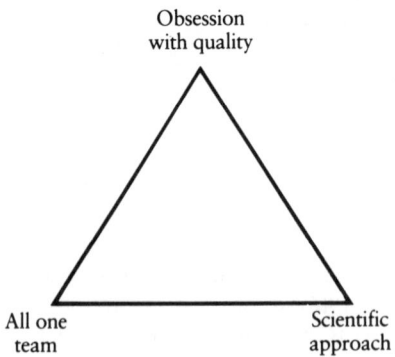

Figure 9.8   *The Joiner Triangle*

consequences of that underlying concept. And they are principles which, I believe, are not shared by other approaches to quality improvement; nor are they more than superficially in place in the majority of organizations that consider themselves as doing pretty well in the quality stakes.

Obsession with quality

At the top of the triangle is 'obsession with quality'. Now, 'obsession' is a striking and maybe controversial choice of word. In its favour, it certainly conveys a sense of the profound and primary importance of quality, as opposed to its familiar role of playing second fiddle to more pressing short-term considerations, crises, and financial expediency. No longer can quality be regarded as something which you may just think of measuring at the end of the line, perhaps with some judgment then being made as to whether it is sufficiently good for the customer not to complain about it. But one might also criticize the choice of word, since 'obsession' also gives the impression of preoccupation which could be described as 'beyond rhyme or reason'. Maybe, however, that's just the point . . .

Let's look again at that Deming 'chain reaction' (Figure 9.2) which, you will recall, was displayed at all Deming's meetings with Japanese top management 'from July 1950 onwards'. Many readers will already have recognized that the Deming chain reaction concerns issues which we have all-too-recently begun to consider under Japanese-sounding titles such as total quality or company-wide quality control.

The core of the chain reaction, and the essence of what makes it different from more familiar notions of quality, is seen in its first and third steps. We could express this by proposing that quality and productivity are *positively* correlated. That is not what we have been brought up to think. We are used to thinking of quality as *costly*, because it is achieved through slowing things down, increasing the amount of inspection, double and triple checking, more detailed and comprehensive paperwork, more expensive machines and materials, greater accountability, more inspection of *people* (do you recall the Lufthansa advertisement proudly claiming that they have people who check the people who check the people that check the aircraft?). All of this is surely detrimental to productivity. Similarly, one can always speed things up, thus increasing productivity; but speeding things up is then likely to be detrimental to quality. This all implies that quality and productivity are *negatively* correlated.

But if we instead consider quality in an all-pervasive way, as indicated by that word 'obsession', then we can begin to understand what the chain reaction is telling us. We are no longer talking just in terms of quality of end-products or services, but of quality of *everything* – all activities, all operations, all processes, all systems which contribute to those end-products and services. If quality improves in *that* kind of dimension, then we start painting a very different picture. In particular, all the things in the second step of the chain reaction begin to happen. There *are* less problems, delays, hassles; there *is* less waste, rework, and confusion. So therefore, step 3 *does* follow from step 1. And if we have both improved quality and improved productivity, surely the bottom line (in two obvious senses of the phrase) follows.

All one team

The second vertex of the Joiner Triangle is represented by the three little words 'all one team' – three little words, but such a wealth of meaning, both of what they involve and of what rewards they can produce. In a similar way as 'obsession with quality' means so much more than just 'quality', so does 'all one team' convey much more than just 'teamwork'. 'All one team' implies working together with common aims, common purposes, common objectives – combining resources for mutual benefit, and surely for the benefit of the organization's customers.

Some people draw a false conclusion from such talk: the conclusion that this must imply loss of individuality, a suppression of whatever makes any person unique. On the contrary, in the 'System of Profound Knowledge', Deming keeps returning to the fact that of course all people are different, and that it is an important part of the job of management to recognize those differences and to use them to the full, thus enriching the system as a whole. Indeed, one of his complaints against much modern management technique is that, in effect, it treats people as inhuman 'things', totally failing to recognize individual needs and to value individual talents, and ignoring the fact that such individual talents need to be channelled toward the general good rather than be used for personal one-upmanship.

Although Deming does not use Joiner's words, he does now frequently speak of 'co-operation: win–win'. In fact, one of his ways of describing the needed transformation is as the change from a society ruled by the ethic of competition: win–lose (if you win, then I lose, or vice-versa) to one guided by co-operation: win–win (with the aim of *everybody* gaining). Co-operation: win–win is one of the concepts that I include under the general heading of 'the new climate' in the tree-ring diagram.

Several of the 14 Points can be seen as directly related to this concept. Point 9 concerns the breaking down of barriers between departments and staff areas, concentrating instead on the need for people from different areas in the organization to work together for improvement. Much modern management builds barriers rather than breaking them down. The theme of Point 4 is to build up genuine customer-supplier relationships – indeed Deming uses the word 'partnership'. That is very different from standard methods of supplier assessment and/or awarding business on the basis of lowest price. In Point 7, the purpose of leadership is defined as to help people do a better job – yet again, working together for mutual benefit.

But 'all one team' – or 'co-operation: win–win' – is rendered impossible by so many common management practices, including some which are relatively modern inventions. Typical are management by objectives (at least in the ways it is usually employed), annual performance appraisals (i.e. judgments of people), and the use of arbitrary numerical goals and targets – all of which foster competition and conflict between people and between groups and whole departments, as opposed to their working together for the true benefit of the company. Such management practices have become common because they *make the best of a bad job* – in an inherently bad situation, they can make things less bad than they would be otherwise. What is unseen by those who do not know or understand the 'new philosophy' (as it is called in Point 2) is that they also constitute massive obstacles to real progress, which could be described as turning the 'bad job' into a good one.

Scientific approach

So finally we reach the third vertex of the Joiner Triangle: use of a scientific approach. Perhaps this is the hardest to discuss, not because it is necessarily more difficult than the other two but because there is so much that can be included under this heading; the other two vertices are relatively specific.

An attempted one-sentence description of the scientific approach might be expressed in terms of using data – and information of more general kinds – in a logical and sensible way. Some would speak in terms of being objective rather than subjective, but I don't wholly go along with that. Subjective feelings and impressions are information of a kind, and as such they should not be ignored. Opinions are informative, and should not be ignored. But opinions, 'gut-feel', and other subjective contributions should also not hold sway when there is good evidence to the contrary view – even if those subjective contributions come from those who are most senior or have the loudest voices.

Variation

Clearly, the work we have already covered on the nature of variation is fundamental to the scientific approach. Indeed, without it, how can we treat data 'in a logical and sensible way'? But the implications of this are likely to be immediately painful to many, especially those used to living by 'crisis management' and 'flying by the seat of their pants'. Financial managers will also find some hard bullets to bite on. Near the end of the previous section, I claimed that 'the understanding of variation affects every facet of management' – a pretty ambitious claim. But consider this. Think how much of management, especially in financial matters and other issues which directly affect them (budgets, sales, profits, costs, for instance), is ruled, or at least guided, by straight comparison of this month's figures with last month's figures, or this week's with last week's, or this year's with last year's. If the figure goes up, we react one way. If it goes down, we react in a different way. But wait! Suppose the underlying process is in statistical control. Except for the rare occasions when consecutive figures are equal, obviously they must go either up or down – *whether the process is in control or not*! Have we learned anything from the Ford tampering example? Remember how, in the short term, every adjustment by the compensation device seemed eminently sensible. But what was the result? *Increased* variation – brought about by all good intentions and best efforts – *and* the willingness to spend money on that compensation device. *Wasted effort, wasted money, poorer quality.*

A consequence of this realization is that a number of companies, both here and in America, have switched from their old past-versus-present comparisons to charting data over a longer period of time. Thus decisions can now be made based on understanding of whether or not processes are in control. If improvement is needed or desired, the managers are thus well-informed as to whether they should be studying data over a relatively long-term, in order to understand and improve the system itself, or whether they are justified in reacting directly to particular low or high points on the chart. This was the purpose of

Shewhart's work: *to offer guidance on appropriate types of action for improvement.*

Operational definitions

But what else is included as part of the scientific approach? One topic which Deming regards as critical in his work with the Japanese in the early 1950s was the use of *operational definitions*. At the start of Chapter 9 in *Out of the Crisis*, he says that 'no requirement of industry is so much neglected' as the use of operational definitions.

What is an operational definition? It is, in essence, a definition which is unambiguous and suitable for an understood purpose. Combining some words of Shewhart and Deming, it is a definition *which reasonable men can agree on and do business with.* Sounds so obvious that it's hard to imagine why anyone would ever use anything different! But we do. Lack of operational definitions lies at the root of a high proportion of arguments and disputes, in and out of court, between people, between sections of a company, between companies, in business, in politics, in insurance, in the laboratory, in the office. We shall not pursue the matter further here: Deming's Chapter 9 and Chapter 7 of *The Deming Dimension* focus on this subject.

Scientific method

A scientific approach must surely include what is often termed 'scientific method'. Deming emphasizes the need not only for experience but for *theory*. Indeed, he warns against depending too much on experience; as we have already seen, 'Experience and examples are of no help in management unless studied with the aid of theory'. What does that mean? Quoting from the 'System of Profound Knowledge',

> Without theory there is nothing to modify or to learn by comparison with experience.

Theory needs to be useful for prediction. If we are aiming to improve the future (and Deming is in no doubt that that *should* be our aim), how can we hope to learn without theory whether or not we are succeeding?

Deming's use of of the word 'theory' is rather specialized: it could in fact be described as '*method* for prediction' – it doesn't have to be *explanation*. Somewhat disconcertingly, he points out that 'No number of examples establishes a theory, yet a single unexplained failure of a theory requires modification or even abandonment of the theory'. He certainly isn't using theory, as some do, as an easy way out to avoid the problems of the real world! In a single sentence, 'scientific method' begins with a theory (which may well have been suggested by previous data) which is then matched against future data and is improved, if necessary, by use of that additional information – and this is an ongoing process. The approach is certainly helpful in avoiding catastrophe which can be caused by imposing experience which has been gained elsewhere onto a different environment where the circumstances may make that experience totally inappropriate.

Processes and systems

But perhaps most important of all concerning a scientific approach is thinking in terms of *processes and systems*. When speaking to an elite gathering of top executives at a special meeting jointly arranged by the British Deming Association and the European Federation for Quality Management in 1990, Deming repeatedly referred to the diagram we have already seen called 'Production Viewed as a System' (Figure 9.3). Indeed, he went so far as to say that

> If you read the report written by the Japanese, I think you will find that the greatest way I accomplished anything there was through that diagram.

One of the huge challenges of the Deming transformation is the organization of management to reflect the unarguable logic of this diagram, as opposed to simply using all that is implied in the traditional hierarchical structure of an organization. The difference is startlingly clear. In the hierarchical structure (Figure 9.4), the most important customer of anything which goes on is the immediate superior of the individual or group concerned; in the horizontal structure seen in Figure 9.3, the most important customer is the one who receives the fruits of the labours of that individual or group, i.e. whose work is helped – or hindered – by them. Information, feedback, communication of any kind – exactly what is needed to aid improvement efforts – is indirect and inefficient unless some strong horizontal lines are drawn through the vertical structure of Figure 9.4. Those who should be the real internal suppliers and customers are otherwise effectively far apart from each other, whether or not they are physically so. And note that the *external* suppliers and customers don't even appear explicitly in the hierarchy diagram. Doesn't that leave the picture rather incomplete? As Deming says in *Out of the Crisis* on the page immediately following the 'Production Viewed as a System' diagram,

> The consumer is the most important part of the production line. Quality should be aimed at the needs of the consumer, present and future.

The concept of a *system* is an enormously strong concept in Deming's current teaching. In this context, he defines a system as 'a network of functions or activities (sub-processes or stages) within an organization that work together for the aim of the organization'. This should immediately ring some bells concerning our earlier discussion on 'all one team'. The aim which Deming suggests for an organization is for everybody to gain (co-operation: win–win again). He interprets much of what is wrong in modern management as suboptimization of sub-systems rather than optimization of complete systems – and suboptimization, by definition, immediately strikes against the concept of 'all one team' or 'co-operation: win–win'.

Management by numbers

I am finishing this section by emphasizing something which the scientific approach is *not*. It is *not* 'management by numbers'. Some management people seem to have become obsessed with numbers (and I am now imputing bad connotations of 'obsession'!): 'Don't bother me unless you can show me the figures'. In these days of supposed quality revolution, many industrial statisticians are told that their job is to 'Show me how to measure quality' or '. . . productivity'. Deming also tackles that idea in the preface to *Out of the Crisis*:

> There are conferences almost any day in this country on the subject of productivity, mostly concerned with gadgets and measures of productivity. As William E Conway said, measurements of productivity are like accident statistics. They tell me that there is a problem, but they don't do anything about accidents. This book is an attempt to improve productivity, not just to measure it.

Another quotation often bandied about is 'If you can't measure it, you can't manage it'. Deming is pretty summary about his dismissal of that one: 'Totally wrong – nonsense!' Maybe that quotation is an adaptation of Lord Kelvin's 'When you cannot measure it, when you cannot express it in numbers, your knowledge is of a meagre and unsatisfactory kind'. But beware! Dependence only on 'visible figures' is actually the subject of the fifth of Deming's so-called 'deadly diseases' of Western world management. Anybody can jack up the figures at the end of an accounting period. Anyone can ship everything at hand, regardless of quality. Anyone can mark something as shipped and show it on accounts receivable. Anyone can cut down on research, education, training. Figures are but tips of icebergs. Actually, one of Deming's favourite sayings, originating from fellow-statistician Dr Lloyd S Nelson, is 'The most important figures needed for management of any organization are unknown and unknowable'.

As I implied, the third vertex of the Joiner Triangle involves rather a lot of issues!

The 14 Points

Many readers who already know something about Dr Deming's work might have expected that, in an article such as this, I would have concentrated most of the space on the 14 Points. Five years ago, that is probably what I *would* have done. But I soon learned that to do so can hardly fail to give the wrong impression that the 14 Points are a set of somewhat autonomous principles, if not mere instructions, on 'how to do Deming'. Nothing could be further from the truth. The Deming philosophy is a *system*, full of interlinking and interdependent components, working together for that previously-expressed aim of *everybody to gain*. Furthermore, the 14 Points are not the Deming philosophy itself, but are more the natural results and consequences of that philosophy.

It is therefore far more important to spend time, as we have now done, learning something of the foundations of the Deming philosophy upon which the 14 Points (along with the deadly diseases and the obstacles etc.) are built. Since some people misleadingly talk in terms of the Deming philosophy being rather like a religion, I usually try to avoid religious analogues – but the need to avoid building castles on sand does spring to mind! Incidentally, the reason I do not like to hear of the Deming philosophy referred to as a 'religion' is that religion depends so much on *faith*. My understanding of 'faith' is as belief unassisted by fact and argument; whereas it was the unarguable logic of the Deming approach, coupled with deep warmth and understanding of humanity, which first attracted me to the Deming philosophy.

In any case, one can hardly do justice to the 14 Points in an article of this length. Agreed, Dr Deming does cover them in a single chapter in *Out of the Crisis*, but that one chapter is about two and a half times as long as this article. Several other writers have produced separate chapters on every one of the 14 Points: see, in particular, Mary Walton's *The Deming Management Method*, Bill Scherkenbach's *The Deming Route to Quality and Productivity*, and Howard and Shelly Gitlow's *The Deming Guide to Quality and Competitive Position*. Further, I have spent some 130 pages doing the same thing in the final Part of *The Deming Dimension*.

Consequently, all I shall do here is give you an initial sight of the 14 Points, with the hope that you will then be willing to embark upon such further reading and study. I might even suggest that you owe it to yourself – and your organization – so to do. I shall precede the statements of the 14 Points with some general comments and follow them with a discussion of just one of the Points to give you a flavour of the depth of thinking which can be involved when one does embark upon such study.

My preliminary comments are mostly comprised of a few warnings. I repeat that this is not a list of instructions. The 14 Points are not techniques. They are not a check-list, to enable you to see what fraction of the Deming philosophy you have accomplished. There is great danger in just obeying the words without understanding deeply why Deming is saying these things and the background which had led to him saying them. To treat the 14 Points as a 'recipe' is a pretty sure recipe for disaster! Only with understanding can people in an organization have the ability to plan how to move toward Deming's thinking in their particular circumstances. For the need is not simply to adopt the 14 Points, individually or collectively – but to create a new environment fully consistent with and conducive to them. This isn't a project, it isn't a programme: it will be never-ending.

A good illustration of the hazard of plunging in without understanding comes again from Ford of America. Apparently, in the early days, a manager became aware of the third of the 14 Points, which refers to elimination of mass inspection. So the story goes, this manager consequently immediately fired all his inspectors. That is not what Deming had in mind regarding that Point!

But there are important lessons to learn from this silly story. Point 3 has now become widely accepted, but imagine nevertheless that you work for an organization in which mass inspection is still the order of the day. What would your reaction to Point 3 be? I suggest you should use it to open up your mind (remember the second section of this article) to the possibility that there might be a very different way of doing things, a way which would be much superior to what is happening now. Imagine a situation in which you wouldn't *need* mass inspection any more. What would it take, and what would it mean to you? It would take substantial improvements in the quality of your processes, procedures, systems, materials, supplies. It would mean greatly improved product and service for your customers, and drastic reductions in waste, scrap, rework. I suggest it would also mean a higher level of morale and pride of workmanship in the workforce: people don't really enjoy manufacturing and handling rubbish.

So surely, the lesson is *not* to take precipitate action but instead to use the Point to help in understanding the new way of doing things, and to appreciate how valuable it could be – and then, armed with that understanding and your knowledge of your particular situation, business, and people, to start carefully designing an appropriate strategy for change. I believe that all the 14 Points can be treated in this way.

Here then is a statement of the 14 Points. There is, incidentally, no 'authentic' and 'correct' version: Deming practises what he preaches in terms of continuous improvement by refining his statements of the Points from time to time. The version presented here contains material from several sources, thus hopefully making these descriptions more comprehensive than briefer statements would be.

Point 1: Constancy of purpose

Create constancy of purpose for continual improvement of products and service, allocating resources to provide for long-range needs rather than only short-term profitability, with a plan to become competitive, to stay in business, and to provide jobs.

This first Point is clearly totally in line with the Joiner Triangle's 'obsession with quality'.

Point 2: The new philosophy

Learn and adopt the new philosophy. We are in a new economic age, created in Japan. We can no longer live with commonly-accepted levels of delays, mistakes, defective materials, and defective workmanship. Transformation of Western management style is necessary to halt the continued decline of industry.

Deming's version is 'created *by* Japan'. It seems to me more correct to say that the new economic age was created *in* Japan by Deming and those who worked with him.

Point 3: Cease dependence on mass inspection

Eliminate the need for mass inspection as the way of life to achieve quality by building quality into the product in the first place. Require statistical evidence of built-in quality in both manufacturing and purchasing functions.

Do not think this doesn't apply to you if you're not in manufacturing. Are not auditing, validating reports, performance appraisal, and proofreading all cases of mass inspection?

Point 4: End lowest-tender contracts

End the practice of awarding business solely on the basis of price tag. Instead, require meaningful measures of quality along with price. Reduce the number of suppliers for the same item by eliminating those that do not qualify with statistical and other evidence of quality. The aim is to minimize *total* cost, not merely *initial* cost, by minimizing variation. This may be achievable by moving toward a single supplier for any one item, on a long-term relationship of loyalty and trust. Purchasing managers have a new job, and must learn it.

This is the Point I have chosen to expand upon in the next section.

Point 5: Improve every process

Improve constantly and forever every process for planning, production, and service. Search continually for problems in order to improve every activity in the company, to improve quality and productivity, and thus to constantly decrease costs. Institute innovation and constant improvement of product, service, and process. It is management's job to work continually to improve the system (design, incoming materials, maintenance, machines, supervision, training, retraining).

Again this is improvement as a principle, as a way of life – rather than letting things ride until they fall.

Point 6: Institute training

Institute modern methods of training on the job for all, including management, to make better use of every employee. New skills are required to keep up with changes in materials, methods, product design, machinery, techniques, and service.

Don't think of investment as applying only to *things*. Training is investment in *people*. It is regrettable that financial statements often regard things as assets but people as costs.

Point 7: Institute leadership

Adopt and institute leadership aimed at helping people to do a better job. The responsibility of managers and supervisors must be changed from sheer numbers to quality. Improvement of quality will automatically improve productivity. Management must ensure that immediate action is taken on reports of inherited defects, maintenance requirements, poor tools, fuzzy operational definitions, and all conditions detrimental to quality.

> Leadership is for helping people, as indeed are all the 14 Points: it is not for judging them since, as we now know, the system within which they live and work causes most of what goes wrong.

Point 8: Drive out fear

Encourage effective two-way communication and other means to drive out fear throughout the organization so that everybody may work effectively and more productively for the company.

> More positively, we might speak of *creating trust*, another vital function of leadership.

Point 9: Break down barriers

Break down barriers between departments and staff areas. People in different areas, such as research, design, sales, administration, and production, must work in teams to tackle problems that may be encountered with products or service.

> 'All one team' and 'Co-operation: win–win'.

Point 10: Eliminate exhortations

Eliminate the use of slogans, posters and exhortations for the workforce, demanding zero defects and new levels of productivity, without providing methods. Such exhortations only create adversarial relationships; the bulk of the causes of low quality and low productivity belong to the system, and thus lie beyond the power of the workforce.

Slogans, posters and exhortations scratch the surface – but the itch and irritation come from well beneath the skin!

Point 11: Eliminate arbitrary numerical targets

Eliminate work standards that prescribe quotas for the workforce and numerical goals for people in management. Substitute aids and helpful leadership in order to achieve continual improvement of quality and productivity.

We have already mentioned the fallacy of management by results. Improve the system and the results will follow.

Point 12: Permit pride of workmanship

Remove the barriers that rob hourly workers, and people in management, of their right to pride of workmanship. This implies, *inter alia*, abolition of the annual merit rating (appraisal of performance) and of management by objective. Again, the responsibility of managers, supervisors, foremen must be changed from sheer numbers to quality.

I can repeat verbatim my comment on Point 11, and also remind you of my comment on Point 3.

Point 13: Encourage education

Institute a vigorous programme of education, and encourage self-improvement for everyone. What an organization needs is not just good people; it needs people that are improving with education. Advances in competitive position will have their roots in knowledge.

Training (Point 6) is for skills; education is for growth – for the person, for the organization, for society.

Point 14: Top management commitment and action

Clearly define top management's permanent commitment to ever-improving quality and productivity, and their obligation to implement all of these principles. Indeed, it is not enough that top management commit themselves for life to quality and productivity. They must know what it is that they are committed to – that is, what they must do. Create a structure in top management that will push every day on the preceding 13 Points, and take action in order to accomplish the transformation. Support is not enough: action is required.

> Think carefully on the following oft-quoted Deming claim: 'quality is made in the boardroom'.

Discussion of Point 4

Although I hope that several of the 14 Points will have immediately intrigued you, it occurs to me that Point 4 might have particular interest to the readers of this book. Consequently, that is the one which I have decided to discuss briefly here, in order to expand upon some of the issues involved, to see how it links in with the fundamental concepts developed earlier, and to illustrate the kind of debate which can develop from indeed any of the Points.

Awareness of the dangers of buying the cheapest is not new. The 19th century art critic, John Ruskin, had some things to say about it:

> It's unwise to pay too much, but it's worse to pay too little. When you pay too much, you lose a little money – that's all. When you pay too little, you sometimes lose everything because the thing you bought was incapable of doing the thing it was bought to do.

And, even more pointedly:

> There is hardly anything in the world that some man cannot make a little shoddier and sell a little cheaper, and people who consider price only are this man's lawful prey.

It is interesting how people who advocate buying on lowest price in their companies do not necessarily follow the same principle in their private lives! In fact, who does – except for the most poverty-stricken in our society who really have no other choice? Ask yourself: how often do *you* buy on lowest price? If you are buying a car, or a meal, or a drink, or a radio, or a theatre ticket, or a spade, or a holiday, or a newspaper, or some curtains, . . . do you really buy the cheapest you can find? I suggest not. You are not ignoring price, but you are attempting to maximize overall *value*. Why then should not your company do the same in its purchasing?

Don't be alarmed by the concept of a 'single supplier' which is mentioned in this Point. This was certainly regarded as one of Deming's more controversial ideas ten years ago, but a lot of companies have now given it a try, and the successes seem to heavily outweigh the failures. (Japanese companies and car manufacturers are particularly well-known for embracing the concept.) Don't forget to read to the end of the sentence: '. . . on a long-term relationship of loyalty and trust'. I get scared when I hear of companies who have 'decided on a single-supplier strategy'. To plunge hastily into single-supplier arrangements is just about as silly as firing the inspectors. As with that case, the first step must be to think hard about the concept so as to understand why Deming is including it amongst his recommendations. What is involved? What would be the rewards – presuming you do it right? (Answer: enormous!) What, on the other hand, would be the damage if you do it wrong? (Answer: horrendous!) All change involves risk, and the risk can be huge unless the change is well understood, well planned, and well prepared for.

The risks are plain for all to see. So let's concentrate on the potential gains which may, at first sight, be less obvious. A good relationship with a single supplier effectively becomes a joint venture: each party has real interest in the other's success. For without it, both lose. The relationship is co-operation (win–win) not competition (win–lose, or possibly lose–lose). There is increasing opportunity for long-term planning and hence security. Supplier and customer can work together on research and development. There is willingness, and eventually perceived necessity, for both to learn more about each other's products, processes and systems. The supplier will learn more about what the customer does with what he supplies, and that guides him on how to make his supplies more suitable, often at no extra cost. The customer learns more about what the supplier could provide, and can thus give him more business. If either gets into some kind of difficulty, or sees trouble ahead, they can work together on it for mutual advantage, rather than hiding it from the other and thus increasing the likely damage.

Paperwork and other administrative costs become only a fraction of what they used to be. Delays, inconvenience and waste through repeated set-up costs disappear. For, irrespective of some set of specifications being met, there can be no denying that different suppliers really are different in just about all respects: different processes, different raw materials, different procedures, different people, different aims, different conventions. Does that not imply unnecessary and undesirable extra variation? Do you still expect to get the same product and/or service, in spite of all that? If you can really honestly answer yes, then maybe *you* have nothing to lose by going for lowest price after all, and maybe *you* don't have much to gain from a single supplier. Maybe you are the exception that proves the rule.

Notice that the single-supplier concept is fully consistent with all three vertices of the Joiner Triangle. An obsession with quality is an obsession for reducing unnecessary and undesirable variation – and you can only go so far in that direction with two or more suppliers before all those obvious differences stop you from going any further. 'All one team' now gets extended into the customer-supplier relationship: why restrict it to within your own company? Similarly, the system of service or production with which you are involved now extends naturally into the supplier, straddling the interface between you and enabling further development of the scientific approach.

Connections with the other Points abound. You are certainly breaking down barriers, driving out fear and creating trust, eliminating the need for mass inspection (because you *know* that your supplier will be doing a good job for you); there is ability and desire to improve together, and help each other so to do; knowledge (training and education) is increased. You are beginning to see something of how the Deming philosophy is a 'system'. And you are, at last, beginning to see something of the new economic age!

The system of profound knowledge

It is probably unfair to occasionally mention *profound knowledge* to you in this article, and leave you without any extra information about it! In fact we have by now touched upon many of the issues in Dr Deming's document. Here is a very brief summary; Chapter 18 of *The Deming Dimension* provides a comprehensive description.

The System of Profound Knowledge is in four parts. Naturally, the concept of 'system' implies that the four parts are all inextricably linked and interdependent. The first part concerns the very understanding of 'system' and of the need for optimization not suboptimization. The second is statistical theory, in which the understanding of variation developed here is a substantial part. The third is the 'theory of knowledge', and we have more than touched on that when discussing operational definitions and the nature of theory *vis-à-vis* experience.

The fourth part is psychology, something which Deming has not said much about until very recent years. Even so, what he now has to say fits right in with the rest of his philosophy. Indeed, one particular issue maybe summarizes vast tracts of that philosophy more comprehensively than anything else which I can think of right now. It is awareness of the importance of intrinsic over extrinsic motivation. Maybe bad management – and bad government – is bad because it only thinks of extrinsic motivation, often with the result of destroying the innate and invaluable intrinsic motivation with which we are born.

With that in mind, I'll finish with a question – a question which perhaps says it all. *Why should anyone do more in their lives and their work than the minimum they can get away with*? Possible answers are

1 fear;
2 financial incentive;
3 because they want to.

Which do you think holds out the most hope?

Bibliography

Out of the Crisis, W Edwards Deming. Massachusetts Institute of Technology, Center for Advanced Engineering Study (1986); Cambridge University Press (1988).

The Deming Dimension, Henry R Neave. SPC Press, Tennessee (1990).

The Deming Management Method, Mary Walton. Dodd, Mead & Co., New York (1986); Mercury Books, London (1989).

The Deming Route to Quality and Productivity, William W Scherkenbach. CEEPress Books. Washington DC (1986); Mercury Books, London (1991).

The Deming Guide to Quality and Competitive Position, Howard S and Shelly J Gitlow. Prentice-Hall Inc., Englewood Cliffs, New Jersey (1987).

The Keys to Excellence, Nancy Mann. Prestwick Books, Los Angeles (1985); Mercury Books, London (1989).

The World of W Edwards Deming, Cecilia S Kilian. CEEPress Books, Washington DC (1988).

Economic Control of Quality of Manufactured Product, Walter A Shewhart. Van Nostrand (1931); American Society for Quality Control (1980); CEEPress Books, Washington DC (1986).

Statistical Method from the Viewpoint of Quality Control, Walter A Shewhart. Graduate School of the Department of Agriculture, Washington (1939); Dover (1986).

10

The quest for total quality at Rank Xerox

Richard Coleman

About Rank Xerox

Rank Xerox is a British-based multi-national joint venture between Rank Organization, a British company, and Xerox Corporation, which is based in Stamford, Connecticut, USA. Rank Xerox operates in over 80 countries, employes 28,000 people and had revenues of approximately 5 billion dollars in 1990. It has extensive research, development, and manufacturing facilities in the European Community, with plants in England, France, the Netherlands and Spain and also conducts research and development in European locations. The Rank Xerox distribution network covers over 80 countries throughout the world.

Rank Xerox is the leading European manufacturer of copiers and office systems to meet customers' needs in the creation, printing, copying, distribution, filing and publishing of paper and electronic documents.

Why change?

In the 1960s Xerox created, then dominated, the modern document copying industry. However, it was hard hit by competition – especially the Japanese – during the 1970s. The product line began to mature, growth slowed and the Corporation saw its market share plummet from dominance to less than 50 per cent by 1980.

Like most monopolies, Xerox had created an expensive infrastructure, one that was no longer affordable. Aggressive competitors had little trouble undercutting Xerox's price levels in the market.

Many companies have found that they have lost focus on the

customer, becoming inwardly focused with overly-complicated processes and too many levels of management, and have been unable to respond to customers' needs effectively. Rank Xerox found itself in just this position.

In the mid 1960s, the then President of Xerox, Joe Wilson, had made this statement – as relevant today as it was then:

> In the long run, our customers are going to determine whether we have a job or whether we do not. Their attitude toward us is going to be the factor determining our success. Every Xerox person must resolve that his most important duty is to our customers.

In the exciting years of tremendous growth, building a new industry, the Corporation started to lose focus on the customer and to lose its way.

Why quality as the vehicle for change?

To understand the power of quality, one need only look toward the Japanese. Since the early 1950s, they have been applying the tools and principles of quality – and with results that are the envy of the industrialized world. In the span of three decades, they became a major force in automobiles and motor cycles, televisions and stereo equipment, calculators and copiers.

Much of their success is attributed to a handful of men, of whom two of the most prominent – Dr W Edwards Deming and Dr Joseph M Juran – both took their messages to Japan in the early 1950s.

Deming firmly believed that by using statistical quality control methods, the quality of manufactured products could be increased dramatically and the number of defects could be decreased dramatically.

Other key principles stressed by Deming are:

- That inspection of products after they have been manufactured is wasteful – the emphasis should be placed on preventing errors, not detecting them after they occur.
- That top management must make the pursuit of quality a corporate goal.

Juran defined quality as 'fitness for use' and maintained that the basic quality mission of a company is 'to make products which meet the needs of the user.' He further believed that 'fitness for use is properly determined from the viewpoint of the user, not the manufacturer.' By Juran's definition, 'users' are not merely the ultimate customers (or consumers) of the product, but most of the individuals involved with the product as it moves from the design stage through to final delivery. Other key points made by Juran include:

- The pursuit of quality is a never-ending process. Consequently, companies must look for 'annual significant improvements in quality.' Put another way, quality improvement is an ongoing process, not a one-shot programme.
- Massive training is a prerequisite of quality. The entire management of a company must be trained in how to attain, control and improve quality.
- Quality requires hands-on leadership by senior management including the chief executive officer. Without that attention and leadership, quality efforts are meaningless.

The success of the Japanese in following the strategies of Deming and Juran in the automotive and electronic industries is well known. Less known is the success that Fuji Xerox – a company jointly owned by Rank Xerox and Fuji Photo Film – has had in implementing a total quality process. Following its founding in 1962, Fuji Xerox experienced a period of phenomenal growth. But in 1975, not only was Japan's economy jolted by the worldwide oil crisis, but also competition became a harsh fact of life and Fuji Xerox lacked adequate new products with which to respond.

Virtually overnight, Fuji Xerox went from the confidence of success to the harsh reality of a competitive marketplace. Sales performance began to slip. Unless something bold was done, the very survival of the company was threatened. In May of 1976, Fuji Xerox announced that it was launching a total quality process under the name 'New Xerox Movement'. The organization responded with enthusiasm and commitment: quality circles flourished, the use of statistical tools became the norm, teamwork was fostered and been rewarded, a participative management style was nurtured, and an absolute dedication to quality improvement and cost reduction became the accepted way of life.

The turnaround was nothing short of phenomenal. In 1980, the highly coveted Deming Prize was presented to Fuji Xerox, and by 1982, revenues were increasing at an annual rate of 25 per cent and profits by 28 per cent. Much of the success was attributable to the New Xerox Movement and its insistence on a never-ending quest for quality improvement.

This provided the rest of the Corporation with evidence that quality does work. Out of that realization, 'Leadership Through Quality', the Corporate approach to total quality, was born.

What is Leadership Through Quality?

Once the decision was made to adopt quality as the basic business principle for Xerox and for Rank Xerox, it became clear that no existing total quality process could be transplanted into the existing environment. As with any large organization, it had its own unique culture, values and philosophy, and its own unique business opportunities and challenges.

It became apparent that if a quality strategy were to succeed, the highest levels of management would have to lead the implementation process and act as examples for the rest of the Corporation. Consequently the decision was made to make the 25 senior operating executives from around the world responsible for the design of the quality strategy. In a series of meetings that spanned a 15-month period, this team developed a quality policy and the broad outlines of a strategy and implementation plan. The policy says simply, but powerfully,

> Rank Xerox is a quality company. Quality is the basic business principle for Rank Xerox. Quality means providing our external and internal customers with innovative products and services that fully satisfy the requirements. Quality improvement is the job of every Rank Xerox employee.

The policy refers specifically to *products and services*. Quality, particularly in terms of quality assurance, has its roots in manufacturing and, for many years, Rank Xerox has been active in improving its manufacturing processes and the resultant quality of its products (for example, through vendor certification and just-in-time practices). However, customers require more than a product, they require a total package, which includes (among other things) delivery, installation, service and query handling. It is the total package to which Rank Xerox relates its quality policy – its products and associated services.

When an organization embarks on the implementation of a total quality process, it is important that the meaning of quality to that organization is fully understood. The Rank Xerox team took great pains to define precisely what was meant by quality, and identified four aspects where it was to differ from the conventional view:

- Whereas the conventional *definition* of quality is often taken to mean 'goodness' or 'luxury,' Rank Xerox defines quality as 'conformance to customer requirements.'
- Whereas the conventional *performance standard* for quality is some acceptable level of defects or errors, the quality performance

standard in Rank Xerox is 'products and services that fully satisfy the requirements of customers.

- Whereas the conventional *system* of achieving quality is to detect and correct errors after products have been manufactured or services provided, Rank Xerox emphasizes the 'prevention of errors.'
- Whereas the conventional system for *measurement* of quality relies on indices, Rank Xerox measures quality by the costs incurred when customer requirements are not met.

A strategy of change

After the broad strategic architecture was developed, the responsibility for the detailed planning was turned over to a quality implementation team. Working for and with senior management, this team designed the long-term strategy and implementation plan for Leadership Through Quality – a strategy and plan unique to Xerox. It laid out the strategic goals for the subsequent five years and developed the key elements or mechanisms for change. These were:

- A common set of tools and measures
- Recognition and reward
- Communications
- Training
- Management behaviour and actions

supported by a

- Transition team

A common set of tools and measures provided all Rank Xerox people with new ways of assessing and performing their work, solving problems, and improving quality. Tools to do this included problem-solving and quality improvement processes, competitive benchmarking, statistical tools, and techniques for determining the cost of quality.

Recognition and reward ensured that Rank Xerox people are encouraged and motivated to practise the behaviours of Leadership Through Quality. Both individuals and groups are recognized for their quality improvements – whether in the form of a simple acknowledgement or a cash bonus.

Communications ensured that all Rank Xerox people are kept informed of the objectives and priorities of the Corporation in general and their work group in particular, and how they are doing in meeting these priorities. Communications includes formal media, such as magazines and films, as well as informal media such as staff meetings.

Training provided every person with an understanding of Leadership Through Quality and a working knowledge of the tools and techniques for quality improvement. Training which took about 5 days, was delivered in 'family groups', consisting of a manager together with his or her direct reports.

Management behaviour and actions ensured that the management team – at all levels of the Corporation – provided the necessary leadership and acted as examples for the successful implementation of Leadership Through Quality. Managers are expected not only to espouse the principles of Leadership Through Quality but also to use them consistently.

The transition team was composed of quality implementation teams at both the Corporate and individual company level with the responsibility of assisting senior management in implementing the strategy. Quality officers report directly to the head of each company within the Corporation.

How is the strategy being implemented?

The role of line management

Since the initial definition of the policy and the strategy, it has been stressed that implementation is the responsibility of line management, with the local quality officer and quality network taking an important, but subsidiary role of promoting and supporting the implementation process. That line management should take this responsibility has proven to be essential, and experience within Rank Xerox shows that implementation has been most effective where local line management is actively, visibly and consistently assuming that responsibility.

Training

In the early days of implementation, a training process was put in place throughout the organization to ensure that people at all levels had a thorough understanding of the tools and processes encompassed within Leadership Through Quality. Following the initial training, application support was provided to ensure that what had been learnt progressively became the natural way of working. Managers experienced the training twice: once as a member of their manager's 'family group' and again as the leader of their own 'family group' (Figure 10.1).

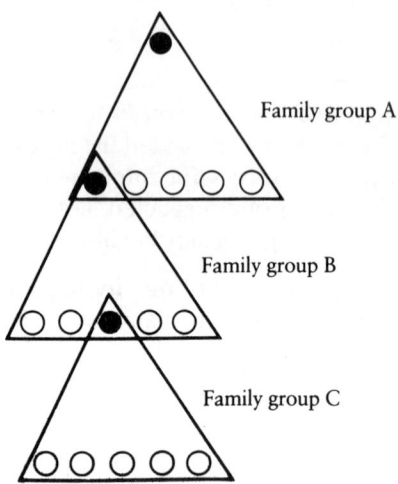

Figure 10.1   *The training process: family group cascade*

During the training (Figure 10.2), the groups selected projects for application of the quality processes and tools. After training, the manager was responsible for guiding and supporting the group in the use of the processes until such time as he or she felt that they were individually ready to lead the training of their own family groups. In this way the training process was cascaded from the top to the bottom of the organization. At each stage professional trainers were involved in delivery of the training, but worked with the active support and involvement of the family group manager in such a way that the ownership of the training process was seen to be with line management rather than with the trainer or the training function.

The basic quality training commenced with a one-day workshop in which the background, goals, concepts and principles of quality were presented and discussed. The key activity of the workshop, however, was to define the mission of the group and the 'outputs' (or 'deliverables') provided to others outside the family group – its 'customers'. An understanding of the 'next customer in line' concept was essential to the training that followed. At the conclusion of this workshop, the group would have defined its mission statement, its

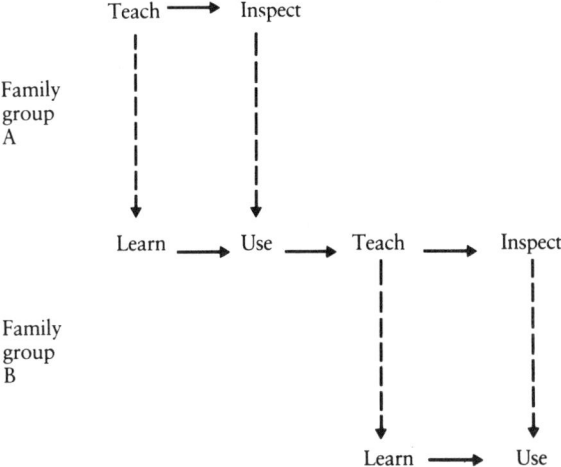

Figure 10.2   *The training process: learn-use-teach-inspect*

'outputs' and the customers for those outputs, thus providing a foundation for the remainder of the training (Figure 10.3).

The major part of the four days of the subsequent basic training was devoted to the problem-solving process and the quality improvement process. In addition, time was given to introducing group process and interactive skills and to estimating and using cost of quality. The final session dealt with the role of the manager – preparing managers for the new demands which a total quality culture would place upon them.

The *problem-solving process* used within Rank Xerox is a 6-step process, which was originally developed in support of an employee involvement initiative. The first step is to identify and quantify the problem (Figure 10.4). This is followed by analysis and data gathering to help develop a clear understanding of causal factors.

The third and fourth steps involve developing possible ways of solving the problem and then selecting and planning the most appropriate solution. Steps five and six relate to developing an implementation plan for the chosen solution and to evaluating its effect.

The *Quality Improvement Process* involves 3 distinct phases – planning for quality, organizing for quality and monitoring for quality – and comprises 9 steps in all (Figure 10.5). A team using this process first identifies the 'output' to be improved. Next is identification of the customer for that work – the person or group for whom it will be done – and what the customer's requirements are.

These requirements form the basis of supplier specifications, which need to be agreed with the customer. This is followed by the identification of the steps in the work process – what has to be done, by whom and when, in order to deliver the output in line with specifications in order to meet the requirements. This is followed by the establishment of measurements which will indicate the extent to which the output meets customer requirements. Next is a check of process capability, to provide an assurance that the process can produce the output consistently to agreed requirements, and finally, after the work process itself, an evaluation of the final output.

Although the training of these two processes was often conducted in separate sessions, in reality they are often used iteratively and in conjunction with each other.

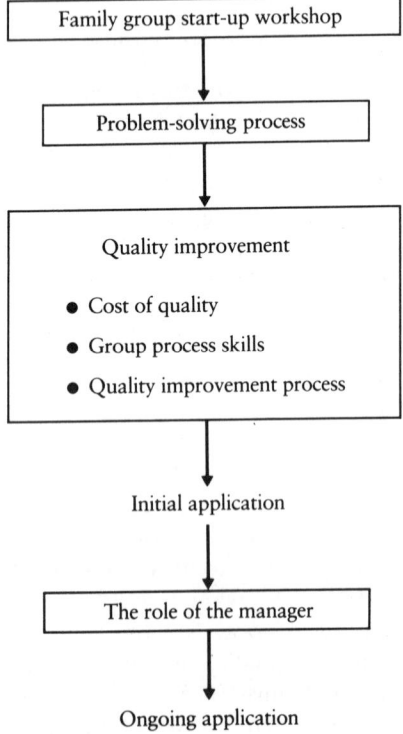

Figure 10.3   *The training process*

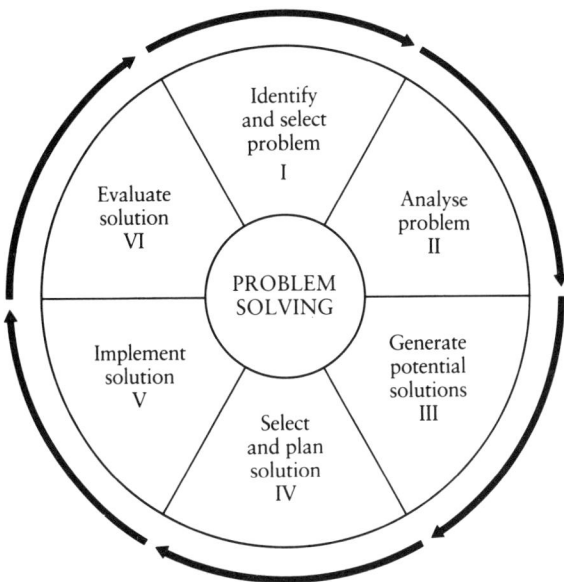

Figure 10.4   *The problem-solving process*

Customer satisfaction focus

One over-riding theme which began to emerge as implementation of the strategy progressed was the need to ensure that efforts were continuously focused on end customers and their requirements.

In response to this, Rank Xerox senior management established and formally communicated customer satisfaction to be the number one priority for the entire organization. This was supported by actions which fell into two main groups: measurement and management.

Measurement

Survey systems, which had been in place for some years aimed at assessing levels of customer satisfaction, have been significantly refined to include surveys of customers who have recently taken delivery of products, as well as regular surveys of samples of existing customers. Information from these surveys enables the company to understand causes of customer dissatisfaction and to put in place action plans to address them. Based on information from these surveys, a set of internal measurements has been developed in order to track performance in known areas of potential customer dissatisfaction, such that action can be taken, hopefully in advance of any impact being felt by the customer.

These methods of assessment – surveys and measurements included – are not regarded as a substitute for talking to the customer directly. All senior managers are expected to visit customers on a regular basis in order to understand their needs and problems, and the agenda of the

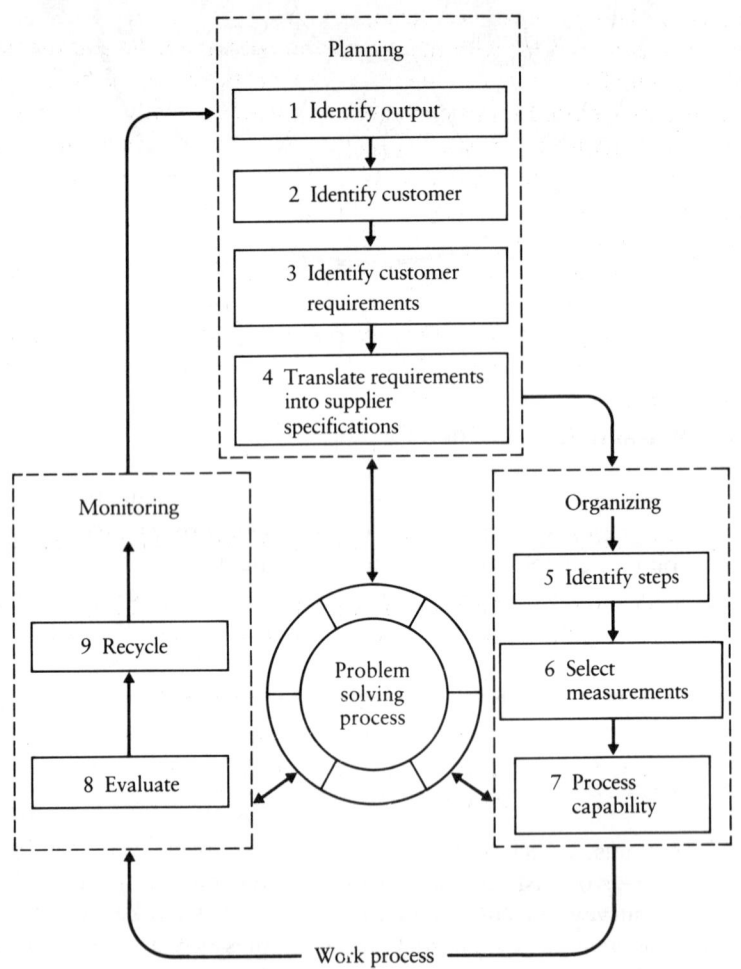

Figure 10.5 *The quality improvement process*

monthly board meeting of Rank Xerox routinely includes time for exchange of views on recent executive visits.

In addition to these activities, the company has been strengthening and extending its activities in the area of market research in order that the products and services offered to the market have the best possible match with customer requirements.

Management

Collecting data on levels of customer satisfaction is, however, of no value if nothing is done with the information obtained. To address this a customer satisfaction management system has been established. This is a systematic, closed-loop management process which provides the necessary structure to ensure that issues affecting customer satisfaction are formally analysed and prioritized and that corrective actions are taken. Progress on this closed-loop cycle is a major agenda item at all business review meetings.

In addition, in order to motivate managers to pay appropriate attention to this critical area, Rank Xerox is well down the track of giving every employee some sort of bonus or compensation based on customer satisfaction performance. In 1990, about 16,000 employees received this type of bonus, based on a combination of survey results and measurements of actual customer loyalty.

Focusing quality on where it matters – Policy Deployment

Policy Deployment is the process whereby the whole company, based on an understanding of the company's strategic direction, and the critical areas where improvement is needed, is involved, through an iterative and participative process, in identifying the actions necessary to achieve that direction and in tracking progress against them.

Rank Xerox has been developing this approach for a couple of years now and the process involves five key steps:

- Diagnosing the reasons for success or failure in achieving the previous year's objectives and action plans.
- Setting an overall direction for the year at top management level.
- Establishing the few fundamental objectives for the total company (Rank Xerox has four of these), based on 3–5 year goals and a company vision.

- A participative cascade of objectives and the direction statement down the entire organization, such that each group develops its own objectives and actions for the year in line with the overall direction; the focus within this step is on actions to achieve improvements or fundamental breakthrough in terms of performance.
- Progressive inspection of progress throughout the year.

The emphasis is on openness and honesty in diagnosing reasons for past failure, clarity in direction, participation in the cascade process and teamwork in its implementation. It is by concentrating on these values that policy deployment is distinguished from other, potentially more authoritarian, management methods.

Early results are very encouraging, and Rank Xerox has found that the approach has gained widespread support from employees in the areas where managers have focused on these values and invested the time it takes with their team to put them into practice. In most operating companies, every employee receives a booklet which includes:

- a clear statement of the direction of the company;
- a clearly documented and logical cascade of objectives down to their own department's quality improvement objectives;
- worksheets for their own family group to use in developing their own actions.

One significant finding has been that the process is very effective at bringing home the complexity of business and highlighting the disruption which had previously, although unwittingly, been caused by management attempting to change far too much from the top.

Quality in manufacturing

When Rank Xerox started its company-wide total quality drive in 1984, the development and manufacturing part of the company had already been introducing a wide range of TQC techniques for over three years, with significant results. Some examples of the tools and strategies that have been used are:

Statistical process control (SPC)

Initiated in 1981, incorporation of SPC has helped the development and manufacturing organization to focus and measure its activities as it drives for continuous improvement. It serves as the vehicle which aids the transition from inspection to prevention and the consequent reduction in the cost of quality.

Taguchi techniques

Experimental designs, using analysis of variance, are yielding improved product design robustness, giving better understanding of manufacturing processes and reducing manufacturing process variability.

Just-in-time

Work simplification projects and set-up time reduction teams use video technology to increase manufacturing flexibility and responsiveness by reducing cycle times, lead times and inventory levels. New measurements such as actual versus theoretical cycle times has been incorporated so as to reinforce the achievability of performance improvements.

Total productive maintenance

Integration of self-diagnostics into manufacturing equipment and processes has helped maintenance staff move to a predictive rather than reactive mode of operation, maximizing machine utilization and improving production planning and control.

Similar techniques have been incorporated into Rank Xerox's product range in the form of remote interactive communication (RIC) where microprocessors, built into the machine itself, assess equipment performance, predict failures and communicate through a modem to the service centre so that preventative measures can be taken before the customer detects a problem.

Supplier quality

More than 80 per cent of the company's production costs are made up of purchased materials, creating a heavy dependence on suppliers for the quality of finished goods. Development of a team relationship with suppliers has been a main part of the quality strategy, with numerous programmes including SPC training, process certification, continuous supplier involvement and Taguchi training, starting in 1981. Early experience with TQC convinced Rank Xerox of its value and as a consequence, since 1986 the company has been supporting suppliers' quality improvement efforts through a team of full-time consultants.

What has been learnt?

As a result of regular assessments of the progress being made in the implementation of their quality strategy, Rank Xerox has found that the most successful of its companies share some, or all, of the following attributes:

- A high degree of *general management leadership*.
- The existence of a rigorous process for *integrating quality into daily work* via the management process.
- A high degree of *management role modelling*, inspection and coaching.
- A strong focus on *satisfying external customer* requirements.
- The effective use of *recognition and reward* to reinforce the use of quality tools and processes.
- The existence of a *sustaining implementation strategy* that has taken the implementation of Leadership Through Quality beyond training.
- The provision of adequate *quality resources*.

What has been achieved so far?

One important learning is that the implementation of the quality strategy is taking longer than had first been anticipated. The company has, however, made considerable progress in a number of areas:

- The strategy is widely supported by employees and is seen as essential to the company's success.
- It has provided an enhanced focus on satisfying external customers' requirements.
- Large numbers of problem-solving and quality improvement projects have been completed or are in progress, addressing critical business issues.
- There are increased levels of co-operation and effectiveness between groups and functions, achieved through teamwork.
- Improvement has been achieved in key management and operational processes.

- Several national quality awards have been won – in Britain, France, the Netherlands, Australia and China; in addition, other parts of Xerox Corporation have won awards in the USA, Canada, and Mexico.

In terms of business results:

- Levels of customer satisfaction have been improved.
- Product development cycle times have been cut.
- Unit manufacturing costs have been reduced.
- Inventory levels have been cut.
- Improvement has been achieved in return on assets.
- Market share has been regained from competition.

The future, quality intensification

Rank Xerox regards quality as a never-ending journey, and despite six years of effort, believes that there is still much to do. As a result of a further recent internal assessment process, a set of actions has been developed which are intended to further intensify effort throughout the company and to assist in the quest for total quality.

In order to focus attention and ease communication across the different parts of the company, these actions have been condensed into six vital areas:

- To ensure, through effective market and customer satisfaction research, that the company has the best possible understanding of the requirements of its market.
- To further develop policy deployment as a basis for setting continuous improvement goals, and to incorporate an understanding of the performance of world-class companies into the establishment of those goals.
- To develop and implement improved work process improvement tools.
- To reinforce further the responsibility of line management visibly and actively to lead the drive for continuous quality improvement.
- To reinforce employee motivation.
- To strengthen training, communications and quality support, with a particular emphasis on training in process management and in the appropriate application of measurement and statistics to achieve performance improvement.

Clearly these are not fundamentally different to the basic principles of the original strategy, they do, nevertheless, bring a new focus to the continuous struggle to achieve total quality.

In summary, Rank Xerox has come a long way, but the story is far from over. The pursuit of quality is never-ending – but the company is well on the road. As Rank Xerox's chairman, David Kearns, said at the start of the change process, '*We are no longer the company we once were, and are not yet the company we want to be*' – hence this major transition.

11

A role for managers in total quality
Brian Plowman

Barriers to change

Exhortations to improve quality only serve to alienate staff from management. To achieve total quality, everyone must be motivated and become involved. Obtaining improvements requires that management create a culture where staff propose change in a structured approach that delivers benefits in an environment without fear. Knowledge then becomes the essential ingredient that reinforces the quality theme and motivates towards continuous improvement. For years, managers have 'managed' without total quality. If total quality is now the route to prosperity, then by definition, managers must learn that they need to manage in a new way. In a total quality company they have a new role.

National action to implement total quality

In a survey undertaken by Develin & Partners, published under the title *The Effectiveness of Quality Improvement Programmes in British Businesses*, it was found that many companies had responded to the threat of low competitiveness by initiating a variety of quality improvement programmes. The awareness of total quality was high but, although much importance was attached to the reasons for starting, it was disturbing to find that despite some notable successes, the average level of improvement was reported as low. A key measure, profitability, only marginally improved. Why was this so? A number of serious concerns were reported which provides clues to the two main underlying causes.

The TQ implementation approach

The first underlying cause of poor reported success is to do with the way total quality is implemented. The respondents in the survey highlighted a number of factors which gave cause for concern (Figure 11.1). These were:

- *Making time.* Starting an improvement process is always a problem as the effort requires additional time and everyone is already very busy. Not all activities in the business add value, but the problem is knowing which activities these are and how to eliminate them.
- *Cannot enhance internal service.* Any request to have another department enhance its service to your own, always seems to get the response that additional resources will be required. As it is difficult to eliminate wasted activity, any request for others to improve their service is often resisted if this is likely to increase costs.
- *Few tangible benefits.* Exhortations to improve quality do not provide a clear focus on the actions needed to provide tangible benefits. When the initiative to improve quality fails to deliver benefits, then the momentum is lost.

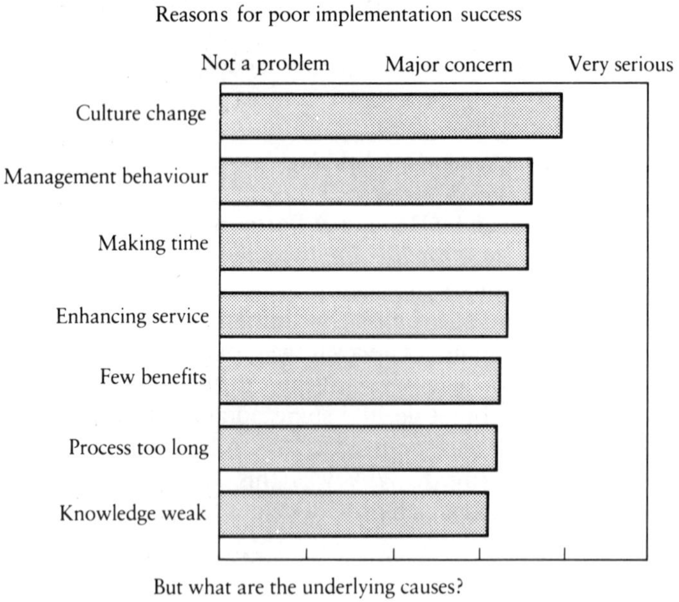

Reasons for poor implementation success

But what are the underlying causes?

Figure 11.1   *Reasons for poor implementation success*

- *Process too long, from the chief executive to staff.* Just focusing on communicating the main message of total quality has taken up to two years to cascade the message in some companies. Only a few people receive the message at the same time, so it is difficult to track failure activities across the business. More importantly, staff know where the problems exist but the business waits too long to obtain that knowledge.
- *Interdepartmental knowledge weak.* Staff have little knowledge of how the whole business works and thus have difficulty in tracing the root causes of problems they experience locally.

There are many approaches to total quality, all of which overcome these concerns to varying degrees. As time passes, worldwide experience increases so companies are better able to use this experience base and choose a process that will be a comfortable fit to suit their own business.

Management issues

The second underlying cause is to do with management. In fact, only addressing the first cause is not enough to achieve the motivation that ensures a permanent result. Culture change and achieving a demonstrable change in management behaviour were found to be the key factors to obtain a successful implementation of total quality.

Much is said and written about 'culture', but what is the culture of a business? It can be summarized as the historical development of the business since the day it started and the influence this has on all its employees. This results in a degree of commonality in the management style and behaviour where beliefs and values are shared. In total, the business will have developed a way in which knowledge is obtained, analysed and interpreted and will have created clear limits to the authority that is held and used by managers. Therefore, to change a culture requires changes to all these factors. The historical inertia within any business is a major constraint when attempting to implement change, and the degree to which total quality challenges the current culture determines the resistance management and staff may well express when the board launch a total quality initiative. Often 'commitment' from the top will be voiced but it this is not supported by action, the rewards and benefits of change will remain an elusive entity. A culture change by management is therefore the turning point.

The lone voice

In foregone days, medicine had been successfully practised without the knowledge of germs. In a pre-germ era, some patients got better, some got worse and some stayed the same; in each case some rationale could be used to explain the outcome. In any event, mistakes were buried and in general we remained none the wiser

Today we take for granted that doctors administer to the needs of their patients according to what they learn through training and experience. They apply what they learn and believe, and interpret what they see through their understanding of the way the body works. As a professional group they do not stray too far from shared beliefs, and current knowledge keeps them on the line of accepted practice. Like doctors, we are all prisoners of our upbringing, culture, and the level of knowledge of our teachers and fellow practitioners in our own areas of skill, and thus draw comfort from sharing common beliefs. We credit ourselves as being intelligent, and in general we believe we know what we are doing.

Even 120 years ago, doctors were using common practice to advise people how to avoid catching malaria. The word comes from the French, mal-aria or bad air and was believed to be carried on the night air, so early colonists took the doctors advice and perfumed the air on retiring to sleep. At the time, their theory of medicine had them looking in the wrong places for the wrong solutions. Other people paid for such mistakes but were sadly silent and unable to join the debate on likely other causes.

In the 1990s, managers still do the same. They look to changes in tax structure, import restrictions, government economic policy, unfair competitor activity – everywhere but to their own businesses to understand what is really happening. Like the early doctors, everything is questioned except their own theory of management.

Let us retrace our steps for a moment. Imagine that you are a young trainee doctor in the 19th century, hoping to become a doctor in your community. You see that doctors are successful, they are respected members of the community and visibly they have profited from the rewards of their labours. They cure some people and lose others, but on balance no one doctor is particularly better than another. In the culture of the society at the time they have the trust of the community.

Let us also imagine that during your learning period, funded by the local community, you came across the work of Pasteur and Lister. You learn of carbolic acid and its use to reduce inflammation during surgery,

Figure 11.2   *'We all did our best'*

and you learn a new word – antiseptic. It dawns on you that these famous physicians, those you respect and have learned from, are killing their patients. Your keenness to bring this new knowledge to their attention steels your resolve to go back and tell them that because they do not wash their hands or sterilize their instruments they are sewing death into every wound. At this point you have greater knowledge, you have a new theory of germs. You resolve to go back and tell them that what they have been taught, what they are still teaching, and what they firmly believe as the accepted wisdom, is completely wrong.

Now imagine you are one of these doctors, listening to this new theory from a young upstart. You are a respected member of the community, you are successful, you follow common practice, you even pass on your accumulated wisdom at some of the most respected colleges in the land. How would you feel if your established edifice was crumbling under this apparent attack, and your patients told that you are a menace to society and unfortunate to be under your professional hands.

In the 1990s, professional managers approach management according to the accepted rules and common practice. Whatever happens there is always a plausible explanation for it. What if managers explained a failure in this way: 'You know, I really don't understand what I am doing and I think that most of what I know is wrong'. Broadcasting such doubts is not usually seen as a route to promotion, and questioning the validity of widely held accepted ideas is not a normal way that managers behave. But in 1870, doctors had a sense of social responsibility, they were sincere in their efforts to do the right things and for centuries they had taken the Oath of Hippocrates. Those early doctors did the best they could with what they knew at the time and so do management today (Figure 11.2).

What the doctors were taught was just not good enough. Some things they did were dangerous and harmful to their patients, but they learned as everyone can, even management. The profound changes in medicine following knowledge of germs need to occur again in business with a change in managerial practice. The changes needed are not a passing fad, they are necessary for survival. If your competitors have started making the changes, they will prosper and at your expense. Where whole nations have made the changes they are leading the world in economic performance, and we ignore the risks at our peril.

A fundamental problem

When a business starts up, its 'pioneer' phase, staff and management pitch in willingly and do each others' jobs as need creates the vital team spirit. Over the years, staff become more specialized and become managed by functional specialists and the business becomes more complex. As problems and process failures occur then a sense of collective defence creates the walls of parochialism and, quite quickly, organizations become functional hierarchies. However, the transactions in the business that provide customers with products and services remain a horizontal flow through the functions and usually at a low level within the organization structure.

As the transactions flow through the business then hiccups arise at the function boundaries. Some things get turned back, others get misinterpreted, others get their priority for action changed. In fact, so many small diversions occur that it becomes just a collective 'noise' that keeps many people busy in most businesses. Should we accept that growth necessarily leads to specialization, complexity and parochialism?

Culture, the way things get done and the behaviour of management, reflects in difficulties experienced in being able, or even allowed, to communicate meaningfully across functional boundaries to resolve inter-functional process problems. Poor communications up a structure are a reflection on the way authority is shared and used, and the way management style inhibits the acceptance of ideas from staff and the implementation of change.

Noise distorts what is really happening

Taking one function, sales, and looking at how the salesmen (the exploded segments of the pie chart, Figure 11.3) and the sales-office staff spend their time it is possible to classify their activities. The salesman travels to 'support' the 'core' activity of a face-to-face visit to an eager customer. He also has to make some visits to react to failures somewhere in the business. These visits are to aggrieved customers who have received too many split deliveries, late deliveries, missing items, incorrect invoices or whatever. Such face-to-face visits have 'diverted' him from 'core' activity somewhere else. On this basis the travel to aggrieved customers is thus also 'diversionary' – it soon mounts up! In the sales office, staff are dealing with noise. Credit notes, special orders, keeping aggrieved dealers happy.

What upsets the sales department is their perception that none of the 'diversionary' activity was their fault. In fact, they create a bit of 'diversionary' activity all by themselves – statistics on other departments' failures. Why not? – the current culture will eventually be looking for people to blame later, as sales decline. For whatever reason, the key process of getting the right goods on time to the customer has failed. A

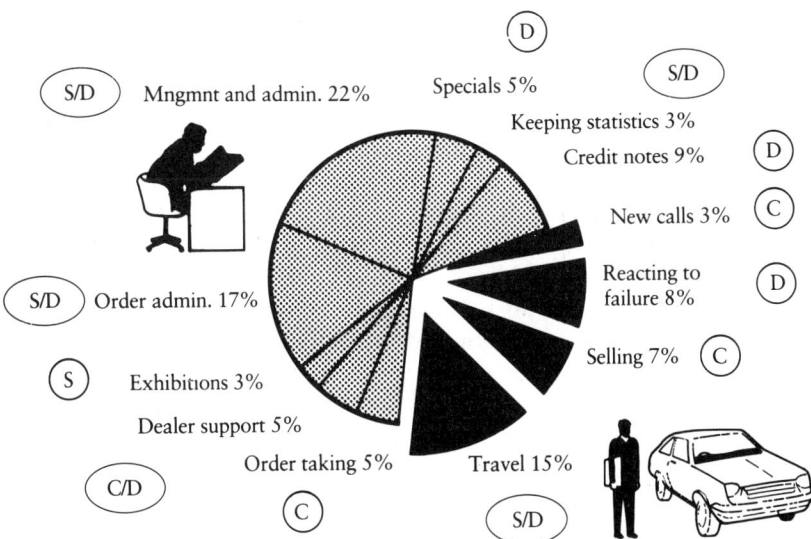

Figure 11.3   *Core, support and diversionary activities*

certain amount of failure is always accepted, it's known as 'business as usual' and is probably built in, and thus buried, in the standard costs.

The failure of a key process in a business can be very costly. A process that is common to most businesses is new product launch. At risk is a lot of expense in terms of the staff resource required; advertising, PR, product development and literature, and the cost should the product fail to capture a market opportunity. Lead time, between the idea being generated and the first sale, needs to be short.

The process can fail for a number of reasons:

- people are already busy with the current business;
- the whole process is not co-ordinated through to the delivery point that affects the customer;
- there exists a poor understanding of the current constraints within the current processes and the effect this will have on launching the new product.

When one investigates each part of the process you find that nobody came to work to screw-up and everyone was doing their best. Staff doing their best in a poor process will always fail to deliver – the process is incapable of delivering.

The virus of variability

If the process is failing then what is causing the failure? Processes become infected with viruses (Figure 11.4). Once a virus is in the system their presence is felt. Viruses cause diversionary activity and if the system is not treated to become immune to their effect, then they escape and re-infect others. A system that contains viruses is one that produces a variable output; the results are no longer predictable, stable or high quality.

Like any illness, though, do we always know what we are treating? The effect of the virus can create serious symptoms, and our response is most often determined by the higher visibility of the symptoms which divert us from attempting to treat the root cause. What is important is to be able to recognize the difference between symptoms and causes, and then with knowledge and sufficient time, treat the root causes. What often mitigates against this is a traditional measure of a good manager; an ability to make snap decisions on little evidence – the 'firefighter'.

All businesses contain the virus of variability. We attempt to do our best but the system consistently beats us; things just do not happen as predicted every time. Whatever we do, the process contains the virus –

Viruses cause diversionary activities

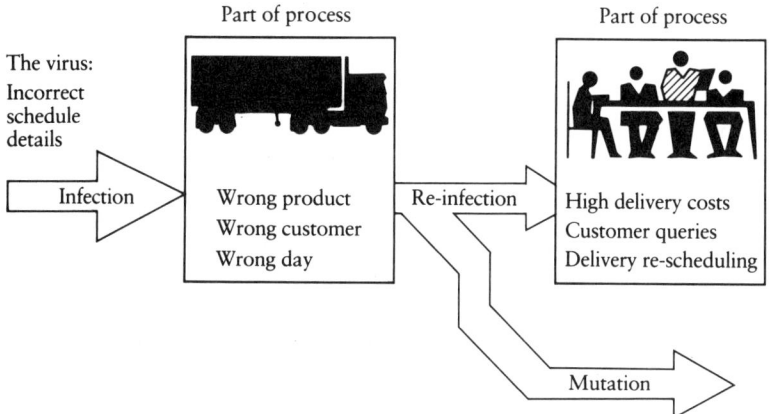

The virus:
Incorrect
schedule
details

Part of process

Part of process

Infection

Wrong product
Wrong customer
Wrong day

Re-infection

High delivery costs
Customer queries
Delivery re-scheduling

Mutation

Figure 11.4 *Viruses cause diversionary activities*

parts don't fit together every time on assembly, invoices have mistakes on them, specifications are incomplete, the computer breaks down, the materials are often inferior, things just keep letting us down.

The processes we are using are not capable of doing the job. And, if the process is not capable then despite our best efforts our output will be variable and, in the broadest sense, of inferior quality. No amount of exhortation, 'to do better', or 'be right first time', can expunge the virus of variability. Only by working on the process can it become capable and its results stable and predictable.

In the medical sense, germs are invisible to the naked eye and thus dangerous and difficult to track down. You know they are there by the symptoms that are all around you. To find the germ you need to know where to look, how to find it, to culture a sample, to analyse it, and in some cases special instruments will be necessary to fully understand its nature and true effect. The virus of variability in companies is just such a germ. Managers must also learn to take data and analyse it so they can understand the effect of the virus, learn how to eradicate it and get the patient back to a healthy and long life.

Germs, though invisible, can be transmitted. So too can the virus of variability. It passes from one department to another and multiplies and takes on other forms, creating symptoms that lead to an incorrect diagnosis. Some departments react to the symptoms and put themselves or others into isolation wards and refuse all contact with the outside world, others resolve to ignore it and not acknowledge its presence.

To remove the virus, reduce its effects and become immune, first requires that everyone acknowledges its existence, recognizes it for what it is, stops treating the symptoms and starts addressing the cause. Doctors had to learn new techniques, they had to believe that it was important to do something new, they had to learn about the causes of infection, they had to learn preventive medicine rather than treating the symptoms – they had to stop killing their patients and burying their mistakes. Doctors did this, now managers must do the same.

One man and his virus

Imagine now that you are the chief buyer in a business, management have set you objectives and your performance is measured against them. You are going to be measured on your ability to screw down suppliers to a low purchase price. There seems nothing wrong with this, after all, you were trained to know what to do, so you set about the task using all your knowledge. Eventually you find two cheap sources of supply for your steel bar, each supplying 50 per cent of the total requirement. You achieve and keep low prices by constantly threatening to move the balance of your orders from one supplier to the other. Both supply to specification but each supplier is at the extreme of the tolerances on material hardness – opposite extremes. The material is infected with variability. To give you a low price, each supplier cannot afford to maintain its consistency close to the mid range of specification.

In your material stores the materials are held in the same place, as they are both to specification and thus pass materials inspection. The material then begins to infect your machine setters, they are forever changing the machining settings to allow for the different material hardness. Tool wear is now unpredictable as are the visits by the maintenance engineers. The safety stocks of tools in the tool stores have to be increased to cover the unpredictable rise in demand; the virus has now infected the stores. The previous preventive and predictable maintenance of the machines now changes to fire fighting, and more skilled men are required to work on the now unpredictable and frequent calls to deal with unusual vibration.

With more skilled men to train on a wider variety of potential problems, some begin to receive more training than others. The training department is now infected with the virus. Eventually, people with variable skills attempt repairs where they have insufficient knowledge and experience and the standard of repair deteriorates.

The virus then infects personnel department who attempt to address a perceived problem of diversity in the ability of the maintenance engineers. Following the appraisals by the supervisors, the personnel records now include details of the below average workers. In the management accounts, tool stocks, usage, maintenance costs have all gone up but as this is a new stable level, the standard costs are adjusted and the root cause of the problem disappears from view.

People have become the victims of a lottery. The virus has created winners and losers but everyone was doing their best. Unseen and unrecognized the virus has wrought havoc – on people and the business.

As one of the buyers, you met your objectives and perform better than your peers, and are justly rewarded through the merit scheme. Soon after, the business goes bust. You sit at home and ponder your life. You did nothing wrong, you did your best, you met the company's objectives, you followed the rules; in fact everyone did.

Let us imagine that you decided to make a fresh start, something different, nothing to do with manufacturing, something simple, something where you can meet people, meet customers, no bureaucracy, somewhere where things can't easily go wrong. When you read the job advertisement it seems ideal so you apply and get the job working in a TV rental showroom.

Things start well as the shop is always full with people and there are always at least three people waiting to see you. A lot of people come and go, maybe they are just browsing. It amuses you to note that some people just cannot seem to be able to wait patiently while others are being served. You seem to be kept busy all day so that must mean you are doing well.

All the time a new virus is in the shop just waiting. The rental forms seem a bit complicated to start with but you help the customers whenever you can. You don't have to help them when they fill in their name and address. If they want a TV set, insurance, credit terms, service arrangements or particular delivery dates, they have to write their name and address six times. Customers get lots of practice writing their names so they are bound to get it right. Unfortunately, that is about all they get right. The pressure of the queue means that you often leave customers to get on with the form-filling bit and the customers don't want to bother you, you seem awfully busy. They do their best to complete the forms, drop them on your desk and then leave the shop. The completeness and correctness of the forms has been infected with the virus of variability and, right at the start, the process of satisfying the customer has gone wrong. You don't know, nobody knew, that across the country a total of 30 per cent of the forms contained errors. You were doing your best, what else could you do.

Unknown to you, the virus then went on and infected the regional offices. The second from bottom copy of the six part order set went to the regional office, so the delivery of the TV could be organized and a check for stock-outs made. Many hours were spent by people dedicated to checking for errors. Although some errors were found, some were not seen as errors, and when the data was keyed into the regional computer, some new errors were created.

The preferred delivery date for the customer was keyed into the computer, but as everyone could not be satisfied, so some delivery dates were changed. In the regional office they hope that someone will be home when the TV is delivered. The virus has infected the regional office and the installation engineer, and now waits to infect the customer.

The failures in the process are now exposed to the customer (Figure 11.5). The costs of these failures have to be paid for by someone – the customer. You may be lucky, all your competitors are just the same – aren't they?

Figure 11.5

Back in the showroom you begin to notice more people seem to be coming in. They don't browse, they don't leave, they wait patiently for their turn to complain until one day your patience breaks. None of the complaints were your fault, you were just doing your best. However, you know better than to complain to your boss as you heard that's why the last person left and the job became vacant in the first place. But you have an idea, when people come to you to complain, give them the phone number of the regional office. Even better, put a big notice in the window. 'Complaints – ring the Regional office'. Soon nobody comes into the shop to complain to you and you forget there was ever a problem.

Meanwhile, in the regions, the virus creates new departments to deal with the symptoms. With so many complaints, someone suggests a complaints department. The staff in this department are dealing directly with customers, and customer loyalty is valuable. Resolving complaints is important and speed of resolution is seen as a key issue when serving the customer. Speed has merit and what has merit can be rewarded, so the growing complaints department introduces individual bonuses. Nobody shares their knowledge of how to resolve problems quickly; why should they, it only reduces their share of the merit bonus. Each one does his best but the problems are varied; some other departments are helpful, most are not. They are all too busy, doing their best.

Some people get the bonus, but those that do not are appraised as being useless. In the personnel department their cards get marked. Once again, the staff have become victims of a lottery and the virus has created winners and losers while everyone was doing their best. Unseen and unrecognized the virus has wrought havoc – on people and the business.

In your shop things get quieter and at last you can cope. You are amused to see a competitor open a similar shop across the street. What a fool, doesn't he know everyone round here has a TV. Shortly afterwards, your shop closes but your competitor's doesn't. You sit at home and ponder your life. You did nothing wrong, you did your best, you met the company's objectives, you followed the rules, in fact everyone did.

You continue to ponder. While you were doing your best, management were doing everything wrong. They didn't realize that their job was to manage the process. Not just the process in their own departments, but the process of the whole business. They had to recognize the virus of variability and how the processes were infected by it, and then manage the process to reduce the variability within it. If they had spoken to other managers they could have tracked the virus, but to do this would have required co-operation across the functional boundaries.

Where fear is the norm, or no two-way communication exists, or where reward schemes mitigate against team work then the chances of finding the faults in the process are very small. Similarly, subordinates are often afraid of highlighting where the process is failing, as it is usually seen as a reflection of their own weakness. Often, managers never invite their subordinates' opinion of the process, after all, they are managers and what could they learn from the people doing the jobs? When mistakes are common, management tell everyone to get things done right-first-time, as if they think everyone came to work just to get things wrong every time. But can you blame management for the attitudes they hold? They do their best with the knowledge they have, they meet the company's objectives, they follow the rules; in fact everyone does.

No knowledge creates victims

Recognizing a virus, its symptoms and root causes is one thing. Making a process robust and immune to its effects is an entirely different matter. Those people with the knowledge of the process failures are not the same people as those with the authority to change the process. Staff gain a high degree of knowledge of functional procedures, after all, they are working with the functional procedures. As someone rises through management then, generally, the detailed knowledge becomes weak but their authority to change the functional procedure increases.

If we now look at two different variables; the authority to change a process and the level of detailed knowledge of the process (Figure 11.6), then the picture worsens. Processes are multifunctional and suffer from noise at the interfaces. The culture, measured by communication failures, may actively discourage gaining a cross-functional awareness and the knowledge base may be so low that nobody is really able to spot

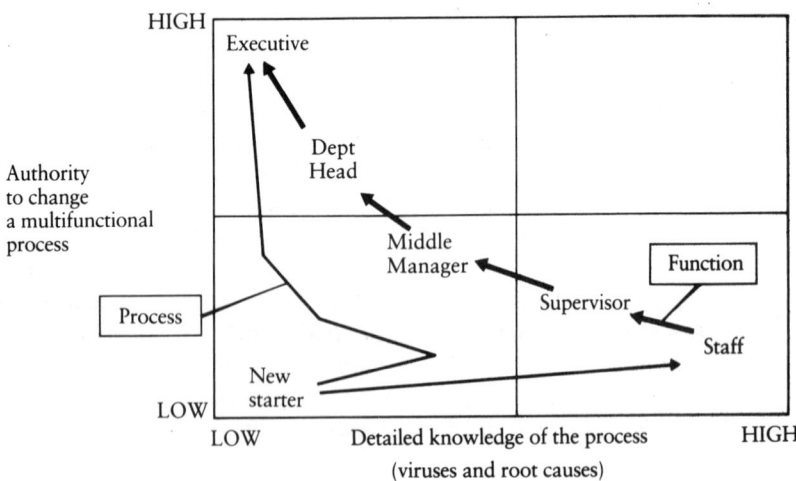

Figure 11.6 *Knowledge and authority*

a virus, its symptoms and root causes. In this scenario, authority to change a process resides with the executive board and few people are able to know how to improve the process.

As parochialism increases and staff have increasing difficulty in communicating across the organization, the chances of understanding and resolving multifunctional problems reduces. More insidious and, in many ways, the more alarming is the constraint on change imposed by the relationship a manager may have with his subordinates. Staff are often not credited with the ability to have ideas for change – 'well, what do they know!' say some managers. This attitude swiftly decouples the manager from the very people who have the most knowledge of the process and particularly its failures.

Ideas for improvement from the staff are often treated with disdain and at worse with contempt. The manager is resentful of such ideas – he never thought of them. After all, isn't he paid to come up with such ideas – he'll come up with them in his own time.

With the manager's profound lack of understanding of the process, he will remain unaware of the entirely statistically predictable variability of all processes. Those processes that lack robustness will be susceptible to the viruses from others. While remaining unaware of this effect he will be acutely aware of the failing outputs of his own staff – his internal customers will be pointing these out, and at the highest level. By appraisal time he will have carefully tracked the errors his staff have been making – 'well, aren't the failures all their fault.'

An impasse. Management blind to the issues, but with maximum authority to improve the process. Staff with knowledge of the issues but unable to break through the constraint of management. Staff have become victims.

The variability of the process, a process the staff have no authority to improve, has created winners and losers. Appraisal is simply a lottery with your chances of losing increasing with the passage of time. Such an environment is one of fear, and although fear conjures up images of someone who is personally frightening, this scenario is worse. This fear is less tangible, it is a cultural issue and represents a behaviour pattern in the whole business that becomes the way of life for everyone. In the end, staff just give up. Why shouldn't they?

Intuition and emotion are not enough

In some companies, the measure of a 'good' manager is the ability to make quick decisions based on the minimum evidence of a solution.

Whatever problems are thrown at them you can get a snap decision back. What was the skill that was used? Was it intuition, emotion, gut feel or just simple experience? If the problems have been around for a long time then was the experience really of any use, particularly if the problems are recurring? Such a style of management avoids the very difficult bit, that is, finding out what is really the root cause of the problem. Intuition and emotion are not the minimum management skills needed to implement total quality. Companies need first to recognize when they have management without knowledge of the damage they are causing, staff without knowledge of why they have become victims, and everyone without knowledge of how to analyse the processes in the business. To understand what is going on now in a business, point the way to the future and to have a clear basis on which to judge the benefits of change, management need knowledge. Gaining knowledge is thus the first step to becoming a total quality business.

Business direction and customer needs

What are those factors that the business must get right in order to be successful? Is the current performance against such measures, adequate, or is the business failing in some areas? Do all employees share the same views as management? Becoming aware of these issues provides a company with the focus for short-term action.

External customer needs surveys establish which elements of the service are important to customers, as viewed by customers rather than as decided by the supplier's management. By establishing the customers' views of the supplier's current performance, particularly compared to the competition, clear measures of serious shortfalls are highlighted.

Internal customer needs surveys will bring out the major interface problems and historical perceptions of the failures of processes that travel across function boundaries.

Key business processes

To overcome the constraint that functional structures impose on our thinking, we should view businesses as containing a number of key processes.

A key business process can be defined as a collection of activities, which from initiation require the diverse skills of a number of functions in order to deliver a predetermined result by a due date to the satisfaction of both the customer and the business.

Key processes, unlike functions, have 'flexible' boundaries and tend to overlap with each other at various points. As business conditions change over a period of time then the boundaries will change. The process reflects the business and its relationship with customers, and as the relationship is dynamic, so the process needs to be dynamic.

When viewing the business as a set of processes, rather than as functions, the essential requirement is to make the processes visible. This can best be achieved by charting all the steps in the process. Furthermore, by determining the points in the process where decisions have to be taken, and by whom, it becomes abundantly clear where the accountabilities lie for the incurred cost of each decision. It also determines the impact each will have on the business and its customers both in timing and cost. By clarifying each step in the process, it is possible to determine where specialist input from outside the main process is needed to bring the necessary quality to a particular stage, and also to avoid wasteful backtracking over previous stages.

As the end result from key processes always directly impacts customers (Figure 11.7), and as there is often little to differentiate one business from another in a particular sector, then any improvement in the deliverables will enhance the customer's perception of the business: all processes therefore provide opportunities for gaining competitive advantage. The business's ability to deliver from its key processes becomes a key determinant of performance, and so variability within processes becomes the measure of the performance.

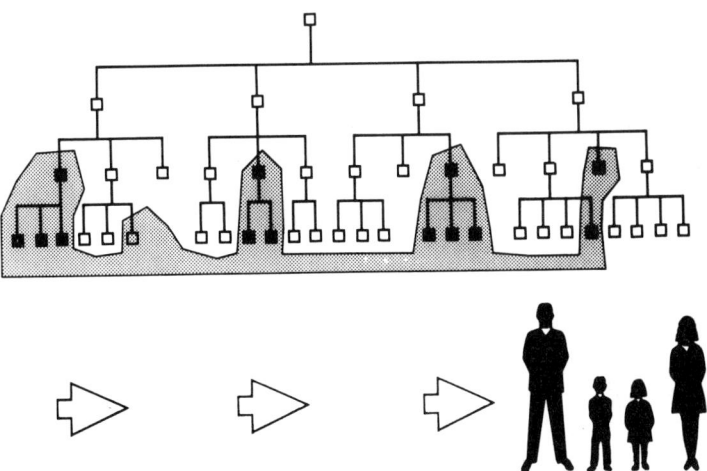

Figure 11.7 *The process impacts customers*

The current process capability

With the help from staff (the victims of the current process failures) the current activities can be quantified and the activities classified. As in the example of the sales department, using a core, support and diversionary analysis, the company will be able to focus on the costs of failures in the process. The way forward is not to exhort people to work harder on their core activities, but rather to re-balance their diversionary activity into core and use better methods. This change requires a change to the process in which the people work and a need for knowledge of the process, its behaviour and limitations. When people are motivated to gain knowledge they will reward the business with many ideas for improvement.

All processes contain inherent variability, things do not go as planned. The processes can be worked on to improve the repeatability, predictability and quality of the outputs. When people identify and quantify failures they will begin to look for viruses and then start to trace root causes. In many cases, ideas for change will impact others and the internal customer/internal supplier relationships will need to become visible. Staff, in these internal customer/supplier relationships, will need to come together in a forum where they can discuss change without the previous emotional conflicts and apportioning of blame.

Most businesses are 'controlled' by visible numbers; those numbers that appear monthly in the accounts. In a total quality company, most measures of process performance will be non-financial and the key measures will be those that impact on customer-perceived performance. Such numbers are often invisible; companies just do not measure the current capability of a process independent from the financial outcome of the process.

A change to real measurement of the processes will be seen by staff as a meaningful method of gaining real knowledge, rather than providing meaningless financial numbers that do not indicate where or how to make process improvements. Such a change in the means of measurement is yet another boost to motivation.

Many people in companies are given targets as a means of motivating them to ever increasing levels of performance. On receipt of a new target what do most people think? First they make a judgement on how reasonable the targets are; a 1 per cent increase they would scorn, a 50 per cent increase they would laugh at as impossible. When the target is around 10 per cent, in a subjective sense, it is reasonable. However, if the individual already knew how to achieve the target then that level of performance would already be being delivered. Without changing the capability then the process will only be capable of delivering the previous result. Setting a higher target is just frustrating to the individual who receives it, unless the means to improve the process are communicated at the same time. To ask the manager how such a new target can be achieved is perceived as admitting likely failure, a common measure of an individuals personal performance. A change to process improvement and away from target setting is yet another boost to motivation.

Any business must be able to provide products and services in response to the market needs, driven either by competitor activity or through internal innovation. Its competitive edge comes from both timing and cost, being able to respond both quickly and cost-effectively. Timing is addressed by everyone understanding and knowing their role in a process, avoiding the need for backtracking or delays. Cost is addressed by doing everything in the 'smartest' way possible, eliminating wherever possible the need for error correction, rework and other diversionary activities.

Measuring the processes

By having staff collect data on the parts of the process in which they work, they will then have:

- a basis for challenging the output or levels of service provided by the existing resources;
- a basis on which the benefits of method improvements can be evaluated;
- basic data on the mix and volumes of transactions and problems between sections;
- insights into the relationships between various functions within the same process.

Such data provides the basis for rational, objective, fair and open discussion and decision-making about improving the effectiveness of the business.

By categorizing activities, everyone will see their own work in relation to the problems that exist in the overall process.

Core activities can be defined as those which use the specific expertise of the section and can be seen to add real value to the business. Core activities are therefore those which provide an essential service to external or internal customers.

Support activities are those that make it possible for core activities to take place.

Diversionary activities are caused by poor quality somewhere within the organization. Such activities include correcting errors and pursuing others who have provided an inadequate service. Diversionary activities have many causes including, for example:

- inadequate training;
- inadequate tools, procedures and systems;
- poor documentation;
- poor communications;
- poor quality suppliers;
- conflicting functional objectives and performance measures;
- inadequate understanding of customer needs.

Poor efficiency and effectiveness can only be eliminated by isolating the root cause of the problem. Frequently, failures cascade through a number of sections, picking up further diversionary activity, and therefore costs. By identifying the source of failure and the associated diversionary activity costs, wherever they occurred, simple cost/benefit analyses can be undertaken. A key outcome must be to change the mix of core, support and diversionary activity within each area of the business – that is, to place more emphasis on core activity to enhance service quality, and so avoid diversionary activity elsewhere.

Staff, the victims, have the knowledge of why things fail and can therefore propose many ideas for improvement. However, any proposals for change inevitably affect other groups, either as receivers of a service provided by a section or as service providers to the section. By exploring the impacts of proposals for change, cross-functional awareness will increase, internal barriers will be removed and the cause and effect of change understood.

Such group sessions provide a forum for symptoms of the problem to emerge, where, typically, such symptoms are expressed as placing 'blame' for failure on other departments.

The willingness of staff to do a good job and always to do their best, is never usually in doubt. However, people can live with the symptoms for many years without addressing the problem and putting something better in its place. Without a structured approach to address process failures and without a thorough understanding of the total process, many *ad hoc* initiatives will occur and a consistent waste of resources then result.

Process performance

Obtaining data creates new insights into the activities within a section allowing the main issues to be evaluated. By aligning the data to the key processes it becomes easier to track the cause and effect of process failures. The resolution of problems within a process and between processes can be achieved by creating a forum, that brings together previous multi-functional 'protagonists' in a natural way of problem-solving without any notion of parochial interest.

Data on activity costs can be used to allocate the costs of all activities to products and services, in order to improve the business's understanding of customer and service profitability. A greater understanding of what type of activity is being undertaken – core, support, or diversionary – can be used to differentiate between the wasted activity created by internal process failure, and those diversionary costs generated by external customers.

Some activities will always be sensitive to volume. However, when volume sensitive activities are also diversionary (failures, error checking, corrections, etc.) they should attract a greater emphasis to ensure their elimination. Most activities, including core activities, are driven by factors outside a particular section. When this is the case, the section will only be able to budget its resources when it has an assessment of the change in these factors somewhere else in the organization. The budget creation process should therefore take into account that costs are driven in this way, as any analysis of activities links directly to the cost of the activities.

As important is the need to know how the activities vary over time, as well as to measure the key non-financial variables that determine the behaviour of parts of key processes. The requirement of a process is that it produces an output that is predictable, repeatable and to specification (high quality). When the process lacks 'robustness' then the output is not predictable or repeatable, and is therefore of lower quality and higher cost. Measuring the outputs provides a measure of the inherent variability of the process. By working on improving the process, the variability will be reduced and the outcome achieved at lower overall cost.

Lack of robustness in a process allows errors to be made: forms are not completed correctly, mistakes in interpreting information are made, incorrect investment appraisals are prepared. In nearly all cases the people in the process have not made the mistakes on purpose. However, where the process is perceived to be designed to a point of maximum robustness, then training in the use of a procedure reduces another source of natural variability.

Measuring the current variability of any process is therefore the first step in understanding how much effort is required to work on making a process robust, and in understanding the potential waste and/or risk to the business of leaving the process as it is. A process that lacks robustness is vulnerable to inputs that are themselves variable, the viruses.

The measurement of dimensional variability is well understood in the manufacturing sector, and statistical process control (SPC) put in place on the shop floor. In the overhead functions the processes are often less amenable to the use of SPC and even greater difficulties seem to occur where the process is very judgemental. However, it is the judgemental processes that can show the greatest variability and often expose the business to the greatest risk.

For example, the lending process is the core activity within the bank. It is likely that the lowest risk, least cost and best competitive advantage, to a bank occurs when the lending judgement is undertaken quickly (least elapsed time from first customer contact to giving a reply and least amount of risk evaluation time). Also, judgement factors must consistently be applied, to ensure that the customer evaluation process produces a high certainty that the loan will be repaid without further intervention by the bank or the bank incurring a loss.

One analysis of a bank's current lending judgement did not give a clear indication of what might be the 'best' mix of judgements, variability existed in the lending process (Figure 11.8). Any opportunity to reduce that variability could improve the process – for example by tracking the judgements made at the outset and matching these to the

0 = Factor not considered		10 = Main factor considered	
Judgement factor	Miniumum	Average	Maximum
Purpose of advance	5	7.5	10
Ability to pay	0	7.5	10
Security for advance	1	5.5	9
Customer's background	2	5.3	8
Amount of advance	0	4.6	10
Quality of management	0	4.2	8
Remuneration to the bank	2	4.0	8
Customer investment	0	3.0	8
Repayment term	0	3.0	8
Borrowing/net worth	0	2.6	9

Figure 11.8 *Variability in making judgements*

outcome of the position. Although reasons for poor lending had a high profile in the bank both as a financial impact and as a measure of the manager's performance, there was little evidence to suggest that active refinement and communication of the factors that create good lending were taking place.

A further example of variability in the lending process, turnround times, did not indicate the reasons for the range of turnround times, but the outcome of the process was variability in customer service (Figure 11.9). The bank had always believed the sole difference that accounted for only two separate periods of delay could be attributed to the two distinct sub-processes, that depended only on the value of the loan. By relating turnround times to variables concerning the lending proposition, such as type of customer, purpose of loan, external economic conditions, and as important, the knowledge of the authorizing manager in the advances department, it became possible to understand both the capability of the current process and the route to improve the process capability (Figure 11.10). Interestingly, both the variability of the internal systems and the lending judgement had become inextricably bound together to obscure the true nature of the process, a lack of visibility that had existed for decades and worsened by continued expansion of the business. Market research and competitor analysis indicated the importance of reducing such variability in gaining competitive edge.

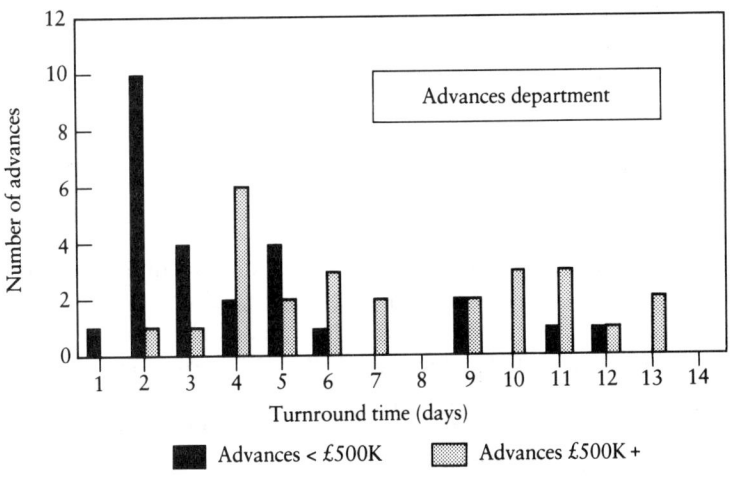

Figure 11.9 *Variability in turnround times*

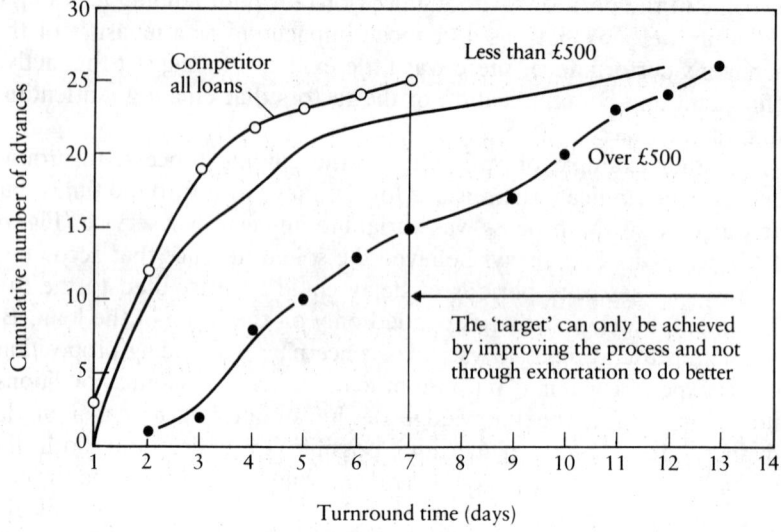

Figure 11.10   *Cumulative performance*

All processes can be measured in terms of variability, and a change to process management naturally creates a focus on measuring the process as the key means to identify the route to improvements, as well as to establish the means of measuring what improvements have actually taken place. The net result of improvements will then track back into the conventional measures as reported in the management accounts.

A manager's role in total quality

The old role

In an ideal business, the objective is for staff to undertake tasks in robust processes. No diversionary activities would be taking place, and all core and support activities would be undertaken in the most cost-effective manner. External factors affecting the business would generate the need to change the internal processes. Measuring and gauging these effects is itself another process, as is the requirement to give the business its overall strategic direction.

As most businesses are far from this ideal, managers have to act on situations that reflect the extent to which the business deviates from the ideal. In addressing these situations, conventional management style then shows a number of common characteristics. These are:

- an expectation that quick decisions are a measure of successful management;
- lack of understanding of variability in the current processes;
- failure to co-operate across functional boundaries;
- firefighting (dealing with symptoms), rather than searching for root causes of problems;
- a widely-held view of subordinates as individuals that make mistakes, rather than as victims of processes that lack robustness;
- appraisal systems that measure an individual's failures primarily as indicators of his performance, rather than as indicators of process weakness;
- appraisal systems that reward individual performance, rather than share the rewards of improved business performance resulting from their behaviour in a team effort;
- a reluctance by staff to propose process improvements or highlight their own failures in a poor process (the fear factor);
- a reluctance by staff to communicate across functional boundaries at their own level, if parochial constraints are in evidence at a higher level (the fear factor).

Over long periods of time these behaviour patterns become the accepted norm for managers. Subordinates take this behaviour as a role-model and the pattern is perpetuated. In all companies elements of the pattern will be found to varying degrees.

The new role
In simplistic terms, the new role will be the opposite of the pattern described above. However, it will not be easy. Because few things go seriously wrong, and as it is difficult to gauge how much better things could be, there is little apparent motivation to make the change. The present culture of the business will have been formed over many years and to some extent will be mirrored throughout the sector. Such comfort therefore creates considerable inertia against change.

In the context of key business processes, the role of a manager is clear:

The role of a manager (for any business, for any manager) is to work continually on improving the processes by:

- involving the people that work in the process;
- co-operating across functional boundaries;
- eliminating fear.

This role requires that managers:

- understand the nature of failure and current levels of correction activity;
- treat subordinates as victims of poor processes, and measure employees' failures as measures of their own failure to reduce process variability;
- tap into their subordinates' detailed knowledge of each part of the key process;
- use their authority to change the processes under their control.

Describing that role seems too simple, surely there is more to it than that. The simplicity hides the difficulty. To change to this role requires demonstrating a real change in behaviour – staff will be surprised, probably suspicious, definitely curious and may well register disbelief. The manager may well feel very much alone if the current culture is against the change.

For many managers, the change required is a moment of truth. They will need to try the acid test, calling their staff together and saying, 'Sorry, victims!' The manager should undertake a standard staff appraisal but treat the outcome as their own appraisal. They will need to work actively with their staff, to understand how the staff are failing in the processes that the manager has authority to change. Managers may well stop and think – even as managers they will also be victims of the failures of the larger processes.

What if you are a victim, how will you convince your own manager to make the change? Although there may be a perception that all levels of management in your company understand the need for change to the new role, subordinates invariably regard their superiors as understanding the requirement less than they do, and less likely to make the change.

Managerial styles

Imagine a chief executive with the highest authority to make changes happen, but who never understood that he must also change to the new role. Such a company has never heard of total quality. If he had some understanding but was committed to the change, there would have been hope. He still realizes there is yet more to learn, and will actively change as he gains knowledge (Figure 11.11).

A manager within the structure, with little authority and no knowledge of the need for change will be harmless, as long as everyone else continues to implement total quality around him. A manager with a

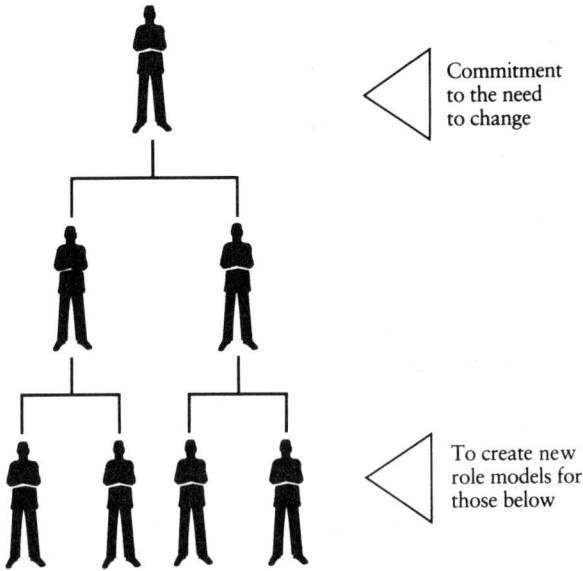

Commitment
to the need
to change

To create new
role models for
those below

Figure 11.11   *Those in authority must be first to change*

full understanding of the need for change and a high commitment to make the change, may still have little authority to make change happen. Such an individual represents the future of the business, the rising star. He was probably an aware person, even before joining the company. The situation can be risky if he perceives a role-model within the company in conflict with his beliefs. How long before he can no longer resist the pressure of the old culture and leaves to join a competitor? A member of staff aspiring to become a manager still has everything to learn, but has more role-models above him than anyone else. Which culture would we want him to have?

Who does what?

Managers always have 'own work', things only they can do. The board are expected to be thinking of the future but they get drawn into daily issues. Senior and middle management are drawn into historical problems and staff are the victims of poor processes. Even with knowledge of the necessary improvements and the right relationship with staff, implementation can be at risk if authority to change the processes is not devolved to lower levels. This is not a blind act of faith, but trust built on the foundation that lower levels of management in a total quality company will actually be capable of handling that authority.

Managers currently spend much of their time managing 'diversions', but they should spend their time 'improving processes'. This will not happen overnight. Not all managers will change to their new role at the same time. Some may not be capable of the change, while for others, the previous culture will still be the stronger force. Managers already perceive they have a difficult job, even before they learn what their job should be in a total quality business. However, managers are just as tired from a day of wasted diversionary activity as they are from a day of core activity. In their new role they will get all the help they need from their staff – the victims will have been freed.

Key process owners (KPO)

To confirm a change in focus to processes, the business can specify that some managers are the 'key process owners' (KPOs). A key process owner owns a specific process through to its final deliverable, even where the process is multi-functional. He will seldom own all the staff within the process, but he will be its focal point and will have authority to make changes within that process. Because all processes interact, the key process owners then actively co-ordinate changes and any cross-functional initiatives to improve processes.

Staff within a function can then be actively educated to see their own role in the process in which they operate. Visible processes also facilitate the induction of new members of staff. They can be shown the whole process and how it fits into the context of the overall business operation, and can spend periods 'upstream' and 'downstream' of their final job within a process. Such an approach provides faster overall awareness of the business, and provides them with a sense of belonging to a process rather than a function.

Taking a longer view, the basis of reward can be adjusted to reflect knowledge of a process, the individual's flexibility to work anywhere within the process, and their readiness and ability to improve the process. The usual progression up a hierarchy as a manager within the limits of a function, can then be changed to becoming a higher-graded individual, without necessarily creating a structure beneath that individual. Increasing knowledge of the process is valuable to the business, as it allows root causes of problems to be identified and solved quickly. Of equal value is the pure specialist who provides a scarce but necessary skill within a process. A change in emphasis reduces the need for promotion to 'manager' as a reward for making the business more effective, and allows the role of a manager to be something more specific in its own right. As a byproduct, this also reduces the trend towards many layers of management.

All one team

Finally, recognition that the business runs by key multi-functional processes will lead the business into focusing its efforts on improving the processes. The importance of a functional structure and of the management hierarchy within the function will start to diminish. The knowledge that the parochial functional barrier can be removed and that all managers and staff can work together as one team, provides the highest motivation to become a total quality company.

Every day, for many years, companies have so easily destroyed everyone's basic underlying desire to be personally successful in a successful business. The knowledge to make the change to a new role as a manager is not secret, but do we have the initial motivation to get the knowledge? On the world stage, perhaps we do not have the choice.

The author is indebted to Myron Tribus for permission to use parts of his paper The Germ Theory of Management presented at the British Deming Association annual conference, 1989.

12

The role of the British Quality Association

Douglas Denyer

In one brief sentence, the role of the British Quality Association is '*to promote a concept*'; this concept is '*total quality*'. In this chapter the author will consider:

- What it is that needs promoting
- Why it should be promoted
- To whom it should be promoted
- Where and when it can be promoted
- The means by which this promotion can be achieved
- The activities involved in such a promotion, their costs and benefits
- The consequences of failure
- The rewards of success

Putting quality into perspective

It is very difficult to analyse the concept of quality and to put its appreciation into perspective. Quality, like beauty, is in the mind of the beholder; what one person will value another will ignore; what one person will bid a large sum of money for another will simply dispose of by putting into an auction! Such are the variations in choice.

However, there are some aspects of quality which seem to meet with general approval and from analysis of these perhaps one can distil a knowledge of what it is that the British Quality Association should be trying to promote.

First, let us analyse quality from three entirely different points of view:

- Aesthetic quality   compliance to fashion
- Functional quality   compliance to need
- Durability   compliance to expectation

Most people would agree that a Rolls Royce is a 'quality car'. It has variously been described as 'elegant and the epitome of good living'; 'a model of engineering excellence' and 'good for a life-time's service' – that is to say it complies with all three criteria.

However, there are many who would not wish to own one and one imagines them saying 'It is too ostentatious for me' or 'It is too heavy and consumes too much fuel' and 'If I kept it that long it would become terribly old fashioned in appearance!' In other words, it would not comply with any of the three criteria listed, yet they would still acknowledge it as a 'quality car'! This is simply because through the years Rolls Royce have built a reputation for gracious appearance, functional excellence and impeccable reliability.

When the 'man in the street' is asked what he looks for in a car, the interviewer will often get as many answers as the number of people he interviews:

- I want something economical to run.
- I want a fast car with good acceleration.
- I want a small car, easy to park and fit in my garage.
- I want an estate, for carrying the tools of my trade.
- I want something to last, I am retiring soon and it may be the last car I buy.
- I want a car that holds its value, because I change it every year or two for my business.
- I am tall so internal headroom is important.
- Being short I must have a high driving position for visibility.
- My top priority is reliability; I often visit remote places and I'm not mechanically minded.
- I want a car with easy access to the engine because I like to service it myself.

Fortunately for the car industry there is a great variation in consumer preferences, leading to many different ways in which the manufacturer may comply with aesthetic quality and functional quality . . . though it must be said that almost everyone expects durability.

This is not the case with other goods or services. A man may want his suit to last for years but most women would prefer variety to durability in their clothes. However, all clothes must be functional, comfortable and affordable. Some purchasers also expect them to be original (or unique) and distinctive (to stand out). In some cases also the expectation is for a windproof or waterproof garment. Once again the consumer choices are almost infinite in variety giving the supplier an almost infinite range to explore.

What are the factors then which would reward a supplier with the accolade 'good quality'? What factors help beat a path to one door, whilst labelling others 'also-rans'?

In the world of clothes these factors are even more difficult to define, even for the 'experts'; choice is often led by the few, but not everyone follows. However, there are distinguishing differences for the discerning purchaser and they are sometimes independent of fashion:

- A level hemline.
- Stitches that do not come apart at the seam.
- Buttons which do not fall off in the first month.
- Materials where the colours are fast.
- Garments which do not shrink or stretch after the first wash.

Just as there are 'changing scenes' in the world of motoring and the world of fashion, so there are changing scenes in the world of food. Who would have forecast 40 years ago that people would go into a restaurant today and eat their meal from a cardboard box or a paper plate with no knife or fork? Who would have foreseen so many young people paying so much to consume fast foods sometimes in the restaurant and sometimes sitting outside on the pavement? There is more to the growth of the fast food industry that first meets the eye.

First and foremost surely is the quality of service. Where else can one be served so quickly by counter hands who are almost always very pleasant as well as very efficient? More often than not, the food is seen to be prepared under very clean conditions. The tables and chairs are easy to clean and the floors easy to wash down at the end of the day. Wrappings are quickly removed from the tables by either the customer or staff, and placed in plastic bags in bins which are frequently emptied.

Secondly, there is the consistent quality. Almost all the fast food chains work as franchises, buying in supplies which look the same, taste the same and cost the same. This suits the mass market and fulfills a need. There are minor variations between one chain and another which in the main consist of a difference in the sauces to go on the burgers, the type of bun and the thickness of the milkshake. There are therefore, small differences of choice.

Putting 'quality' into perspective is thus a case of recognizing both the diversity of customer perception within a diverse range of products and the varieties available from suppliers.

Emphasis on the future for British industry

For years many businesses have been run in a style which has prevented managers from realizing the full potential of their staff. This now dated approach required managers to set achievable performance standards and encouraged employees to adjust performance to meet numerical targets.

Many companies now find that they have to operate differently to survive in an ever more competitive world. They have to build quality excellence into every aspect of company activity. Simply providing a service must be replaced by providing a service which not only meets but surpasses the customer expectations. To deliver such a level of quality requires the creation of a work environment which encourages everyone in the company to contribute. It involves the creation of new policies, behaviour, management styles and ideas so that everyone in an organization is obsessed with quality and efficient working practices. To achieve this state will mean:

- The breakdown of traditional barriers so that worthwhile innovation is made a way of life for everyone.
- Determining those critical factors which will maximize the effects of contemplated improvements and identifying key opinion leaders to help in initiating changes and in maintaining the impetus necessary to keep quality initiatives firmly 'in sight'.
- Gaining willing acceptance by all involved.
- Achieving organizational flexibility by empowering people to initiate change.
- Linking change to the direction and overall activities of the company.

Why promote quality?

Dealing first with the questions of national pride and national identity there are very good reasons to promote quality in sectors of industry involved with trade.

Before World War II Great Britain had a name for good quality. 'Buying British' generally meant getting the best, the most reliable, good value for money, honest dealing and other attributes. Our industries had a fine reputation and even local names like 'Made in Birmingham' for toys and other manufactured goods, 'Lancashire

Cottons', 'Yorkshire Woollens' and 'Harris Tweeds' were names which were valued world wide.

After the war a feeling of complacency crept in. Machinery was old fashioned and worn out and was not replaced fast enough. Materials were in short supply and often overpriced. Labour became more concerned with financial rewards than with pride in workmanship. In short, things went downhill and Britain lost market after market. Ship building went to countries with new yards and no demarcation disputes; cottons to cheaper labour abroad; motor cycles to efficient manufacture on new machines in new Japanese factories; radios and televisions to other far eastern countries where labour was cheap; our car industry nearly disappeared but fortunately was partly saved in time.

British industry turned to other products and services: the electrical industry, the computing industry, anything with a high-tech content and a greater 'added value' to pay for rising standards of living. In doing so Britain promoted its service industries: banking, which aided the ever increasing investment of British money abroad; insurance, tourism. All call for different concepts of quality.

There is a very great need to promote the good name of 'Great Britain Ltd', to restore confidence in the quality of British goods and to gain increased confidence in reliability of the service industries and new growth areas like tourism and pop music.

Promoting quality to producers, distributors and consumers

It is easy to understand that quality is everybody's business: the producer because without quality his goods will not sell (or be accepted); the distributor because it is imperative to maintain good quality during distribution; and the customer who must learn to be discerning.

But how can BQA help and at what level in various organizations should help be given?

The key lies in standards. The application of standards is but one step on the ladder to total quality management but it is a key step. Taking BS 5750, part 1, for example and considering each section in turn demonstrates how essential it is to comply with standards in all walks of business life.

Management responsibility

It is absolutely essential that top management accept responsibility for quality and be seen to participate in achieving it.

Organization

The organization shall be arranged so that each person's quality responsibilities are clear to all and the quality manager shall be senior enough to stop defects getting through even to the point of stopping production to do so.

Contract review

This is the important stage in business where a supplier communicates fully with the purchaser, not only to ensure that both parties are completely aware of the specifications for the product or service which forms the 'substance' of the contract but also that the supplier does have the equipment, knowledge and skills to complete the contract to the purchaser's satisfaction – that is to say to a quality standard acceptable to both parties.

Document control

Documents are very important throughout the production process – job cards, office records, labelling, etc. – but they are also important from start to finish of the contract itself, any amendments to specifications, documents concerned with testing and with packaging and despatch. It is vital that all personnel are well informed and to ensure that this is so, it is not only important to give out full instructions but also to remove any obsolete documents from point of issue or use.

A document register should be kept listing all operating instructions and standard documents in use. This should be readily available to all personnel on a 'need to know' basis.

Purchasing

Perhaps the most important aspect of quality management in purchasing lies in the placing of sub-contracts. In sophisticated manufactured articles today, like aircraft, cars, televisions, radios and a multitude of less conspicious items like manufacturing machinery, power and sub-stations, and oil refineries, it is impossible to manufacture an item from start to finish. Many components and sub-assemblies are bought in and quality controls and documentation must cover all aspects of the components and their history.

Product identification and traceability

What could be more important than ensuring that individual parts, sub-assemblies and assemblies are clearly identified as they progress through processes in a factory to ensure that any fault found subsequently can be traced back to source? It is very important to impress upon employees at all levels that identification is clear and traceable; not only back through processes but forward through the processes in case any other sub-assemblies or assemblies have been affected.

Process control

Here perhaps the most important factor is the availability of clear documented work instructions defining both installation and production practices. Criteria for workmanship should be stipulated in written standards or presented in representative samples.

Inspection and testing

It goes without saying that inspection is important throughout all stages of production or service. Testing also must be vigorously adhered to using well-maintained and regularly calibrated equipment, testing of incoming materials, in-process items and assemblies and finished goods prior to dispatch. It is also important to inspect packing materials and documentation concerned with delivery.

Control of non-conforming products

Here it is essential to ensure that any item out of specification is segregated, identified and evaluated for possible reworking, regrading, acceptance by concession or scrapping. Re-inspection after reworking or regrading is also very important.

Corrective action

When non-conforming products occur it is necessary to evolve a procedure for ensuring there is no recurrence. This is accomplished by analysis of processes and operations, initiating preventive action, applying controls to ensure that corrective actions are taken and are effective and implementing and recording changes in the resulting procedures.

Handling, storage, packaging and delivery

In establishing and documenting procedures for these operations it is necessary to ensure that no damage or deterioration can occur. Appropriate methods for authorizing receipt and despatch between areas should be stipulated and conformance to specified requirements ascertained at each stage. Where contractually specified, protection of the quality of the product is extended to include delivery to destination.

Quality records

Quality records must be maintained to demonstrate achievement of the required standard at all locations and times. Where stated contractually these should be retained and made available for evaluation by the purchaser or his representative for an agreed period.

Internal quality audits

Manufacturers should carry out a comprehensive system of planned, documented, internal quality audits, scheduled on the basis of status and importance of the activity concerned. Many audits are annual but may be more frequent in special cases.

Training

Suppliers should establish and maintain procedures for:

- identifying training needs for all levels of staff;
- providing training according to personal needs and also according to any changes in practices or procedures;
- recording training courses, internal and external as required;
- keeping individual records of training and performance before and after receipt of training.

How does the BQA stand in respect of the 14 foregoing sections listing the requirements of BS5750 pt.1?

This is the very heart of the management system in a production or service environment. If the management system is not controlled and there is no quality manual recording all the plant operations and controls, what hope is there of achieving total quality management? None!

There is a considerable danger of companies thinking that they can skip such stages as compliance to British Standards. Strictly speaking it is not absolutely essential for a company to be certificated but it is certainly advisable and it is an extremely good discipline to have an assessor in to go through all the operations of the organization and comment in detail on the findings.

The BQA recommends certification. Its 'sister organization', the Governing Board for the National Assessor Registration Scheme is there to ensure that all assessors adhere to standards and that a high degree of professionalism is maintained.

Promoting quality

Quality is an enduring attribute. At no time should quality be forgotten or even allowed to slip. Quality is part of life and there is no place where standards are not applicable.

The British Quality Association must use all the media in its effort to promote quality: papers and journals, the radio and television, exhibitions and conferences. All exponents of quality should promote the British Quality Association through personal contacts.

The BQA is organized into sectors headed by special 'sector quality committees' such as:

- The Automotive Sector Quality Committee
- The Local Authority Sector Quality Committee
- The Food and Drink Sector Quality Committee

Through these sector committees various attributes of quality can be analysed and the best features promoted. Such committees can prepare reports, make recommendations, hold seminars and even big national conferences and run training courses for staff involved in their industries.

When promoting quality, as stated at the beginning of this chapter, it can be regarded from three points of view:

- Aesthetic quality   compliance to fashion
- Functional quality   compliance to need
- Durability   compliance to expectation

Let us consider the opportunities to promote each of these:

Aesthetic quality

We judge quality with all five senses.

(a) We see it.   Beauty is in the eye of the beholder. We must make sure that when advertising quality, our visual display material is the best available.

(b) We hear it.   Judging music, no matter whether one's personal taste is for a classical or popular style, each of us can apply standards of sound; the same applies to listening to lectures. Spoken material should also be of the highest order.

(c) We touch it. Whether judging furniture or cloth for a suit, a car seat or a cup and saucer, the sense of feel is another area of human judgement.

(d) We taste it. Again the scope for personal choice is wide-ranging but the care and presentation of food and drink is just as important as that of more durable commodities. Who would give praise to overboiled cabbage thrown haphazardly on the plate or to a flat beer?

(e) We smell it. In this environmentally conscious world the often neglected sense of smell has come more to the fore and certainly all that can be done to suppress malodorous emissions must warrant support from the BQA.

Functional quality

We also judge quality by our assessment of the way in which a product or service succeeds or fails in its stated (advertised) functions.

Here is where the critical judgement of the consumer is an important criterion to be encouraged and where there are many instances of purchasers being misled by sales ploys directed at stimulating senses rather than inviting critical appraisal of a function.

One example is the now rather hackneyed technique of selling cars at motor shows by 'decorating' them with bikini-clad models – clouding technical judgements of possible road or race performance with lascivious bedroom contemplation!

Another is in the technique for selling time-share apartments where the picture painted is one of a continuous dream holiday in ideal surroundings of permanent 'luxury in the sun' through a one-offpayment, which (it is often claimed) would cost more in future years because of world inflation . . . etc., etc. The reality is frequently a brief 2-week stay, an annual bill for maintenance almost equal to the cost of renting an apartment of one's choice, a depreciation in value (in many cases), the only chance of a re-sale being at a loss and the loss of several thousand pounds of capital which would have earned a considerable bank interest.

The BQA endeavours to encourage membership from consumers organizations on its various committees and is always keen to listen to and consider the consumer point of view.

Greater customer satisfaction means increased sales, leading to increased profit – and greater customer satisfaction is not accomplished by achieving sales through misleading claims. In the longer term, truthful attention to the function the customer or client expects from his purchase or advice, achieves a lasting satisfaction and enhances the likelihood of repeat business.

Durability

To a certain extent and in many cases, but not exclusively, 'durability' is synonymous with 'functional quality'.

We may buy a product to last only a short time but to perform its intended function well – examples are increasingly common in today's society of 'throw-away' torches, paper handkerchieves and serviettes, plastic glasses, plates and coffee mugs; functionally adequate but certainly not durable.

However, now that 'green' issues are coming to the front of public consideration one is tempted to consider a rather different balance sheet of values:

> . . . a generation ago everyone had linen tablecloths, cotton or silk handkerchieves, ate food from earthenware or china plates and drank from real glass glasses. Now we destroy rain forests, clog waste dumps and makes thousands of workers unemployed in potteries, cotton mills and glass foundries – for what? A better standard of living? is this the 'ultimate'? to save washing up? especially since there are now available sophisticated washing-up machines!

However, the main emphasis on 'durability' must lie in our assessment of those goods and services we reckon to buy only once or twice in a lifetime:

> The house, built to 10 year guarantee periods (but why not 20 or 50?) Furniture is at least chosen to last one generation – 20–25 years, the best china – 50 years (but with guaranteed stocks for replacement of breakages). Tools – admittedly the craftsman expects to replace and update the tools of his trade several times in a working career but the 'DIY' enthusiast (one of a rapidly growing number) surely expects a 'life-times' use from his tools?

How is the British Quality Association organized?

What the BQA is

The British Quality Association (BQA) is an association of companies and organizations, all based in the UK, who have recognized that quality is a vital factor in the achievement of commercial success. The Association acts as the UK focal point for national activities in the field of quality. It is committed to furthering the interest of UK industry and commerce into 1992 and beyond, through the advancement of their quality competitiveness.

The BQA is affiliated to the Institute of Quality Assurance (IQA) from which it derives its secretariat and executive support. It is bound by a published Constitution and Rules which is accepted by all member companies and organizations. It is a non-profit making association, supporting itself financially almost entirely from its member subscriptions.

The objectives of the BQA

To provide:

- A focal point for national quality activities.
- An opportunity for the interchange of quality knowledge.
- A contribution to national and international standards.
- A range of special services to its members.

To represent:

- UK interests in the international quality field.
- Member interests in national and international quality activities.

To promote:

- Best practices in quality management.
- Total quality management (TQM).
- The UK's quality image.

To co-operate with:

- The IQA in its professional activities.
- The DTI in its quality initiatives.
- All bodies contributing to UK quality improvement.

To sponsor:

- The annual British Quality Award Scheme.

Benefits of membership

Publications:

- BQA Newsletter, quarterly.
- Quality News, monthly magazine.
- Quality Forum, quarterly journal.
- The opportunity to purchase European Organisation for Quality (EOQ) and American Society for Quality Control (ASQC) journals.
- BQA Yearbook, articles and member listings.

Discounts:

- Preferential fees for certain conferences and courses.
- Discounts on selected technical books.

Services:

- A forum for personal contacts in the field of quality.
- Participation in various BQA committees.
- Involvement in national and international quality activities.

Programmes:

- Experience Exchange (Ex-Ex) programme.
- Benchmarking programme.

And also:

- Use of BQA logo.
- Affiliate membership of the IQA.
- Invitation to the BQA Annual Dinner.

Grouping of members into sectors

Each year the BQA publishes a yearbook with member bodies listed under their main industrial/commercial sectors.

Sector quality committees have been formed to provide specialized services for member bodies in eleven of these sectors and more are planned. Some members are listed in more than one grouping.

Aerospace	Inspection/Testing
Automotive	Instruments
Building/Construction/Roads	Local Authorities
Chemical	Mechanical Eng-Heavy
Commerical Services	Mechanical Eng-Light
Computers/Software	Medical
Consultancy	Metal Industries
Defence	Non-Destructive Testing
Distributive Trade	Offshore Structures
Domestic Appliances	Petro-Chemicals
Education & Training	Pharmaceutical
Electronics	Printing
Electrical Eng-Heavy	Process Industries
Electrical Eng-Light	Raw Materials
Energy	R & D Design
Financial Institutions	Rubber & Plastics
Food & Drink	Service Industries
Hotels/Catering	Social Care Agencies
Hospitals & Health Services	Textiles
	Others . . .

The eleven sectors for which special 'sector quality committees' have already been formed are:

Automotive	Building & Construction
Chemical	Education & Training
Electronics	Energy
Food & Drink	Health Services
Local Authorities	Pharmaceutical
Social Care Agencies	

and others are being formed at an increasing rate as interest in the 'quality culture' percolates through British society.

The BQA statement on 'total quality management'

This is a 'definition' arrived at after several meetings of the special Total Quality Management Executive Committee.

> Total Quality Management (TQM) is a corporate business management philosophy which recognizes that customer needs and business goals are inseparable. It is applicable within both industry and commerce.
>
> It ensures maximum effectiveness and efficiency within a business and secures commercial leadership by putting in place processes and systems which will promote excellence, prevent errors and ensure that every aspect of the business is aligned to customer needs and the advancement of business goals without duplication or waste of effort.
>
> The commitment to TQM originates at the chief executive level in a business and is promoted in all human activities. The accomplishment of quality is thus achieved by personal involvement and accountability, devoted to a continuous improvement process, with measurable levels of performance by all concerned.
>
> It involves every department, function and process in a business and the active commitment of all employees to meeting customer needs. In this regard the 'customers' of each employee are separately and individually identified.

The BQA services

How the BQA can help

One key to high quality is teamwork, there is a real need for teamwork in quality management and the consequences of failing to build a team are often fatal. Why?

Years ago when most goods were made by a single craftsman or by a family of craftspeople, pride of accomplishment (of 'quality') became a matter of competitiveness, of striving to achieve the best for the customer, for one's own satisfaction or for the family name. There was little need to write down procedures or standards, or test for functionality. The craftsmen passed on their skills by example, by word of mouth and by the apprentice learning the 'feel of the job'.

Time moved on and the small groups of craftsmen were replaced by larger groups (in workshops and factories) to increase the rate of production in making items such as furniture, the manufacture of hundreds of complex units of equipment for radios, televisions, computers, etc., and in 'gangs' for the building of roads and houses. This 'rush' increased the opportunities for making mistakes, for failure in communication and for lack of understanding. There is now a great need for training, for documentation and above all for co-operation by everyone within each team.

If one person in a group misunderstands instructions or is careless in their work, a small error, possibly not clearly apparent before sale or despatch can have many and varied repercussions.

How often has the purchaser of a new car had to take it back to the garage and complain?

- the water seeps in through the corner light on the driver's side;
- the lock on the boot has stuck, and will not open;
- it is difficult to change down from third to second gear.

All these complaints cost money to put right, perhaps not always large amounts individually but they all add up and have to be borne by the supplier under the terms of the guarantee. The greater the number of defects the lower the profits and the greater the chance that the customer will look elsewhere in the future.

If a company cannot maintain or increase its market share, its profitability is at risk, it may not be able to pay its shareholders, attract investors, pay enough to attract the best employees. It will be on the 'downward slope'.

How can the BQA help to avoid these pitfalls? By:

- running courses and conferences on quality techniques;
- running World Quality Day;
- encouraging Experience Exchange;
- promoting benchmarking;
- sponsoring the Annual British Quality Awards competition.

Fees

As with most Associations and Institutions the British Quality Association relies on the members for funding. Membership subscriptions are based on the size of the organization and many of the larger member organizations participate in the activities of the BOA thus creating a higher standard of service and 'greater value for money' for all the members.

Supporting the Institute of Quality Assurance

The BQA provides regular public relations 'promotion' exercises for quality issues which usually show a surplus of income over expenditure. This surplus supports the Institute of Quality Assurance with running training courses and seminars. These vary both in size and complexity; a typical spread of courses run by the IQA is shown in Table 12.1.

The BQA also supports the IQA in providing a range of conferences, typical issues covered within a year have been:

Bahrain	The quality challenge
London	Software engineering and quality assurance working together
Coventry	Quality in Europe
London	Audit and assessment standards
London	The food act – safety first (a BQA food and drink sector seminar)
London	Managing change – mobilizing for success (world quality day)
London	Disaster control conference
London	Reliability
London	Towards a European certification system

Other seminars

As was mentioned earlier, each Sector Quality Committee runs the 'routine' business of the Association. Most SQCs meet four times a year but also foster sub-committees which meet more frequently and organize various special quality events ranging from full national conferences to seminars at a local level.

Table 12.1

Level to which material covered

- Introduction to subject
- ○ A full session on the subject
- ● Subject covered in depth

Approximate time

½ hour
1–2 hours
½–2 days

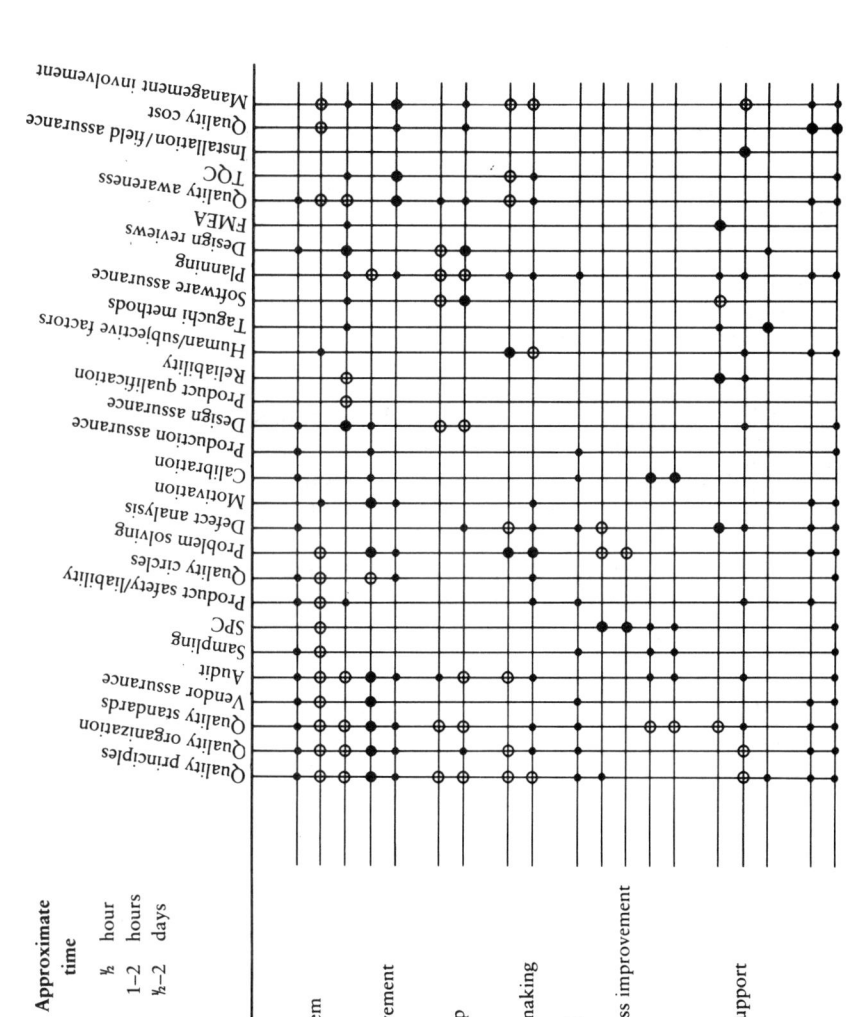

Module   Courses

A Quality assurance
A1 General introduction to QA
A2 Organizing an effective Q system
A3 Design assurance
A4 Preparing for a Q assessment
A5 Introduction to total Q improvement

B Software assurance
B1 Introduction to software QA
B2 Quality for software work shop

C Human involvement
C1 Managing human error
C2 Problem solving and decision making

D Quality control
D1 Quality in an inspection world
D2 Statistical process control
D3 Statistical techniques for process improvement
D4 Calibration mechanical
D5 Calibration electrical

E Reliability
E1 Practical reliability
E2 Quality assurance in product support
E3 Taguchi methods

F Quality costs
F1 An introduction to Q costing
F2 Reducing quality costs

Column headers (subjects):
Quality principles · Quality organization · Quality standards · Vendor assurance · Audit · Sampling · SPC · Product safety/liability · Quality circles · Problem solving · Defect analysis · Motivation · Calibration · Production assurance · Design assurance · Product qualification · Reliability · Human/subjective factors · Taguchi methods · Software assurance · Planning · Design reviews · FMEA · Quality awareness · TQC · Installation/field assurance · Quality cost · Management involvement

The TQM Committee also has a special sub-committee which organizes a number of 'road shows' where the quality message is taken to various provincial towns by a group of its members who give lectures on quality, presenting material evidence of quality techniques, quality improvement plans and getting area delegates involved in discussions on various aspects of total quality management.

Publishing

One of the functions of an association such as the BQA is to publish the best possible information available on various topics for its members. In particular where there is no easily understood standard or clearly described interpretation of particular documents.

Examples are government regulations; British, European and International Standards and even a complex treatise.

Two recently published reports are described in the next section and it is interesting to note how these came to be written.

The work of recently formed Sector Quality Committees

In the last few years quality assurance concepts have spread away from the engineering and scientific industries into the service sector and public sector of British working life.

Through the formation of the Local Authorities Sector Quality Committee in January 1988, one of the first special Sector Committee reports was published – *Quality Assurance, Cleansing Services, Grounds Maintenance and Leisure Facilities. A guidance document on the use of BS5750: 1987.*

A 1988 report on the work of the Local Authorities Sector Quality Committee chaired by Clive Bone of the London Borough of Wandsworth.

Despite its long title it proved to be a 'best seller' and the first edition was sold out between September 1988 and March 1989, when a second edition was printed. Extracts from the foreword to that report are reproduced here:

'The British Quality Association acts as a focal point for quality matters at national level and provides a forum for examining the fundamentals of quality in every sector of the economy. The advent of the Local Government Bill stimulated much interest in quality assurance, and following informal discussions with senior local government officers the

British Quality Association established a Local Authorities Sector Quality Committee to disseminate information on quality assurance, initially in the contexts of cleansing and grounds maintenance.

The Sector Committee first met in January 1988 and today with its sub-committees comprises over seventy individuals and representative organizations drawn from local government, the contracting industry and quality assurance. Whilst much of the committee's work was impelled by the Local Government Act 1988, the British Quality Association has no views as to the political context of the Act. It is also neutral regarding the use of contractors or direct labour and has no views as to the structures authorities might use vis-à-vis the client function and Direct Service Organizations (DSOs). Quality Assurance is equally applicable to contractors and DSOs and can be accommodated in a wide range of organizational structures.

This slightly revised guidance document is essentially a reprint of the now sold out edition that followed the consultative document published in May 1988. As before, this document's task is to illustrate how BS5750: Part 2. can be applied to cleansing, grounds maintenance and leisure facilities. Little of substance has changed in this document which attests to the quality of advice received following the consultative document's publication. As soon as is practical, advice regarding catering, vehicle maintenance, construction, education, social services, etc., will be produced and work will be done on the monitoring implications of the impending environmental legislation. The advice and interpretations given in these guidance notes and any future such notes are, of course, those of the committee and they may not necessarily correspond with the views of the individual bodies represented on it.

Shortly after the work of the Local Authorities Sector Quality Committee (LASQC) had begun it was apparent that there was a need for sub-committees of some of the very wide-ranging activities represented by local authorities and the first of these, the Social Services Sub-Committee soon developed into a full-blown Sector Committee entitled 'The Social Care Agencies SOC' – an interesting variation in titles brought about by national changes in the three means of providing care in the community.

- The public sector (local authority social services departments).
- The private sector (e.g. private nursing homes).
- The voluntary sector (e.g. the Spastic Society & MENCAP).

Social care agencies are responsible for co-ordinating and providing care to members of the community, but in any society the citizens do have a responsibility to promote their own welfare and that of their family and fellow citizens. Much of the assistance of the social care agencies will, therefore, be in partnership with individuals and their families.

It is expected that the services offered by social care agencies should be qualitative and flexible enough to cater for people who have encountered difficulties in their personal lives where professional assistance is needed and asked for.

Apart from statutory obligations, the social care agencies must accept that adult citizens have a right to reject offers of assistance, even if this means the continuance of a life-style which is disturbing to fellow citizens.

It also means that if the agencies are to encourage independence and freedom in their clients/customers, they will be exposed to the same physical and emotional risks as other members of society. It should be noted that people cannot be protected from every risk. Whatever care workers do should be credible and defendable; decisions not to intervene need to be taken as carefully as those to take action.

Social care agencies must commit themselves to create a positive climate by promoting the concept of quality assurance within their own organizations. It is necessary that a minimum acceptable standard is set within the agency, below which it must not fall, in order to provide a good and consistent service to clients/customers. As the Minister of Health said, 'to define good quality is not always easy but one can begin by listening to clients and customers'.

Quality assurance is a customer-created philosophy and at its core is the belief that the quality of goods and services cannot be simply 'inspected in' but only 'built in' by the people who are doing the job. This lesson has been painfully driven home in the industrial and commercial services sectors of the economy by international competition – the resultant unemployment too often placing a further burden on social care provision.

Underpinning the operation of any effective quality system is a set of documented procedures that ensure that staff know what to do in all conceivable situations. For this to work, staff must be well trained and committed to their work. These guidance notes clearly cannot address the broader subject of management, but suffice to say that quality assurance is not a substitute for poor management or low morale, the remedies for that lie elsewhere. Quality assurance is people-centred and organizations with a remote managerial culture will probably not succeed in introducing soundly-based quality management.

The international standard ISO9000 – known as BS5750 in the United Kingdom – simply sets out the facets of organizational practice that should be addressed to ensure the maintenance of agreed standards. ISO9000 has been derived empirically and enshrines some thirty years experience, often obtained the hard way, from the more advanced economies. Whilst industrial in origin, ISO9000's use in the services field is now a well-established trend in both Europe and North America.

The industrial origins of ISO9000 have given rise to some scepticism as to its relevance. This is best answered by a clause by clause examination of its provisions. It requires, for example, that important documents be kept up to date – who would suggest that that does not apply to them? It requires purchasing procedures that ensure that goods are traceable back to the supplier and that performance be monitored – who feels that social care agencies do not need to provide for this?

Nor must ISO9000 necessarily be seen as the best system. It is a sound yardstick and one that has been recognized by certification bodies for the purposes of auditing the quality systems of providing organizations but some industries have more exacting systems. Nevertheless, the Social Care Agencies Working Party believes that this Standard offers a basis for managing social care and that 'Benefit will be derived in terms of less wastage of time and effort due to poor organizations, with consequent advantages for those we seek to serve.'

In developing the report for Social Care Agencies, the team had to contend with the language of ISO9000/BS5750, a language which betrays its industrial origins – those who wrote ISO9000 did not have social care in mind. They got on with the job and simply recognized and identified those facets common to all organizations which, when addressed in a systematic and commonsense way, will reduce the waste and distress caused by service failure.

World Quality Day

'World Quality Day' is a relatively new initiative which was very much the 'brain child' of Professor Asjørn Aune, the Norwegian 'Vice President for External Affairs' of the European Organization for Quality (EOQ) and supported by the BQA and IQA.

The first events were launched in Europe in 1989 in most of the EEC countries and the British event, organized by the BQA, had as a theme 'Total Quality Management'; it was a most prestigious symposium catering for chief executives and senior management and attended by 450 delegates.

In 1989, also at an International Conference of the United Nations, called by the American Society for Quality Control (ASQC) there was a unanimous decision of all the countries represented to make World Quality Day a regular 'institution' and for simplicity of planning it was proclaimed that it will be held on the second thursday in November, every year.

The 1990 British event was a first class 'state-of-the-art' event with 380 delegates attending. Such events are unique and the theme 'Managing Change – mobilizing for success' was itself a resounding success with high calibre speakers from leading British and multi-national companies. The BQA will ensure that, in Britain at least, World Quality Day will always be at the top of the list of priorities for prestigious information change events.

Co-operating with other professional bodies

With the objective of promoting UK quality always in the forefront, there is no need for the BQA (or the IQA for that matter) to take a partisan stance: quality is not the sole prerogative of any one institute or association: in fact, quite the reverse; it is BQA's duty to co-operate with any other association or professional group which dedicates its purposes (or some of its objectives) to encouraging its members to improve the quality of the products or services they provide.

One instance of such help was assistance given to the Association of Local Authorities Business Consultants (ALABC) at a 1-day seminar they sponsored as part of a national conference mounted by the journal *ITLG* (*Information Technology in Local Government*).

The Seminar was entitled:

Quality Assurance in Local Authority IT

and three of the four speakers for the event came from the IT Delivery Sub-Committee of the Local Authorities Sector Quality Committee of BQA. The event was chaired by BQA's Secretary who also secured the fourth speaker.

A speaker from Essex Social Services referred to the benefits of certification and accreditation and included case histories of experience in Essex and Norfolk County Councils. He emphasized the importance of getting specifications for contracts 'right first time'. He also emphasized the need for software buyers to be 'streetwise' and to get hands-on knowledge. 'There are no IT quality standards' he said – and some hospital systems could be better run with an abacus or coloured tokens than to rely on their obviously faulty computer systems! He also spoke of software (and hardware) having a 'life-cycle' and he pressed users to define what they expect from a quality system, drawing on BS5887 and BS5115 as well as 5750.

'Costs may be high' he said 'but it is worth putting effort and investment into drawing up a sound specification before commissioning a system.'

The Head of Technology Services, Kent County Council, then spoke on the 'Quality of IT delivery in a County'. Despite pressures to quote low for the Community Charge, Kent is so well established in giving a high quality IT service to County departments that the staff succeeded in retaining 85 per cent of the County IT business against competition from private companies. This was done by assuring that the 'service level agreement' (SLA) is reviewed annually and each client department completes a very comprehensive questionnaire to ensure that the IT service given is not only that which was asked for but is perceived by the user to be as good as or better than the previous year's delivery!

In true TQM fashion the County has changed from being:

Supplier orientated	to Consumer orientated
Centralized	to Devolved
Professionally organized	to Functionally organized

These changes have meant a great deal of delegation of responsibility down to first line managers who prepare budgets and are then accountable for expenditure and control.

In each of the three years since these changes were introduced, the staff have changed their attitudes and become more accountable, more flexible and more motivated; the results have shown improvements in departmental responses to the services provided by:

The services desk	On-line services
Batch system service	Output quality
Data preparation service	General issues

These factors have been analysed each year by the professional computer staff by aggregation using structured systems analysis and design method (SSADM).

The speaker left the audience with one suggestion: 'The use of performance indicators' he said 'is the one yardstick needed to assess quality of IT – you must always welcome new ideas, from whatever source.'

There followed a presentation from the computer services customer support manager of Braintree D.C., a relatively small authority, entitled 'Satisfying Client Departments in a District Council' and sub-titled 'Quality of IT Service on a Low Budget'. His motto is 'Braintree means business' and one of the political policies of the authority is 'to aim for quality'. The authority's corporate plan lists the Council's 'core values':

- We are *customer orientated*
- We believe in the *abilities* of the *individual*
- We must be *responsive* and *responsible*
- We believe in *quality*
- We are *action orientated*

To ensure that the reality matches the promises, this authority carries out a monthly evaluation of plans and performance and an annual review which checks that service standards are assessed using 'SWOT' – strengths, weaknesses, opportunities and training. Staff ask for training – training is very important as it builds up staff expertise.

At Braintree, 86 per cent of departmental users of the IT service expressed a degree of satisfaction 'Equal to or better than last year'.

Finally, the last speaker, from Surrey County Council described what had been happening with the introduction of tighter quality control:

- Population   1 million and increasing.
- Budget   £550 million and increasing.
- Staff   currently 21,000 and decreasing.

This had been achieved by the IT department and through devolution of management and a move towards business orientation. Surrey too had carried out its third 'Information System Services Survey' and confirmed an absolute need for quality in IT. To gain contracts for direct services staff, Surrey not only had to compete on price but had to be better than the competition. Mere equality in competitive situations does not necessarily guarantee securing the contract; clients are often tempted by the 'other side of the fence' syndrome!

Quality in Surrey has become an *individual* responsibility. Only through transforming 'goals' through the idea of 'ownership' can quality be truly achieved. To encourage personnel development and through it improve customer care, Surrey spent an average of 2 per cent of salaries p.a. on professional staff training. The County's 'Advanced Management Training Programme' commenced in 1986 and 96 of the top 250 staff attended their in-house courses in the first year designed to:

- help managers accelerate their own development;
- improve their own and their team's performance;
- enable the County Council to offer an improved service.

One very surprising result to the observers was:

- Reduced stress – perhaps coming from increased delegation.

The composition of the new training courses were angled towards *skills* and at all stages the training target had to match or exceed job requirements. The modules included: marketing, selling, business planning, personal communications, financial managment, understanding Surrey County Council and appraisal and motivation – all plus customer care!

The experience – exchange programme (Ex-Ex)

Ex-Ex is a programme for the mutual exchange of experience on quality matters between BQA member companies. The programme, proposed by one of the BQA's member companies, is very simple in concept and has very considerable potential benefits for participating companies.

The BQA has, as two of its primary aims, the encouragement of cost-effective quality management and control practices and promoting improvement in product and service quality. The Ex-Ex programme makes a substantial contribution to both these aims.

Every BQA member company is encouraged to participate and thus benefit under the programme by receiving, on request from other members, information they may require on particular areas of expertise or experience in the QA field. The programme's viability is based on this commitment. Examples of such areas are listed in questionnaires available to members. The programme was implemented in two phases:

(a)   The first phase was a 'pilot programme', during which time provisions were refined in the light of early experience, and the viability of the programme proven.
(b)   The second phase, the programme proper, is now in place.

The principal activity in the pilot programme was establishing the 'database' of participating member companies, recording the areas of expertise and/or experience on which they were prepared to provide information under the programme. The Ex-Ex database is kept by the BQA secretariat, which provides an information service in support of the programme. Information about the database is published in the BQA Year Book and updated periodically in the BQA Newsletter.

The BQA benchmarking programme

Benchmarking in the context of quality management, is the process of identifying the best industrial or commercial 'performer' in respect of a product, service, or practice and using its 'performance' as a standard (or benchmark) against which to measure one's own. The objective is then for one's own company (or department) to achieve, or preferably surpass, the benchmark as part of an ongoing quality improvement process.

Such benchmarks will normally be external ones derived from another company, sometimes a competitor. They may also, however, be internal ones, derived from another department within one's own company at the same or a remote location.

The subject of benchmarking is introduced extremely well in the DTI booklet *Best Practice Benchmarking* a copy of which may be obtained free of charge from: The Department of Trade & Industry, (DTI) c/o Mediascene, Hengoed, South Glamorgan. (Mediascene acts as the DTI's distribution agent for free literature and for videos on free loan.)

The BQA recognizes benchmarking as an important tool in any continuous quality improvement programme. It aims to help BQA member companies to assist one another in the effective use of this tool.

The programme operates in parallel with and in a similar manner to the Ex-Ex programme, i.e:

Donors

Member companies which already employ benchmarking as a tool for quality management, are invited to act as 'donor' companies for the programme, i.e. they are invited to offer to make available to other member companies benchmarks of their choice which they currently employ.

Database

The National Quality Information Centre (NQIC) maintains a database, listing each benchmark offered, with particulars of the donor company representative to whom requests for data concerning the benchmark should be addressed. The list of benchmarks in the database is published and updated for the attention of BQA members through the media of the BQA Year Book and BQA Newsletter.

Requests

All BQA member companies are eligible to request benchmark data under the programme. Requests are made in the first instance to the NQIC Staff who then provide particulars of the appropriate donor company representative. The company requesting benchmark data then deals directly with the donor company representative.

Programme implementation

Questionnaires listing potential areas of activity for benchmarks are available to members. The BQA runs an advisory service on benchmarking which includes occasional seminars on the subject.

The annual BQA awards

There is one special event which the British Quality Association organizes every year. It incorporates the judging of entries, the decision on worthiness and the presentation in November of the British Quality Awards.

The award is given for significant improvements in quality sustained over the previous four years in a product, service or process.

This scheme is the 'jewel in the crown' of BQA publicity. It was introduced to encourage quality improvement in commercial, industrial and corporate organizations based in Britain, including public and private companies, trade and professional associations and educational and research establishments.

There is no constraint to grant only one such award in any given year; in fact, since 1984 when the scheme was launched, the number awarded has varied from one to four; a total of 18 were presented in the first 7 years.

Financial assistance has been received on occasions and is gratefully acknowledged, from:

British Telecom
British Gas Corporation
Marks and Spencers PLC
RG Abercrombie and Company Ltd
CMTC – Training Division EEWMA

Eligibility
Any group or individual working in the United Kingdom may be nominated for an award. Membership of the BQA is not necessary.

Conditions

- The BQA accepts no liability for any loss or damage resulting from the disclosure of information concerning the entry, though all reasonable precautions will be taken to maintain security.
- The BQA cannot undertake to return documents or supplementary material submitted with an entry.
- The BQA reserves the right to alter the rules of the award scheme. The decision of the president of the BQA is final and no correspondence is entered into.

Confidentiality

All entries are treated in strict confidence.

The BQA reserves the right, subsequent to the award presentation and with the winner's approval, to publish details of the winning quality improvement scheme.

Judging criteria

The entrant must, during the preceding four years have significantly improved the standard of quality in:

- product design and/or manufacture;
- or planning and/or operation of a service;
- or development and/or operation of a process;
- quality is defined as fitness for purpose and conformity to customers' requirements at a competitive cost.

Improvement is measured by any or all of the following:

- technological innovation;
- motivation and education of personnel to improve quality standards;
- better product or service performance;
- commercial success (e.g. bigger market share, increased profitability).

Following the improvement in quality, the standard represented by the submission must be substantially higher than that prevalent in the relevant industrial sector:

- proven operational success.

Method of entry

Nominations may be made only by individuals or groups authorized by a corporate organization in Britain.

A completed entry form, accompanied by two copies of a detailed report on the quality improvement achieved should reach the BQA by May 1, in the year of entry.

The report, typed in double line spacing, should include:

- position or affiliation of person making the nomination;
- the job titles and responsibilities of the entrant(s);
- a description of the improved product, process or service and its intended markets;
- details of the changes made to improve the quality and time taken to complete them;
- an evaluation of the results;
- a comparison, where possible, between the original and improved

operation including: market share, profitability and reduction of reject or failure rate.

In the following paragraphs are named some of the winners since the scheme started in 1984. They are listed in alphabetical order with the judges' citation in each case.

3M United Kingdom plc:
As an already successful company, for introducing and operating a total quality managment system which has led to higher quality products and for their enthusiasm in carrying the quality message into the performance of jobs at all levels.

British Steel General Steels Teesside Works. Redcar Coke Ovens:
For significant improvements in the production of coke of consistent quality for use in iron making.

Cameron-Price Ltd, Birmingham:
For outstanding achievements in the manufacture of moulded thermo-plastic products of the highest quality, at competitive cost and with zero defects.

Express Engineering Ltd, Gateshead:
For outstanding achievement in proving that quality is profitable, ensures ongoing success and secures the continuation of the whole organization.

Ford Motor Company Ltd.   Dagenham Engine Plant:
For outstanding success in motivating the whole workforce to operate as a team and in developing improved methods of automated production to achieve higher quality in automotive engines.

GPT – Liverpool Manufacturing Unit:
For dedication to the application of the principle of total quality in the production and utilization of telecommunication equipment.

GPT's Liverpool plant manufactures the System X telephone exchange equipment which also won a Queen's Award for Technological Achievement.

IBM (UK) Ltd. Greenock Plant:
For outstanding achievements in implementing total quality management principles to improve quality and manufacturing effectiveness.

IBM (UK) Ltd. Havant Plant:
For outstanding success in involving the entire workforce in improving the quality of products and services.

ICI Chemical Products, Billingham:
For achievements in introducing and operating a quality improvement process against the background of an old established site and in developing the enthusiasm of their workforce for improved quality resulting in the successful reshaping of their business.

International Computers Limited – Ashton Manufacturing Plant:
For implementing an effective total quality process and achieving outstanding business improvements through quality in the highly competitive computer market.
J.C. Bamford Excavators Ltd   New Product Introduction Group:
For the implementation of new and imaginative quality assurance methods.
Lucas Aerospace Limited – Engineering and Heating Systems Division:
For the introduction and implementation of a total quality culture which has been recognised worldwide.

Lucas Aerospace's Engineering and Heating Systems Division manufactures aircraft cockpit and cabin windows.
Mullard Blackburn, Blackburn.
For outstanding achievement in overall business quality and, in particular, the achievement of zero defects in the supply of delay lines for export.
Plessey Office Systems   CDSS/Monarch Business Division:
For outstanding achievement in the quality of design and manufacture of a computerized digital switching system.
Rank Xerox, Mitcheldean Plant   Management Team:
For applying a highly successful corporate quality improvement programme involving all departments and employees.
Rank Xerox, Welwyn Garden City Plant:
For outstanding achievements in overall business quality and in raising to world state-of-the-art, the manufacture of electronic systems of the highest quality.
Schweppes International Ltd   The Citrus Fruit Comminution Process Technology Team:
For outstanding achievements in responding to a market need by developing an improved process for the production of a citrus fruit drink of enhanced quality.
Sony (UK) Ltd. Bridgend Plant:
For outstanding achievement in quality improvement which has led to the plant becoming the most efficient vertically integrated works for colour television screens in Sony Corporation, with exports to countries worldwide including Japan.
Whessoe Heavy Engineering Ltd   Nuclear Reactor Division:
For innovative methods of manufacture to improve the quality of nuclear pressure vessels.

In a series of events in which there have only been 18 winners to date (and between one and four (the maximum) in any single year) it is also worth noting companies who came very close to winning and were awarded special 'highly recommended' certificates. These include:

Duracell Batteries Ltd   Gatwick Road Assembly Division:
For outstanding achievements in improving the design and manufacture of speciality cells and implementing methods of quality assessment and control.

GPT Switching Networks. Ballynahinch:
For their achievement in involving all staff in the improvement of quality in manufacture.

J.C. Bamford Excavators Ltd:
For exceptional improvements in the quality of a product (JCB 3CX), its in-service maintenance and support.

Rank Taylor Hobson Ltd. Leicester:
For major advances in the technology for the measurement of surface geometry.

Santa Fe UK. Edinburgh:
For improved quality in the complicated and technically advanced process of laying steel pipe in deep water.

Swan Housewares Ltd. Birmingham:
For their achievement in the design of kitchenware and electrical kitchen equipment which has enabled them to improve their share of the market.

Tokheim Limited:
In recognition of consistent improvement in quality and performance, forming a platform which should drive further progress.
   Tokheim manufactures electrical and mechanical fuel dispensers for garage forecourts.

The Wellcome Foundation Ltd. Dartford:
For the replacement of the use of animals for the quality control of insulin by high performance liquid chromatography.

Winning a quality award is not easy but the rewards are considerable and are not restricted to official presentations of cups. Winners speak of the stages through which their companies progress in their aspirations to achieve total quality management and describe at the presentation how other 'rewards' are also gradually achieved on the way, as well as at the goal.

   It is apparent in each company which wins the BQA award that the quality concept is all-pervading from the chief executive to the shop floor. To achieve this requires a lot of staff training, careful study of the customers' needs, close examination of the companies' systems and their improvement, the elimination of barriers between departments and gradually everyone adopting an approach (a unified approach) to the implementation of total quality management.

The main result, all recipients agree on, is their companies' successes, resulting in higher profits, a greatly enhanced reputation and with it – job satisfaction for all employees, from top to bottom.

These are the fruits of total quality management.

BQA's ongoing plans

The British Quality Association is constantly looking to the future; new ideas may be initiated in the affiliated Institute of Quality Assurance or the National Scheme for Registered Assessors but in either case there is, and it is right that there should be both, interest and support by BQA committees and staff.

Two examples of co-operative initiatives, one linked to each of the above-mentioned associated bodies, are given here:

The TickIT scheme

The BQA provides representatives to sit on the various committees which establish British Standards for products, processes and quality systems. One such standard, as mentioned earlier is BS5750 (equivalent to EN29001/2/3 in Europe and ISO9001/2/3 internationally) – the standard for quality management systems.

BQA also liaises in the work of the Assessor Registration Board, drawing up the list of qualifications and experience required by an assessor who is authorized under the National Scheme for Assessors (and Lead Assessors) to perform all or part of a quality system assessment.

It has also provided help in updating and re-issuing new requirements documents and new forms for applications to become assessors. As time goes on there have been demands for special categories of assessors and particularly for assessors ideally qualified to assess and report on companies supplying and servicing software. For this to be possible a special scheme has been drawn up in co-operation with the British Computer Society on behalf of the Department of Trade and Industry and is run by the IQA (Assessor Registration Board) using resources of the BQA, ARB and BCS for selecting, checking and appointing TickIT Assessors as they are called.

This trend towards specialized assessments is likely to continue with possible specialisms like pharmaceutical knowledge being brought into the specifications for persons auditing pharmaceutical companies. BQA companies may require to use these services and/or they may wish to employ these specialist assessors to check suppliers (a 2nd-party assessment) or to check any firm supplying another (3rd-party assessments).

National vocational qualifications (NVQs)

As part of a service to its 'parent' body, the Institute of Quality Assurance, the BQA was represented at the Mapping Workshop to set up a Lead Body to help the National Council for Vocational Qualifications establish NVQs in quality.

NVQs are performance-based qualifications which run in parallel with traditional 'time-based' qualifications such as O-levels, A-levels, Higher National Certificates and Degrees. Unlike time-based qualifications NVQs do not have to be sat in one extended series of examinations but can be taken 'at leisure', as it were, by way of a series of interlinking modules of training and can be built upon from level I standard (such as an operator would pass) after a performance check to ensure competence and the ability to complete satisfactory standards under guidance.

They have been introduced for a number of reasons:

- To give an opportunity to obtain recognized qualifications to the 60 per cent of the workforce who have had nothing hiterto by way of a certificate to prove their value.
- To enable people who change occupations entirely from one industry to another to take across with them proof of competence at one of five management levels, judged against prescribed performance standards.
- To enable employers to rely on this new form of modular qualifications which tell whether a person actually has done a type of work and really has reached a specified level of competence, both at operational, supervisory and managerial levels in the hierarchy of business and commerce.

Most of the NVQs are related to specific disciplines in certain vertically integrated activities but quality, like personnel and training, accounting and other types of occupation act in a horizontal manner, cutting a swathe, as it were, through the sectors of industry and commerce. Quality, as has been emphasized in this chapter is for everyone to create and maintain. Considerations of quality principles and quality matters may be 100 per cent of a person's job as for example the quality manager

(or any other quality professional) or it may form only part of a person's
time at work, as for example the

managing director	perhaps 5–10 per cent
the section manager	perhaps 10–20 per cent
the supervisor	perhaps 20–30 per cent
the operator perhaps upwards of	30–50 per cent

but in every case there are being established, updated and maintained,
NQVs in quality for all the grades of staff mentioned. BQA member
companies will benefit from the establishment of quality NVQs and
eventually, recruitment will improve by the evidence of quality
performance by the holders of such NVQs.

13

Communicating quality
Bill Quirke

Introduction

There is a growing awareness among organizations that pursuing total quality is the way for the future. While different schools of pursuing quality are debated, all agree that there is an essentially important role to be played in the communication of any quality initiative and the central role of communication in creating a quality culture. Against this background of universal agreement on the importance of communication, companies are learning painful lessons about the poor quality of their own communication. Many are learning that the rules by which they ran their communication in the past are inadequate for the cultures they are creating for the future.

Total quality management is a strategy which focuses on the change of fundamental beliefs, values and attitudes of an organization, and on redirecting its culture to enhance the enthusiasm and participation of everyone. While companies have recognized the need to identify and satisfy customer needs, there is only a slowly growing awareness that the same respect and care has to be applied to the employee as an 'internal' customer. Organizations are finding it much more difficult to manage and serve the employee in the same way that they serve the customer.

A foundation for creating a TQM culture is an effective management of internal communication. The development of a competitive advantage through people requires a relationship focus, a thorough understanding of the relationships inside an organization and the way people operate.

There is an increasing move toward generating commitment among employees. The demand is now for caring – about service, about quality. This differs markedly from the employment contract of old – which only required understanding and compliance. This move toward 'emotional labour' demands new ways of dealing with employees to win their hearts and minds.

Experiences show that many organizations' understanding of what creates a competitive advantage is based on a heavily task-focused approach. The dilemma that organizations face is that while internal communication is central to success, managers tend to regard it as peripheral, or as an optional 'bolt on' to their real job. There is a low understanding of what communication involves and low commitment to getting it right.

One of the main causes of failure of total quality programmes is employees' growing disillusionment. Employees' suspicion that another ill-thought-through 'flavour of the month' is being unleashed on them is confirmed by management's preoccupation with the hard, measurable aspects of the programme, and the neglect of softer issues such as employees' values and commitment.

Internal communication cannot by itself create and sustain substantive change. But by itself it can de-rail and undermine change initiatives.

This chapter looks at the catch-22s of internal communication of quality. It suggests that quality and communication are inextricably linked. It also suggests that the issue of internal communication can be used by champions of quality to highlight and remove typical barriers to the success of TQM programmes. Given that everybody recognizes communication is the central symptom to success, and they also recognize the problems in dealing with it, why is internal communication such a problematic area?

One of the answers is that there is no general agreement about what precisely communication constitutes. Discussing communication with managers inside a organization is like giving them the Rorsach ink blot test. One may talk of communication in terms of memos and notice boards, while another will range more widely over issues of management style and cultural attitudes of the organization.

It is worth looking at what communication is supposed to *do* within the organization – what are the requirements made of it. One way to approach this is to look at what behaviour and attitudes are needed from the employees to achieve business objectives. Cascade briefings have been successful in the past because the requirement was for informed employees who understood how their job fitted into the whole. The need was for an efficient, downward, one-way means of communication which efficiently distributed information. All it aimed at was creating awareness and understanding, not feedback, discussion or consultation. Now the range of objectives for communication is wider – from creating awareness and understanding through to creating involvement, ownership and commitment. Figure 13.1 divides the objectives for communication according to what an organization is trying to create within employees.

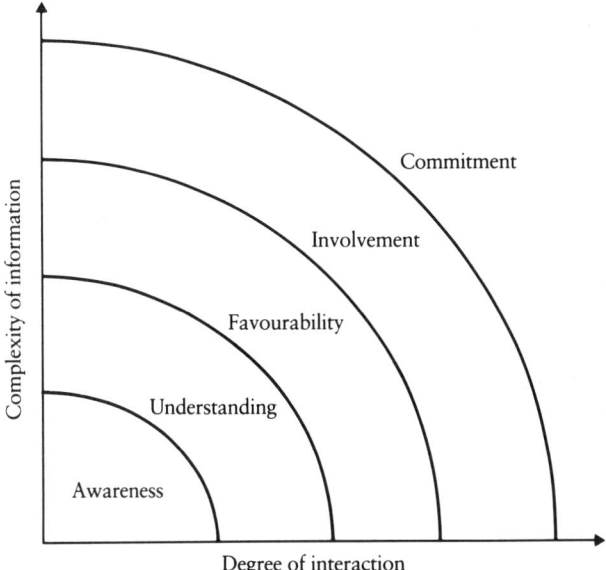

Figure 13.1   *Objectives for communication*

Different means of communication fulfil different objectives. Newsletters, brochures and videos are useful for creating awareness and understanding – but less useful in creating involvement and commitment. Recipients of these vehicles of communication tend to be in passive mode, consuming information. Where the objective is to create involvement and commitment, there is a far greater need for employees to be actively involved in face-to-face meetings, where managers will be doing more listening than talking, and where employees are encouraged to feel safe to vent their feelings and reactions.

Senior management often translates communication simply as 'telling'. It is the provision and the dissemination of information, exhortation and instruction. There tends to be an inbuilt assumption that the right to communicate lies with those at the top of the organization. Senior management often see internal communication as a low priority, or as a simple and straightforward means of mechanically disseminating information. The majority of communication audits of organizations focus on a simple truth – whatever the sophistication or otherwise of the mechanics of sending and receiving information, internal communication is founded on the relationship between individuals, between managers and the managed.

The first step for creating a strategy for effective employee communications is to create awareness of communications as a strategic issue. Senior management commitment is vital to success and unless communication is raised up the senior management agenda as a strategic issue it will be difficult to make it effective.

Most of the employee communications methods we have today are out of date and inadequate. They are based on a perception that we have a workforce in our organization which is largely blue collar. They are also based on underlying assumptions that the military model of communicating down the line management chain will ensure that the employees will comply with instructions. You can no longer rely on hierarchical power to deliver dictates from the top.

Sixty per cent of employees today are white collar and describe themselves as managers – though it is unclear what exactly it is that they are managing. They are better educated and have higher aspirations. That would be change enough if we had leaders at the top of the organization who knew every job that had to be done and could hand out the appropriate orders. Most organizations today are in markets and environments that have changed radically and rely far more on their people at the bottom to feed up to the top what should be done.

The central skill has gone from 'telling the troops' to fostering and facilitating communication.

Most employee communications is like sending people their New Year's resolutions through the post and expecting them to keep them.

Communicating for quality means bringing the same respect and disciplines to communicating with the employee as is brought to communicating with the customer. It is a question of *attitude* rather than of technique.

In the external market we stay close to the customer, listen to his needs, segment and target the market, and adapt our offer to his requirements and aspirations. In the internal market, we have to more than simply tell employees what is expected of them.

The focus of communications change and involvement programmes is often simply on the wrong people. Senior management too often sees those lower down the company as the problem. Whatever happens in any company is usually a reflection of the leaders at the top. Our research shows that all formal efforts can be undermined by the behaviour of managers, that employees receive mixed messages from watching their leaders, and that management behaviour is the most powerful communicator – that you have to be seen to be practising what you preach.

When formal communications stray too far from the truth, they become worthless; newsletters are seen as management tools, and management statements as propaganda. When the formal channels of communication lose their value, informal channels spring up to replace them. Communication is continual, it is just the means of communication that change. The grapevine becomes the most powerful and most credible source of information, and in one company employees took their information from graffiti in the bathrooms. When a company loses control of the communication channels, it has no way of restoring the balance, short of writing graffiti itself.

Unless traditional attitudes change, it is almost impossible to get people to make the strategy succeed. It is almost always because underlying cultural attitudes aren't addressed that initiatives like total quality management run into the sand after eighteen months to two years.

The irony is that the methods and habits designed for effective downward communication are almost exactly wrong for the strong upward and horizontal communication that a quality culture demands. While it is useful to talk of the chain of internal customers as an 'internal market' requiring internal marketing, there is a fundamental difference between the external market and the internal. Employees see their managers as holding their futures in their hands. Beneath the 'we are all each other's customers' lies the perception of a master/servant relationship which actually determines day-to-day behaviour. Communication, therefore, is not seen to be between equals. Subordinates will feel free to give feedback only up to a point. The manager who encourages involvement and feedback can be stung by an unpalatable truth into 'playing the hierarchy card' – reminding everyone just who's in charge here and in the process confirming everyone's suspicions about what management actually wants to hear. This doesn't apply simply to the stiff-necked status conscious manager. When employees are asked to say what they actually think, and feel safe from any threat of retribution, managers are inevitably in for an uncomfortable time. It takes training and self-discipline to avoid being triggered into defensively rebutting what employees say. Anyone who leads a team needs training in facilitation skills, listening and self-control.

Companies reviewing their communication spend too much time deciding what it is they want to say, what are their core messages that they want their employees to receive. They do not spend enough time trying to understand how their employees *listen* to the messages. Without an understanding of employees, *listening*, companies, however efficient their dissemination of information is, are only in control of half the communication equation. Employees 'decode' all communication they receive, listening for the 'real' message. How people listen depends on the organization's culture. In the public sector, for example, there is an acute sensitivity to 'business speak' – and the suspicion that it shows a betrayal of old values. Culture 'refracts' communication. You might say one thing – but they hear another. If you do not know how your employees listen, you're not in control of your communication.

In many organizations, quality programmes fail when employees buy into the culture change they provide, but then find management more interested in the costs and production performance, 'bottom line' benefits. Where there is little attention paid to the organization's bedrock attitudes and values, there is little chance of getting employees' and management objectives aligned.

Internal communication can fail due to the lack of understanding about the prevailing values by which a company abides. People will resist going in any direction that they feel violates their concept of professionalism. The failure to explain how new company objectives are in harmony with the company's traditional values is a recipe for misunderstanding, resistance and conflict.

Culture is a mental programming, the building up of a belief system which is all the more powerful because it is built up unconsciously. It is the lack of that consciousness which makes the culture so powerful. On joining a company, people very quickly learn the unwritten and the unspoken rules of the game. As long as the culture is aligned with the day-to-day workings of the organization, the culture remains quietly in the background. It is when management attempts to shift the goals of the company or tries to adopt new work methods, that the power and the separateness of the culture become evident very quickly.

Strategy is a projection of the future – culture is a force for preserving the status quo. They pull in opposite directions – and usually the culture defeats the strategy for change. While culture conducts guerilla warfare, management conducts set piece communication.

The hierarchy mindset is the biggest problem to communication. A Chinese proverb has it that 'the fish is the last to discover the water' – it's so immersed in it, it doesn't know it's there. Most organizations are so immersed in their hierarchical approach to life they don't know that their communication is unconsciously defeating them.

At the outset of change, the board goes away for a three day off-site retreat. They are the best informed, the most strategically minded and take the long view. When the change is decided they come back to present the future to their employees. Directors who are best informed get three days away to grapple with, and own, the strategy. Employees who are least well informed, least involved in the background thinking and critical to the strategy's success get only a two hour presentation. Why is that? – because it's assumed 'that's all they need to know'.

One lesson we have learned is that people need to know a whole lot more than their level in the hierarchy apparently entitles them to.

Quality is about 'connectedness', where people have a sense of the whole relationships with their internal and external customers, and an understanding of how the process of which they are a part fits together to produce the desired result. Employees want more information about parts of their organization beyond their immediate work area. They want to know what, exactly, other parts of the organization do, and feedback on how they're performing. The division of the organization into functional boxes, and communication only about employees' strictly local work area, works against the sense of connectedness. In some organizations, having been told for so long that all they need to know is information about their immediate area, employees have turned off and no longer want to know, or be bothered about, the wider picture.

There is usually a 'refractive layer' of people in any organization – a layer where information coming down from above is modified or bent before being passed on, and where information from below is similarly bent before being passed up. Identifying the refractive layer is important to ensuring the communication flows up and down the company. Typically, middle managers are blamed for withholding information and 'bending' the truth. This is often as much the result of wanting to protect their people from the vagaries and inconsistencies of those above them, as it is of a desire to hang on to information and power. The complaint made about the refractive layer and of middle management in particular, is that they are resistant to change. They do not accept the torch of change handed to them, or hand it on, in turn, to their own people. Ask a middle manager and he will see things differently. While he accepts the general need for change, while he may like the stirring title chosen for the quality campaign, he would like some more specifics about how this is all going to work.

He is not necessarily being resistant, he may simply be asking for clarification. The problem is that it is difficult to identify if resistance is the issue. The approach to communicating with managers only serves to confuse the issue. Some quality initiatives are launched at management meetings or conferences – whether with dry ice and lasers or not – and then cascaded down the organization. Senior management, like corporate actors, tread the boards and make the speeches – while the audience of managers sits passively taking all this in. It is not hard for them to be resistant. There is no opportunity for them to voice their reactions, and there is no real action for them to undertake.

One approach is to identify those in the 'refractive layer' and then use them as key communicators. Resistance is better than apathy, since at least it shows people are still engaged and interested and have not switched off totally.

One organization identified its junior middle management tier as the most cynical and resistant. They were 'volunteered' as communicators and gathered off site for a 5-day communication training programme. It was the first time they had attended a training event off site, and suspicions were high that this was to be a brainwashing exercise where they would be forced to parrot the management line. However, while they did receive some skills training in how to talk and listen to groups of their people, the event was designed to make them feel safe to say what they really thought.

Experience has shown that people can't listen to what is being said to them if their heads are already full of questions, suspicions and objections. The strategy behind the communication programme was to use employee briefing sessions to 'empty out' more questions so that people could take new ideas on board.

People listen to communication about quality to decipher the 'code'. What do management *really* mean, where are they really going?

Participants were trained to run groups in communication sessions, with a simple principle in mind – people are more trusting of and convinced by, their colleagues and peers, than they are by their managers. Rather than being a one-way top-down presentation, the communication sessions focused on getting the whole group to participate in a discussion, each member contributing his perspective as a piece of a jigsaw, until the group saw the whole picture that made sense. The end result was people understanding not what management was trying to do *to* them, but what they could do for each other.

This new environment for internal communications demands turning the traditional view of employee communications on its head. Given the complexity of the internal audiences in any organization today, it is no longer meaningful to measure the effectiveness of internal communication in terms of whether employees are happy – they may never be. What organizations now need to do is to move away from asking what employees want, and to ask themselves what is it that is required from employees to make the business strategy a success? What attitudes and behaviours are needed from employees to meet the organization's objectives? It is then a logical step to define what communication is needed to achieve the necessary attitude and behaviours among employees.

Research shows that while employees may agree that quality should be got right first time, their feeling is often that senior management will sacrifice quality to expediency, that getting the job done and out is more important than getting it completely right. This points to a difference in definition of what quality actually is inside the organization. Employees believe that if managers were serious about quality they would be investing more heavily in equipment, tools and training. In companies where there is no agreed shared definition of what quality is, people tend to supply their own definitions, and judge management harshly by those criteria. This points to a common dilemma within organizations. Employees see a contradiction between published management ideals for customer service and quality, and the traditional values of service that they have pursued. This is a particular issue in the public sector where differences are perceived between the values of public service and those of customer service. At the heart of the problem of mixed messages is a familiar issue – what we aspire to be versus how we actually behave. There are few thorough-going hypocrites inside organizations. Managers are usually genuinely sincere about changing the culture – even though they themselves are seen to embody the very characteristics they claim are barriers to progress.

Senior managers are usually the ones with the understanding to make change. However, they are senior because they have succeeded under the rules of the old culture. It is no wonder that most initiatives for change eventually take on all the characteristics of the culture they were designed to change. Senior management's task focus, the drive to make change happen and the inbuilt response we all have that it's someone else that needs to change, all serve to undermine programmes to create a quality culture. How do you go about breaking the vicious circle? The first step is to make the unconscious rules of the culture *conscious* – get the unspoken issues acknowledge and recognized.

It is difficult, if not impossible to change someone else. Individual's reactions to change vary, but they are united in this view – that change is a wonderful thing for someone else. Individuals resist being told by others that they must change. Each individual must be brought to a point of self-realization of the need to change. The value of conducting internal research is that it brings people to that point. Managers are asked to identify a management style appropriate to the desired new culture they then rate themselves against that style. Their subordinates are then asked to identify the ideal style of management, and then rate their bosses against it. Presenting managers with the results of this exercise challenges their perception of themselves, without resorting to accusation.

If you don't know what the problem is – you haven't got a solution.

Find out how communication already works inside your organization. Map out the current channels, the degree of coverage and credibility they have and how they measure up to employees' preferences for communication. Employees are not all the same, and they should not be communicated with as an undifferentiated mass. It is best to regard them as internal market and to apply some internal market research discipline. Diagnosis is the key to an effective communication strategy. You need to know what the people's concerns are, and how they get their communication. Without this information you might as well be broadcasting into outer space. Internal research allows you to set benchmarks to measure performance and return on investment, and to target your communication more effectively. Internal research doesn't have to be in the form of questionnaire surveys. It can simply take the form of bringing groups of employees together and listening to them. We learn as much from the jokes that people make, and the graffiti in the loos about the state of communication, as much as anything else. A piece of graffiti on a hand dryer on one organization read 'For a 30 second message from the chairman, please press'.

Even where organizations suspect they already know what research will show, the process of conducting it is invaluable – if only because it is one of the few upward communication vehicles available.

Second, segment your internal audiences by their key concerns. An engineer will have different concerns from a customer service person, a first line supervisor will have different concerns from a director. It is worthwhile making a matrix of these. What does this give you? It gives you an effective way of using specific preferred communication channels, to get direct to a target audience, and address their specific concerns.

Thirdly, decide what you want from your employees – clarity and understanding? Involvement? Commitment? The IABC conducted research into culture change initiatives being pursued by companies. They discovered that 80 per cent of culture change communication programmes consisted simply of a newsletter.

This allows you to choose what is the most effective communication *process*. Arm's-length media, like newsletters or videos are fine for creating clarity and awareness. If what you are trying to create is commitment and involvement there is a greater need for face-to-face methods and for varying the format and style with which those are conducted.

We tend to talk about 'employees' without addressing senior management levels. It is often senior managers who have to communicate, and deal with communication, without *themselves* having being able to have the opportunity to test the truth of what they are hearing. The problems that are most difficult to handle and the objections it's hardest to counter are those that the manager secretly agrees with. While there is permission for employees to ask questions, there is far less permission for senior management to raise issues, scepticism and doubts.

The catch-22s that affect internal communication will multiply. As organizations become leaner and employees' appetite for information and involvement increases, there will be a clash between the amount of communication required and the resources needed to communicate. Increasingly, employees who are already stretched just getting their job done are being deluged with paper. Communication on paper is rapidly becoming less effective and is being put more quickly into the waste-paper basket. Face-to-face communication is most effective but takes most time. Formal meetings, seminars and conferences will be limited by time available. Some organizations are already creating networks of nominated 'lead communicators' who can be used to feed into informal 'corridor communication'.

As the importance of communication inside companies receives more and more recognition, the task will be to create a further understanding of what communication actually entails. What will be required for future success is a significant shift in the relationships between people inside an organization. What will affect this shift in relationships is communication – where the focus for management will be far more on listening and acknowledging than on telling or sending messages. The most effective communication is face-to-face and the most believed communication is behaviour, most visible through the management style. Managers are people who have succeeded by the rules of the old culture. The skills they have may not all be appropriate. They need *training* – communication doesn't come naturally and learning to listen comes painfully.

The fundamental task of the employee communicator is to change the attitude of senior management to communicating with their people. In the drive for better communication, we shouldn't be concentrating on building new roads – we should be looking at removing existing road blocks.

Index